Also by this author:

Whittlesey Straw Bear (1989: Peterborough Library Publications)

Grovely! Grovely! and All Grovely! – History of Oak Apple Day in Great Wishford (1992: York, Quacks Printers)

More Honoured in the Breach than the Observance – Molly Dancing and other Plough Monday Customs in Cambridgeshire (1999: Marden, Frampton Publications)

Lenham Camp – 18th Century Dance Music from Harrietsham (2010: Faversham Papers)

Arise and Hail the Happy Day – Traditional Christmas Carols from Kent (2014: Faversham Papers)

Blackberry Folk Revisited – The Life and Music of George Spicer (2014: Faversham Papers)

George Frampton

DISCORDANT COMICALS

THE HOODEN HORSE OF EAST KENT

Ôzaru
Books

Discordant Comicals – The Hooden Horse of East Kent
by George Frampton
edited by Ben Jones

Published by Ōzaru Books, an imprint of BJ Translations Ltd
Street Acre, St Nicholas-at-Wade, BIRCHINGTON, CT7 0NG, U.K.
https://ozaru.net/ozarubooks

This edition published 1 December 2018 (minor revisions made in 2023)
ISBN: 978-0-9931587-7-3

CONTENTS

LIST OF ILLUSTRATIONS

Several horses are also illustrated in Appendix E

11

FOREWORD

In February 1910, 303 copies of Percy Maylam's book The Hooden Horse arrived at the homes of its subscribers. It detailed this East Kent Christmas custom in which he was interested. Few other works have augmented this, except for one chapter by Dr E.C. Cawte in his book 'Ritual Animal Disguise' published by the Folklore Society in 1978, and Geoff and Fran Doel in their booklet 'Mumming, Howling and Hoodening: Midwinter Rituals in Sussex, Kent and Surrey' published in 1992, which made any attempt. Mention must be made of the republication as 'Percy Maylam's The Kent Hooden Horse' with added notes by Richard Maylam of Collier Street (Percy's great-nephew), Geoff Doel and Mick Lynn in 2009 published by The History Press four years after my own effort (courtesy of The Faversham Society). Commentators of comparative studies, most notably Keith Chandler and Mike Heaney, in their work on the Morris dance, have examined not just what took place, but also who participated. – and even why! It is my aim to emulate these mentors and infuse "a little history into folklore."

This work scrutinizes Maylam's book, to try and add value to his and other people's findings. In doing so, it will put into context the custom in Kent from the eighteenth to twenty-first century, find more about its actors and sponsors, and examine the repertoire in a typical performance. We shall then look at the various revivals up until 1960, then afterwards, to put into place how the past was used to inspire modern-day performance.

After my publication in 2005 by Faversham Papers, I thought little of any serious request for any future edition, despite critics of the publisher's practice of accepting un-subedited scripts, photocopying and printing the same in A4 format to demand, thus eliminating problems of over-supply to minimize costs. I'm therefore grateful to Ben Jones of the St Nicholas Hoodeners and Ōzaru Books, who pursued me to write a new edition – albeit with my insistence that it be updated to the present day – and his forensic subediting which has given me many a sleepless night! Again, it was his inspiration in creating a website in the early stages of web development, into which he poured his father's research notes which led to the St Nicholas team's 1966 revival – one which has now celebrated its golden jubilee!

However, thanks must further go to all those who helped in both the first and later edition. To Lawrence Heath, for his Christmas card design on the first edition's front cover (originally as part of an English Folk Dance & Song Society fundraiser in the 1980s). To Zonia Bateman, Doreen Benham, Gail Duff, Mark Lawson, Gill & Chris Nixon, Ron Shuttleworth, Steve & Pat Grayland, and many many more willing correspondents who have answered my emails and 'snailmail' concerning the recent revival and lapsed teams out there. I am also indebted to the various librarians and archivists in and around Kent who have taken an interest in this book, as well as seeking out requests for information – sometimes beyond the call of duty. I must pay tribute to each of you who have emailed me and made me aware of the revival's progression since February 2015 when I relocated northwards. Lastly, I must pay tribute to the late Arthur Percival MBE, without whose 'warts and all' assistance over 14 years ago gave birth to the first edition of this work.

Once again, I declare this book to be complete in covering all knowledge available at the time of writing. I must also add that any outstanding mistakes are my own. Any contradictions resulting from people living or passed away, were left in deliberately so the reader can pass judgement. I shall also welcome any further news and photographs from anyone else sharing an interest.

George Frampton
Whitley Bay
August 2018

Percy Maylam (1865-1939)

Author of The Hooden Horse – an East Kent Custom published in 1909

CHAPTER 1: INTRODUCING PERCY MAYLAM AND THE HOODEN HORSE

It is Christmas Eve, outside the sound of bells mingled with a clapping noise, and the crunching sound of footsteps in snow are heard. The children stop their game and listen. Mother and father look at each other and smile, and the two girls in the corner hastily pack up their work, push it into a cupboard and join the group by the fire.

The sound grows louder. Whatever-it-is stops at the door. Some discussion follows and a good deal of stamping of feet; then music from an accordion and a Christmas song. The clapping and bells break out with renewed vigour, and a knock at the door sends the eldest girl timidly towards it. As she opens the door the youngsters gasp and draw nearer to their mother. There in the dim light which falls across the door, is a most awe-inspiring creature. In the half-light, one might think it to be a horse or the ghost of a horse…[1]

In fact, what Miss Doreen Bennett, the honorary secretary for the Kentish district of the English Folk Dance and Song Society, was about to describe back in 1939, was the witnessing of a hooden horse and his entourage by a typical farm family from the east of the county. As Miss Bennett's horse entered the room, she went on to describe it:

…The horse does not look so ghostly now. His head is made of wood, and his clamping teeth are polished hob-nails. The body is covered with a horse cloth. The older girls suddenly catch a glimpse of boots beneath the cloth when the horse rears on his hind legs and think that they look extremely like boots they have cleaned on more than one occasion.

Then the fun begins. The horse careers and curvets around the room dragging the patient wagoner. Another of the group makes frequent but fruitless attempts to mount the beast, but the gentlest of pleadings and strokings only seem to send him chasing off again. An old woman who had been standing unobtrusively by the door suddenly attracts attention by leaping out of the way of the horse to turn a fine somersault across the room – revealing her lingerie as a pair of good mannish trousers…

Although this account is deduced to be an original essay based on accounts from Percy Maylam's book The Hooden Horse published in 1909, it amply describes its key character, that of the horse itself, and the pageant he leads. Quite simply, the hooden

---

[1] Doreen Bennett, English Dance & Song, Vol. 4, No. 2, p14 (December 1939)

horse was an effigy skilfully carved from wood, with a jaw usually made to open and shut by operating a string from inside the cloth, used by a team of farm workers (the hoodeners) in an effort to elicit alms. If only because there are so few eighteenth-century records of the custom, one is led to assume that its heyday was the period between 1800 and 1860 throughout East Kent. As the century wore on, the custom became less prevalent and, by 1900, survived in only a few villages in the Isle of Thanet, and along the east coast as far south as Deal and Walmer.

The custom appears to be unique to southeast England, lying as it does in a sharply defined area in East Kent. Once more, due to the dearth of information, we are unable to deduce whether the region concerned was once wider, only shrunk with time; or more focused expanding to the limits found when Percy Maylam was conducting his research. The nearest parallel we have to any other kind of Christmas custom in the county is the Mummers' play, known more locally as that of the 'Seven Champions'. This is more widespread in the west of the county and across southern England, especially in the Darent Valley and around Maidstone, although examples are found in East Kent at Milton Regis, with one possibly at Dover, and another definitely at Harbledown (near Canterbury). This latter example is interesting since Maylam reported how James Browning, one of his informants, witnessed hoodening at around the same time, and this is the only known instance where separate Mummers and hoodening parties coincided in locus, if not in time. Milton Regis too, had a separate party of masquers in addition to its Mummers, but there appears to be no other occasion of this along the North Sea coast. Apart from instances of carollers or psalm singers going around at Christmas time, there is no other Christmas custom with which hoodening can compare in Kent, or indeed, in the south of England. To find this, one needs to explore the East or North Midlands and Wales to find anything by way of the wooing play, Derby Tup, or Mari Lwyd, respectively.

No rational treatise on the subject would be complete without attempting to survey the life, motives, infatuations, resources and methods used by Percy Maylam in compiling *The Hooden Horse – an East Kent Christmas Custom*. The book itself was eventually published by subscription in February 1910, in a solitary print run comprising 303 copies – which, over a century later, has an asking price in excess of £200 in the rare, antiquarian and second-hand book market. So, who was the man?

Parish records tell us that Percy Maylam was baptised at Pluckley Parish Church on 9 April 1865. He was one of the four children of William and Jane Maylam of Pivington Farm, Pluckley, which lies five miles northwest of the market town of Ashford, between Pluckley itself and the neighbouring village of Egerton. William (1826-1908) was born at nearby Lenham, and married Jane Bensted (1829-1925) of Ulcombe in Autumn 1850 in the Isle of Thanet. His obituary notes that he took over the tenancy of Pivington in 1850 until his retirement in 1888. He was a hop-grower, member of the West Ashford Board of Guardians, churchwarden, and active campaigner for the Conservative Party. He was obviously successful in business, since Kelly's Directory for the year 1891 states that his addresses at Pivington was supplemented by a town house at 4 Watling Street, Canterbury to where he finally moved.[2] Whether by coincidence or not, Percy first set up in business as a solicitor in 1894 at 9 Watling Street, before moving on a year later to 39 Watling Street – only just

---

[2]Kentish Express, 30 May 1908, p2

round the corner from Mowll and Mowll's Canterbury office in 73 Castle Street for whom he had once worked during his training.[3]

Percy's older brother, Clark opted for life in agriculture, moving to the family home at Lenham where he started a business centred around traction engine maintenance. Percy showed little interest in either of these careers and, after schooling at Sandwich under the tutelage of Alfred John Wyatt,[4] served articles with solicitors Sydney Cheale at Tunbridge Wells, then James Fraser at Ashford, and finally at the Dover offices of Messrs Mowll and Mowll, before beginning his Canterbury practice.[5] His obituary continues that 'at the age of five years, he began collecting books in an attic at Pivington and the hobby has been a lifelong one. His taste was very eclectic, ranging from the most learned tomes on more or less abstruse aspects of archaeology, to cowboy stories and detective fiction. He had a remarkable collection of both types of literature.' In April 1901, he married Miss Kate Pearch of West Hill House, Hastings[6], having two children: Robert Clark and Morris James, the former of whom joined his father in partnership as a solicitor in the firm Maylam and Maylam. At the start of the century, his legal practice was carried out in Kentish county and petty sessional courts. Before the Great War, he was commissioned as solicitor to the Canterbury Chamber of Trade. He was also a founder member of the Canterbury Mutual Plate Glass Assurance Society. Percy Maylam died on the 4 March 1939 at his home which he had named 'Pivington' in Old Dover Road, Canterbury.

He had published two other books that were privately printed. One was The Custom of Gavelkind in Kent published in 1913, describing how the property of a deceased person was distributed equally among his or her children instead of going to the eldest – a practice abolished by the Law of Property Act of 1925. The other book was Maylam Family Records: First Series. Gravestone Inscriptions published in 1932. He had spent a considerable time tracing the history of his family, finding a direct line to the 17th century. This latter book included the Maylam pedigree, with Percy's own brothers and sisters featuring almost anonymously in the bottom left hand corner. Yet another fascination for him lay in the works of Rudyard Kipling, being a member of the Kipling Society. He was also a member of the Folklore Society and the Kent Archaeological Society.[7]

His work into family history research gives one clue as to his research methods into the Hooden Horse. He saw his first hoodening on Christmas Eve 1888 whilst staying at Gore Street Farm, Monkton with his uncle Francis de Berckem Collard

---

[3] Pike's Blue Book and Local Directory for 1894-95 cites this information. Interestingly, it registered both William and Percy as resident at 9 Watling Street – the other addresses affected are noted as having been occupied by other residents (although Kelly's Directory for 1891 has William dwelling at Number 4). A year later, Percy moved on to larger premises at number 39, and William to number 4. Both locations were bombed during the Second World War. Watling Street and Castle Street are each distinguished now by the pre-eminence of solicitors' residences; 39 Watling Street is today a modern Evangelical temple and coffee shop!

[4] Census Returns for Pluckley, 1881 state that Maylam was resident at Sandwich at the time, cross-referring his status as a scholar when aged 15 years.

[5] Kentish Gazette, 11 March 1939, p7

[6] Hastings & St Leonards Observer, 13 April 1901, p5

[7] Kentish Express, 10 March 1939, p7

(1842-1928) and aunt Betsy (his mother's sister), witnessing similar events during the next four years. It is unknown whether that acted as a catalyst for a 23 year old who was still in training for the legal profession, but when he did begin researching the subject in earnest over 15 years later, he acknowledged the role played by his uncle who made enquiries among the East Kent farming fraternity on his behalf.[8] As it is, Percy Maylam's book is littered with eye-witness accounts from his near and distant relatives, other farmers whom his uncle may have sounded out, and certainly business clients who must have been questioned. There was a small amount of newspaper research – mostly conducted via third parties, and a trawl through local history sources to discover the antiquity of the custom, which suggests that he would have conducted work at least at the Beaney Institute (now Canterbury Public Library) and possibly also at the British Library.[9] Certainly, this notion is supported by the fact that the cathedral city librarian at one time (if not the time he conducted his research) was Joseph Meadows Cowper, who contributed to Maylam a memory of seeing a hooden horse party in the Margate environs in 1855.

Maylam never stated when he began working on his book. In his foreword, he hints that it took place 'during a period of several years', and the earliest 'field trip' mentioned was in early Summer 1905 which led to the photographs of the Hale Farm company from St Nicholas-at-Wade taken at Bolingbroke Farm, Sarre by the Canterbury photographer Henry Beauchamp Collis. The only other question posed at this stage is, how did his fascination with the Hooden Horse result in the book he was to write on the subject? That has already been answered with the acknowledgement in his preoccupation with literature from an early age, amplified by the newspaper obituaries which note his interests in folklore and history. To put events in a wider context, the Folklore Society (of which Maylam was a member) was founded in 1878 for the 'systematic comparative study of oral traditions and cultures, material cultures, folksong and dance and folktales, etc.'[10] The Folk Song Society was formed in 1898. Also, the first attempts at notating ceremonial and social dance in a modern context were attempted from midway through the next decade, culminating in what was to become the English Folk Dance Society in 1911. Punctuated throughout this were the enthusiasm for 'Merrie England' and the boom in pageantry at this time. Locally, this included Louis N. Parker's National Pageant at Dover in 1908, although the countywide fervour for such things was enough to give anything perceived as folkloric a platform at that time. There was also a movement among some to survey national and global folklore in a context epitomized by James Frazer in his meisterwerk The Golden Bough – a Study in Magic and Religion which induced researchers of the day

---

[8]Percy Maylam, The Hooden Horse, pxv, p6 (Canterbury: 1909)

[9]Paula Tempest, Canterbury Library: The Local Studies Collection – leaflet (1995). The Beaney Institute was opened in 1899 following a bequest of Dr J.G. Beaney, 'a native of Canterbury who had made a fortune in Australia (and) had left money to establish an institute for working men in Canterbury' – thus, Maylam must have used this as a primary source for his research. The rest follows, because of the author's belief that Maylam's sources could not have resulted from research in the county alone. The current day public library still holds bound hard copy of the Kentish Gazette and some (but not all) of the texts which Maylam reported in The Hooden Horse.

[10]Folklore, 1992-i, p2 – citing the 'mission statement' on the inside cover

to derive subjects having only a 400 year (or less) proven historical record from something far earlier based on supposition and scanty evidence.

Maylam's book itself came in six chapters. The first chapter served as an introduction, dealing with the spelling and pronunciation of the words 'Hooden' and 'Hoodening', before progressing to the few survivals that Maylam knew to exist. Chapter Two went on to cite printed references to the custom. This, as we shall see, and with the benefit of hindsight, could never be exhaustive. For example, there were no thorough searches through newspapers of the day, although Maylam must be congratulated on some of the surprising results he did find. The third chapter is headed 'Districts in Kent where the custom is still practised, or where tradition of it remain.' Maylam then added to that 'Causes of decay. Suggestion as to preservation'. Chapter Four could be listed as 'comparative studies', including hobby horse customs in other parts of England. The list was selective, and comprised examples at Abbots Bromley in Staffordshire, Revesby in Lincolnshire, Salisbury in Wiltshire, Minehead in Somerset and Padstow in Cornwall, where carpentered horses were (and in many cases are still) used. He also surveyed instances where heads were crafted using a horse's skull, such as the Mari Lwyd of South Wales, that used in Soul Caking in Cheshire, and the grotesque animal masks, such as the Wooser/Ooser from Dorset, and Christmas Bull from Wiltshire.

Mari Lwyd[11]

---

[11] From Wikimedia Commons; location/identity unknown, and actually a **cow** skull!

Dorset Ooser in 1891

In Chapter Five, Maylam attempted to guess at the origins of the custom and its name by comparison with place-names in East Kent, together with a consideration of the Germanic settlers who brought along their own traditions and religions into the county. As will become apparent, Maylam leant heavily on nationwide sources since those specific to Kent alone were few and far between. As if to substantiate the suggestion that the Hooden Horse had its origins in the customs of Northern European settlers, Maylam concludes his book by describing 'German customs of a similar kind' and especially the 'Schimmelreiter' in some detail in the Westphalian region along the River Weser. This compared the taking round of an animal's head whose jaws are made to open and shut, accompanied by the characters of the 'rider' and 'men dressed as women'.[12]

Writing a century after publication, one has to stand back and admire the depths that Maylam went to in conducting his pioneering research. There were few key texts of the day from which he could work, other than William Hone's Everyday Book and Year Book, and William Chambers' Book of Days to name but three. A hundred years on, authors have benefited from more recent research by Alex Helm, Violet Alford, and especially Dr E.C. Cawte. The latter's Ritual Animal Disguise is something of a bible of tradition involving the hobby horse and suchlike creatures. A newspaper search in Maylam's day would comprise combing through any hard copy that was stored in public libraries or elsewhere, years before there was a dedicated national archive at Colindale Avenue in Hendon. Today, many public libraries hold microfilm copies of newspapers. In re-editing for the second edition, it is noted that all provincial newspapers are currently being placed online – a project guaranteed to last into the next decade! Powerful too, is the internet as a resource, from which material as diverse

---

[12]Maylam, p109

as Theodore's Penitential, German calendar customs, and the genealogy of villagers living along the Wye Downs may be drawn – and all used in this present compilation. These research tools would have been thought fanciful in Maylam's day.

It seems possible that Percy Maylam was responsible for unintentionally reviving the custom with his interest. Certainly, his intervention at St Nicholas-at-Wade in 1905 prompted the local builder whom he asked to collect together a local hoodening team so he could photograph them, acted as a spur for Bert Miles to begin one at Hoath. Seemingly, Maylam's interest seemed to act as a spur for Bob Skardon of North Deal to retrieve his own interest in the custom after the Great War, until the time he retired. Writing in *The Hooden Horse*, the author commented enthusiastically on an 1868 newspaper report: "Let us hope that another (horse) will come out for the same purpose (as that) at Minster in 1968." In fact, Percy Maylam's wish came true, but it was the adjoining village of St Nicholas-at-Wade that was responsible with its own revival two years earlier. In the third millennium, teams are carving out their own interpretations of hoodening as a means of entertainment. At the time of writing, there are eight established clubs who hooden at Christmas, and at least five morris dance groups who have a hooden horse as a supernumerary. Long may it continue!

CHAPTER 2: ORIGINS AND POSSIBLE GERMANIC CONNECTIONS

As we shall see, the earliest reference specifically to 'hoodening' comes from the mid-eighteenth century, with the first definite mention of a 'hooden horse' nearly fifty years later – unless we can validate that the custom at the earlier time involved the use of an equine effigy. Now, let us assume for the sake of argument, that the Kentish farm labourer has no ingenuity himself spontaneously to initiate such a Christmastide pageant. The question has to be asked, how did this come about? Did somebody see something elsewhere and think it worth copying, and if so, where and when in time was this? Is the custom older than was thought and a continuation of this and, if so, can we forge a link back to the Restoration or before using historical documentation? Was the custom more recent, and imported from elsewhere in Britain, or even from the continent? In a nutshell, we need to indulge ourselves in some comparative studies to define a geographical and temporal distribution of similar customs, both in Britain and abroad in an attempt to surmise its origin. In fact, Percy Maylam did this using what tools he had at his disposal. The deduction is also made, there is no hard and fast evidence to support the notion that the hooden horse custom is any the less unique than we first thought!

Definition

The earliest citation of the term 'hoodening' was in 1735-6 when the Rev. Samuel Pegge, vicar of Godmersham, referred to it in his Alphabet of Kenticisms as 'Hooding (houding): a country masquerade at Christmas time, which in Derbyshire they call guising (I suppose a contraction of dis-guising) and in other places mumming.' Only one piece of independent evidence suggests the custom was extant at Godmersham or so far west of Canterbury at that or any other time, so we are speaking of a geographical rarity here.[13] That said, Pegge at least knew of the custom even if he had never witnessed it himself. No more attempts are made at a dictionary definition of hoodening until 1857, when Thomas Wright described 'Hodening' as 'an old custom in Kent, on Christmas Eve, when a horse's head was carried in procession; it is now discontinued, but the singing of carols is still called hodening'.[14]

It seems to be the case that in some parts of East Kent, the word 'hoodening' was synonymous with carolling; ironically, those parts where the hooden horse never or seldom gambolled! There was also a custom known as 'Goodening' on St Thomas's Day (21 December) which involved the poor going around the big houses soliciting alms; only in that respect and in name only. Alfred Moore from Eythorne wrote a weekly column for the Kentish Express during the 1890s. He also wrote about goodening, allying it with his own concept of hoodening as a carolling custom, although he was aware of its wider context:

---

[13]Maylam, p12
[14]Maylam, p18

'I suppose almost every native of this county has heard the old Kentish word 'hoodenin' and knows the sense in which it is used today. But as a good many who are not of Kentish birth are kind enough to read these papers I may as well say that the word means going round singing carols or songs or shouting good wishes at Christmas and New Year's Tide for a consideration, of course, though I hope that does not necessarily make them the less kindly meant. Formerly, however, the word had a somewhat different meaning, for a century or so ago it was used for Yuletide mumming or masquerading rather than carol-singing. In East Kent, it was then an annual custom for each farmer to send his best horse round the parish in which he lived. Its tail and mane were always gaily decorated, and the animal was in charge of the wagoner, to whom drink and money were given as New Year's perquisites. Sometimes too, the farm labourers would take their 'horse' around, this latter being a rudely cut wooden (pronounced 'ooden' or 'hooden' by the older Kentish folk) figure of a horse's head with moveable mouth having rows of hob-nails for teeth, which, opening and shutting by means of a string, closed with a loud sharp snap. It was furnished with a flowing mane and the whole arrangement was worn upon the head of a ploughman, who, supplied with an ample tail to represent the equine caudal appendage, was called the 'hoodener', while his house-to-house visitation of the parish was known as 'hoodenin.' And today, although the horse-head mumming custom is forgotten, the old word is still used by us Kentish folks, with an altered meaning, certainly, yet (like almost every vocable in our fine old dialect) carrying us back to bygone days and linking us indissolubly with the Kent of olden times.

I have just had a visit from some lads, presumably at Eythorne, who tell me they are 'out hoodenin' and who have shouted loudly

We wish ye a murry Chri'mus
An' a 'appy New Year,
A pocketful a money, an'
A cellarful o' beer'!

a wish which comes rather late for the former season but is in good time for the year we have just entered upon. The words are simple ones – simple in the worst sense, many of us may say, perhaps – but yet they are very old, this particular form of greeting having been in the mouths of Mummers and carol-singers not only here in Kent but also over the greater part of England for at least three or four centuries, I am told. But at any rate, when I heard them just now on this January evening they set me thinking about Yuletide and New Year's customs in old days, when, as it seems to be, people were heartier in the outward expression of their good wishes than they are now'...[15]

---

[15]Alfred Moore, in the Kentish Express, 5 January 1895 p3

Origins

One cannot progress without commenting briefly on the animistic and quasi-religious practices of our Ancient British ancestors.

In Percy Maylam's search for information, an unnamed correspondent to the Church Times in January 1891 cited the Penitential of Theodore. This condemned and charged 'those who go about at the kalends of January garbed as a stag or an old woman, taking the form of beasts, clad in the skin of beasts and assuming the heads of beasts; who transform themselves into animals, three years' penance, for the thing is devilish.' Maylam seemed to have included this in his book as a suggestion that hoodening may have had a seventh century or earlier origin. Let us examine exactly what comprised this edict, then put it into context.

Theodore was the seventh Archbishop of Canterbury who was born at Tarsus in Cicilia circa 602, and who died in Canterbury in 690. He was appointed to the See of Canterbury by Pope Vitalian in 667. He was described as a monk of Greek origin and extraordinary learning, who shaped the English church into a structure, and the first archbishop whose authority the whole English church was willing to acknowledge. His Penitential was a list of rules for Christian living, including as it did penances for drinking and drunkenness in monasteries, sexual intercourse, menstruating women in churches, veneration of saintly relics, and funeral practices. It seems that any bestial practice throughout the jurisdiction of the See was another factor worthy of penance, and not just restricted to the immediate locality of Canterbury. Historically, the 'kalends of January' was the day on which interest payments were due in Rome, and traditionally thought of as the first day of the month although not of the calendar year, which began on 1 March. It seems that some kind of midwinter celebration was current at that time, and Theodore sought to impose penalties for its procreation rather than incorporate it into a Christian calendar – all this before the celebration of the Feast of the Nativity was to be brought into play. The Church Times correspondent then went on to postulate hoodening (or 'odening') as a custom having Odin and Nordic roots, of which more later.

The Penitential seems to amplify two earlier reports by indirectly or directly quoting from them, which would lend the idea a further air of antiquity if not authenticity. One of these comes from St Augustine of Hippo (354-430) who once inveighed against men who clothed themselves in women's garments at the feast of Janus.[16] Although unconfirmed, it was also said he condemned the 'filthy practice of dressing up like a horse or stag' in the 5th century.[17] Also, ecclesiastical authorities in Scotland later forbade 'any man from dressing as a horse or wild beast and dancing widdershins *(i.e. anti-clockwise)* in the kalends of January, for this is devilish'.[18] Both these comments are invoked by Archbishop Theodore, and seem to be confused with his text.

If this is to be interpreted as a primeval instance of hoodening in Kent, then the trick now is to bridge a 1000-year gap before the next item of documentation in 1735 when Percy Maylam first cites evidence for the hooden horse as mentioned in the

---

[16] Jacobus de Voragine, The Golden Legend, chapter 13

[17] Quoted on Ben Jones's hoodening.org.uk website, but the ultimate source is unclear

[18] George O. Howell (ed.), The Kentish Note Book, vol. 2, pp19-20 (14 February 1891)

European Magazine[19]. To do this, one must resort to comparative studies of similar customs extant in southeast England and elsewhere from as long ago as necessary.

Maylam surveyed many British customs practised at Christmas and/or those that involved the use of a 'hobby horse' of whatever type. Many of the hobby horses mentioned can be described as 'tourney' horses, into which a rider would climb and appear as though he was riding it, as opposed to one that entirely shields its wearer from public view and, inside which he can animate it at will as an alter ego. One example of the tourney horse cited by Maylam is that of Hob-nob at Salisbury, whose existence can be traced back until at least the sixteenth century.

Hob-nob, pictured with St Christopher the Salisbury Giant from 1904

---

[19]Maylam, p12

He was a companion to a processional giant known as St Christopher, and formerly owned by the Guild of Merchant Tailors in the city. Their pageant was celebrated annually on Midsummer Eve until the Guild went bankrupt in the eighteenth century. Thereafter, it was taken into custody by the town museum and used to celebrate days of national rejoicing such as royal coronations, jubilees, and weddings, peace celebrations after wars, etc. At the time that Maylam was preparing his text for *The Hooden Horse*, the Giant and Hob-nob had gone out in August 1902 to celebrate the coronation of Edward VII.[20] But it wasn't only Salisbury that had such a custom: the City of London, Norwich, Coventry and Chester, for example, each had similar pageant characters. At Norwich Castle Museum today, you may see two 'snapdragons' – a sort of tourney in the shape of a dragon.

The Civic Snapdragon from Norwich

These were once used by the city Guild of St George up until 1835, and thereafter informally in a mock mayoral procession up until the First World War.[21] The

---

[20]George Frampton, St Christopher, Hobnob, and the Salisbury Morris, in English Dance and Song, vol. 45, no. 3 (Autumn 1983)

[21]Richard Lane, Snap – the Norwich Dragon (Norwich: 1976)

Corporation of London has revived the passage of the giants Gog and Magog through the city streets on Lord Mayor's Show day, as inflatable effigies on a motorized truck rather than a robust frame-worked image carried on the shoulders of one or more persons. The irony here is that, in 1985, a body called the Graund Order of Guisers was set up who, among other aims, designed a 24 feet high processional giant for carriage by a team of supporters which, they hoped, would be adopted by the pageant master in the Lord Mayor's Show. The giant was built, a hydraulic spine constructed so that it could successfully be raised and lowered to go under the two railway bridges en route, but the offer was declined![22]

So, with these sixteenth century precedents, is there any evidence that some similar custom was ever practised at Canterbury or elsewhere in Kent? Fortunately, there are a number of good sources that indicate that such an equally feisty affair held sway in Canterbury itself, although no mention of a hobby horse character is made!

The Betley Window with a range of Merry May performers

The detail shows a tourney horse (evidence of which is absent from any known example in Kent)

[22]George Frampton collection

Pageantry and Performance in Sixteenth Century Kent

The best account of such a procession in Canterbury is that of the 'marching watch' with its pageant of St Thomas. Records show that a similar civic procession was in use beforehand, but it wasn't until 1490 that any such show was acknowledged to be dedicated to the martyrdom and celebration of Thomas a' Becket. Giles Dawson gives the fine details of money paid in support of this between 1501 and 1543. In summary, he states that: 'This show, enacted annually on a pageant-wagon at least as early as 1504-05, was almost certainly a debased survival or revival of an old St Thomas play. In the show, the saint was represented by an effigy, and a mechanical angel (always called 'the vice') probably flapped his wings as the swords of the knights or tormentors drew a gush of blood from the insensitive torso.'[23] It also brings to mind pageants in catholic countries where the effigy of a patron saint is chaired through the streets, such as at Beaune in the burgundy wine-growing region of France in February every year. A representative and detailed set of accounts for the year 1520-21 for the Canterbury marching watch is quoted thus:

Expenc' Repacois pagiant' sci Thome m'tire	
Itm' paied to Willm Bradle for xx fote of tymber for the new making of Seynt Thomas pagent	*iijs iiijd*
Itm' paied to Brusshyng & his mate for sawyng of the seid tymber	*xvd*
Itm' for beryng of the seid tymber to the Sawstage	*jd*
Itm' paied to Willm Haryson yoynor & hys ij mates for iij five dayes working vppon the pagent taking by the day for eu'y of them iij vijd Sma	*viijs ixd*
Itm' paied to the same willm Haryson & hys seid ij mates for v dayes & half more on the same worke taking by the day for them iij xxjd Sma	*ixs vijd*
Itm' paied for CC of iij peny naile	*vjd*
Itm' for C & di' of iiij peny naile	*vjd*
Itm' paied for ij elle & a quarter of cloth for a surples for ye ymage p'ce the ell vijd ob Sma	*xvjd ob*
Itm' paied to Richard Colbrond for a new cart & new whele for the pagent	*ijd ob*
Itm' for ij li of Sope	*ijd ob*
Itm' paied for v quarter pece of asshe for stanchonyng of the pagent	*xvjd*
Itm' to my lady of Seynt Sepulcres for the standing of the pagent in her barne	
	xxd
Itm' paied to Henry Gyldwyn for di' C of bord for the pagent	*xvjd*
Itm' for iij yarde of wyre for the vyce	*ijd*
Itm' for whipcord taket naile & teynt' hooke	*ijd*
Itm' for ij asshe hoopys to bere vp the clothes ou' the hors bak	*jd*
Itm' for turning of the vyce	*ijd*
Itm' for mete & dryng for the knyghte and other that holp convey the pagent	*xijd*
Itm' paied to trussell for caryage of the pagent a boute the tyme of the watch	*xijd*
Itm' paied to mreʒ Symon for ij elle half of white clothe for an alter cloth p'ce the ell vijd Sma	*xvijd ob*

---

[23]George Dawson, Records of Plays and Players in Kent, 1450-1642 (Malone Society: 1965)

Itm' paied to her for making of the surplice afore wreten	*iiijd*
Itm' paied for a dosen & di' of gold tyn foyle for mending of the harness	*iiijd ob*
Itm' for half a dosen of gold foyle	*ijd*
Itm' for j li & half of glue	*iiijd ob*
Itm' paied to Iohn Colyn for mending of the seid harness	*xijd*
Itm' for candell & wasshyng of the clothes of the pagent	*Ijd*

Modern translation[24]:

Expenses for repairs to the pageant of St Thomas the Martyr		(pence)
• Paid to William Bradle for 20 feet of timber for making the new St Thomas pageant	3s 4d	40p
• Paid to Brushing & his mate for sawing the timber	15d	15p
• For bearing the timber to the sawstage	1d	1p
• Paid to William Harrison, joiner & his 2 mates for 3x 5 days' working on the pageant, taking 3x 7d per day for each of them in sum	8s 9d	105p
• Paid to same William Harrison & his said 2 mates for 5½ more days on the same work, taking 3x per day for them, 21d in sum	9s 7d	115p
• 200 3-penny nails	6d	6p
• 110 4-penny nails	6d	6p
• 2¼ ells of cloth for a surplice for the image, 7½d per ell in sum	16½d	16.5p
• Paid to Richard Colbrond for a new cart & new wheels for the pageant	2½d	2.5p
• 2 pounds of soap	2½d	2.5p
• 5 quarter pieces of ash for propping the pageant	16d	16p
• To my lady of St Sepulcres for standing the pageant in her barn		
•	20d	20p
• Paid to Henry Goldwin for 10x 100 boards for the pageant	16d	16p
• 3 yards of wire for the vice	2d	2p
• Whipcord tacked nails & tenterhooks	2d	2p
• 2 ash hoops to bear the cloth(e)s over the horse's back	1d	1p
• Turning the vice	2d	2p
• Meat and drink for the knights and others that helped convey the pageant	12d	12p

[24]*This is an amateur effort – expert corrections would be most welcome! (ed.)*

•	Paid to Trussell for carrying the pageant around at the time of the watch	12d	12p
•	Paid to Miss Simon for 2½ ells of white cloth for an altarcloth, 7d per ell in sum	17½d	17.5p
•			
•	Paid to her for making the surplice described above	4d	4p
•	A dozen & ten gold tin foils for mending the harness	4½d	4.5p
•	Half a dozen gold foils	2d	2p
•	1½ pounds of glue	4½d	4.5p
•	Paid to John Colyn for mending the harness	12d	12p
•	Candles & washing the pageant's cloth(e)s	2d	2p

At other times, payments were made to a drummer, trumpeter and other 'waits', and the mayor and city aldermen are noted as having taken part. The accounts for the years 1504 through till 1529 detail what was spent on costumes, paints, gunpowder, horse harness (for real horses!), tools, food and drink for the participants. The pageant was maintained until 1541, when Henry VIII removed the shrine and 'scattered the martyr's dust to the winds.' But the pageant continued in different guise, which Brigstocke Sheppard likens to the Midsummer Watch in London.[25] The entry which announces the change runs this:

> *Payd for fetchyng the Gyaunts and the gonnes from the store house to the Court Hall*   *ijd*
> *(Paid for fetching the Giants and guns from the storehouse to Court Hall*   2d)

The giants made their annual progress until the first year of Mary in 1553 when, to prepare the way for a revival of the old pageant, 'two charyotts', gaily decorated, marched with the Watch. With the accession of Elizabeth in 1558, the pageant lapsed and transformed itself into an adjunct to the Watch procession – perhaps it was thought too popish as she strove to cajole the hard-line puritan movement with the followers of her half-sister Mary into a united nation. Brigstocke Sheppard suggests this was because of the effort to create a 'more efficient organization for national defence' at a time when there was no formal body such as the British (or English) Army The marches were superseded by 'musters' at which civic payments would be made for food and drinks, and also for musicians such as fife and drum players. So it was, that a Canterbury-based processional custom existed on a scale similar to that at Salisbury. However, its currency was for a shorter time, although on a civic scale rather than the preserve of one of its Guilds or Companies. And although one is tempted to feel there might be a template for a later custom emulating the Giant and Hob-Nob, there is little evidence in Kentish records to support this notion.

Dawson takes great pains to cite possible examples of Tudor entertainment in Kent that could be allied to our central subject. He tells us that 'Lydd had a St George play in 1455-56, and again or still in 1531-32. In 1532-33 Hythe had Robin Hood

---

[25]J. Brigstocke Sheppard, 'The Canterbury Marching Watch with its Pageant of St Thomas', in Archaeologia Cantiana, vol. 12, p27 (1878); Dorothy Gardiner, Canterbury, p67 (Canterbury: 1950 edition)

players, Old Romney had a lord of misrule in 1525-26, both Folkestone and Sandgate in 1542-43, and Sandwich in 1550-51. New Romney sent a bishop of St Nicholas to Lydd almost every year from 1450 to 1485 and probably longer.' There is a sole reference to the 'morisdauncere of Winchelsey' in the Lydd accounts of 1518-19, and many references to professional minstrels and players, with sundry citations of bear wards, bear baiting and dancing bears, sword players, jugglers, and much more of what today would be called street theatre. W.A. Scott Robertson described the passion play and interludes specifically at New Romney using the same data in 1880, focusing on the drama provided rather than the nature of the actors reported by Dawson. The former highlighted how 'local brotherhoods or fraternities seem generally to have furnished the actors. At Canterbury, the Corpus Christi brotherhood, otherwise called the Fraternity of Jesu's Mass, seems to have furnished the players, at the joint cost of all the crafts and mysteries in the city.' So, all in all, the factors that created the Giant and Hob-Nob at Salisbury were also present as Canterbury and the Kentish market towns. The Flemish woollen trade would have been one factor that could have provided fiscal back up for all this.

The morris dance specifically could also be thought of as a harbourer of such a man-beast, either as a tourney horse or other effigy. The Salisbury pageant already noted included morris dancers, although their mode of performance throughout the centuries can only be guessed at.

Detail from "The Thames at Richmond"

One example is the seventeenth century painting 'the Thames at Richmond' on view at the Fitzwilliam Museum at Cambridge, which portrays four in a line dancing to the music of a pipe and tabor player. The team comprises a man-woman character, a collector and a tourney horse. In Kent, there are few references to the Morris in history. The best description we have took place in May 1589, when nine dancers hired a Mr Ager of Bourne (sic) to play his fiddle for them on a tour which included Reculver, Herne, Chislet, Hoath, Hackington, and Canterbury, on and around Ascension Day. One of the characters was dressed as a 'Maid Marrion' and references are made to bells as part of the dancers' apparel. The dancers are named as J. Turfrey, N. Saint, J. Lichfield, James Barley, H. Seers, Timothy Dimkyn, Thomas Young, H. Parkes, and J.

Rose.[26] There is sadly no reference to such a supernumerary as a hobby horse in this case, which might have proved a precedent for the hooden horse. The performance also took place in spring, not Christmas, but historically, it could be argued that hoodening may have been an amalgam of the two separate entities.

Philological Considerations

Maylam took great pains in surmising the philology of the words 'hooden' and 'hoodening', wondering if they derived from Germanic sources e.g. from the evidence that Woodnesborough could imply an affinity with Woden, and the word 'hoodening' be similarly rooted. He also pondered whether an as yet unidentified predecessor of its custom came from the Kyng Ale such as at Kingston-upon-Thames in the sixteenth century, which included a Robin Hood character. One parallel, or at least some kind of diversion, comes from the East Midlands plough play performed on Plough Monday.

By coincidence, 'hoodeners' were referred to in four places in this area: Selston in Nottinghamshire, Pagets Bromley (Abbots Bromley) in Staffordshire, as well as two unidentified locations in North Nottinghamshire and Derbyshire. The authority for this was the journalist Arthur Sharp who worked for the Nottingham Evening Post. In three separate articles spaced over fifteen years, he describes Mummers' plays whose performances included a 'hooden horse' and players who were described as 'hoodeners'. Before leaping to the conclusion of a common root, Peter Millington, a key researcher in the Plough Play of the East Midlands, suggests that this misnomer came about with Sharp's presumption that the word 'hoodening' – possibly discovered by Sharp in a book on folklore – was thought to be nationally applicable to any similar custom. The native terms for the actors in the Nottinghamshire plough play were 'plough bullocks' or 'ploughboys', and 'guysers' for the Mummers' plays on the western edge of the county. [27] There is also the supposition that, since Nottinghamshire is identified with Robin Hood, this could provide some form of explanation for one or both usages of the words. There are plenty of Christmas-based or Plough Monday-based customs such as the Derby Tup, Mari Lwyd of Wales, or Christmas Bull of Wiltshire, that involves the use of animal disguise, but none come near any direct comparison with the East Kent hooden horse.[28]

The Schimmelreiter of Northern Germany

And lastly, lateral thought would have it that, were the Hooden Horse to have had its origins with the Angle, Saxon or Jute invaders of the fifth century, then a comparison with calendar customs of a similar kind in that country might support the notion of commonality. Percy Maylam conducted searches in regions of Saxony, obtaining translations from a number of nineteenth century sources. Commentators say that tradition in modern-day Germany is a fascinating amalgam of Teutonic

---

[26]Philip Edmonds, in The Morris Dancer, vol. 2 no. 6, p91 (1988), citing Canterbury Cathedral Library JQ 1589 Nos. 221-228

[27]Peter Millington, personal communication to the author, 11 July 2001; citing Arthur Sharp, Nottingham Evening Post, 3 January 1929, Nottingham Evening Post, 30 December 1936, p6, Nottingham Evening Post, 23 December 1944

[28]Maylam, pp61-71

mythology with Catholic festivity. The case study central to these discussions is the role of the Nordic god Woden's steed: the white horse, or 'schimmel'.

The Schimmel is introduced at Demmin in Pomerania, 1930[29]

In defining a German Christmas custom, the obvious target would be the pageantry surrounding St Nicholas. In many parts of northern Europe, the custom took place on 6 December or Christmas when St Nicholas (or his delegate) would go around visiting children to enquire whether they had been good boys or girls during the year (and/or could say their prayers). He might be accompanied by an alter ego, who was often named Knecht Ruprecht. In some instances, this character was fantastically attired, in some cases entirely swathed in straw as a 'straw bear'. They might be further accompanied by 'fays' or 'feien' – young lads with blackened faces, and clad in women's clothes. There might be the 'schimmel' or white horse operated by his 'schimmelreiter' (rider). Maylam quotes his source saying: "In several places...to the lower jaw of a horse's head a string is fastened in such a way, that the rider is able, by pulling and loosening the string to make a snapping noise." Nowhere does he elucidate how this is precisely done. Is the 'schimmelreiter' and 'schimmel' a single unitary figure comparable to a tourney horse such as Hob-Nob or the sixteenth century Morris dance hobby horse, where the rider carries the frame of the horse with options on reins, that might enable the 'rider' to the jaw action noted? Or is he more akin to the Hooden Horse, where the 'horse' and rider or wagoner would be separate performers. How was the horse's head constructed? Clues may be gauged from the

---

[29] Image found during research at Cecil Sharp House

accompanying illustrations that show their diversity: a tourney horse in one part of northern Germany, and a hoodenesque beast in another. Let us begin by assuming the best comparison would lie with a carpentered head that was made to open and close its mouth with a loud snapping noise, rather than an animal's skull that might have a restricted shelf-life. In that case the best example Maylam found appeared in a book dated 1845 from the Isle of Usedom on the Baltic coast next to the Polish border. The custom there featured three characters. The first, Ruprecht, held a big stick and an ash bag, and was concealed in pea haulm. The second carried the Klapperbock (or clapping goat), a staff over which a goat's skin was stretched and to which a wooden head was fastened with an arrangement for making a snapping noise similar to the hooden horse. Ruprecht and the Klapperbock pushed about the children who had not said their prayers. The last figure present was a Rider on a White Horse.[30]

On the mainland there was greater pageantry. Maylam, in translating a text from Prussian dialect dated 1841, commented on the custom at Ruppin. In this young men and women assembled during the evening in the week next before Christmas. One of the lads imitated the rider on a white horse (Schimmel), having a sieve fastened to his chest and another onto his back, over which a white linen cloth was hung. Another lad called the Christmann or the Christ-puppe, was also clad in white and decorated with ribbons, and carried a big bag. The Feien (or Fays) dressed themselves as old women and blackened their faces. The procession went from house to house with music, children joining in with shouts of glee. On entering the living room, a chair was set before the Rider, over which he was expected to jump. This done, the Christ-puppe and his assembly came in without the Fays. The girls sang a song, the tune of which was always the same, but whose words varied, although elsewhere a standard form of words would be used. The Rider then chose one of these to accompany him in a dance. This entailed standing opposite one another, each making all sorts of improvised twists and turns. During this, the Christ-puppe went around among the children and asked whether they had said their prayers. If they repeated a verse from the bible or prayer book, they were rewarded with a gingerbread from the bag, but if not, they were beaten with it. After this, the Rider and Christ-puppe danced with some of the crowd then left, the dance closing the chief part of the ceremony. During the whole of this, the Fays have tried to force their way in, but each time they have been driven back with jokes and ridicule. When the Rider and Christ-puppe have left the room, they burst in frightening all and sundry, jumping around wildly and boisterously, beating the children. This is repeated at every house visited in an evening, depending how many there were in the village.[31]

Maylam cited articles authored by Adalbert Kuhn (1812-1881), who suggested a Teutonic origin for the custom. However, there is an allusion to the 'Schimmel' being more than just a Christmas-related custom: Shrovetide and weddings being cited as other occasions that featured the beast. Nor was the Schimmel necessarily the focus in the affair – the author suggesting the Fays had an equally significant role to play. In an article written in 1848, Kuhn and his co-author Schwartz widened the scope of the

---

[30]Maylam, p104 (citing Moriz Haupt in Zeitschrift für Deutsches Alterthum (Leipzig, 1845)

[31]Maylam, p98 (citing Adalbert Kuhn in 'Ueber das VerhältnißMärkischer Sagen und Gebräuche zur Altdeutschen Mythologie' in'Märkische Forschungen' vol. 1 (pub. Verein für Geschichte der Mark Brandenburg, Berlin, 1841)

Christmas custom itself beyond the two locations mentioned above. One custom took place as far north as Thüringia where a horse's head was often kept ready for the purpose. Its construction comprised a string fastened to the lower jaw, which the rider pulled to cause a clapping noise. At Köterberg near Höxter, a bear appeared with the Schimmel.[32]

St Nicholas appears with his companions in Bavaria, 1958[33]

More examples intertwine Shrovetide and Christmas appearances of the Schimmel, steering us away from drawing direct comparisons with the hooden horse of East Kent. In the Mittelmark and wider afield, the central character was known

---

[32]Maylam, p107 (citing A. Kuhn and W. Schwartz in Norddeutsche Sagen, Märchen und Gebräuche (Leipzig, 1848))

[33] Image found during research at Cecil Sharp House

variously as Holy Christ, Knecht Ruprecht, Hans Ruprecht or Rumpknecht. In Mecklenburg, he was called Ru Clas or Rauhe Clas. In the Altmark, Brunswick and Hanover and East Friesland, he was Clas, Clawes, Clas Bur, and Bullerclas. As well as carrying a long staff and an ash bag, in Mellin he had bells on his clothes. Where he held an ash bag to beat children who had not said their prayers, he was also called Aschenclas. At Otternhagen near Hanover, Deetz near Brandenburg, and Schorau near Zerbst, he rode around on a white horse, sometimes accompanied by a Platzmeister (i.e. a man whose duty it was to make room for the performers and keep the crowds off). At Hohennauen near Rathenow he was accompanied by Fays. At Elm and Cremlingen, he appeared with a bear who is covered with pea haulm and led on a long chain. At Chemnitz, parts of Westphalia and Osnabrück, 'the holy Christ' was a maiden clad in white who called for prayers to be said, and was separate to the Schimmelreiter. At Osnabrück, the Schimmel also appeared at New Year and was known as the Spanish stallion.

Two heads described as 'Schnabbukstangen[34]' from Pomerania

Over fifty years later, Georg Rietschel gave a fuller account broadening the costumery and topography of the occasion, but without really adding to the story. However, he did describe one instance in Silesia, where the schimmel was represented by three young men, each of whom put his arms on the shoulders of the one in front. All three were covered with a cloth, to represent the horse's head and neck. A fourth

---

[34] Confusingly, the Schnabbuk is also spelt Schnabuk, Schnabbuck and Schnabuck, and there is a totally separate 'beast' in southern Germany/Austria called the Schabbock! Thanks to the Vaughan Williams Memorial Library and the Goethe-Institut.

lad was seated as the Rider on the shoulders of the middle one of the three lads who are covered with the cloth.[35]

What is clear at this stage is, that there was a pool of characters, functions and calendar customs that seemed to be shared around Northern Germany. The 'klapperbock' at Usedom in this instance has quite clearly adopted the role of Knecht Ruprecht, but is at odds with what Kuhn and Schwartz had written earlier that it was the latter character who had this role. The use of the Schimmel for Shrovetide and wedding customs has already been mentioned, and note has already been made of Teutonic myth. One use cited where Knecht Ruprecht was dressed as a straw bear ('Erbsbär') is interesting. This character is found much further west in Germany today, where he is part of a revival that has taken place since the Second World War. This is the Shrovetide custom of 'Karneval' (also known as 'Fasnet', 'Fasching' or 'Fassenacht' depending on the region where it takes place).[36] Although not entirely relevant, photographs of two hobby horse characters used in the Fasnet custom are included in a book on the subject written by Johannes Künzig published in 1950, which mainly cites the Kuhn and Schwartz article of 1848.[37]

There seems little evidence that the custom in Germany survived beyond around 1930. Supposition has it that the new-found materialism of the Third Reich and later German Democratic Republic put paid to that. Violet Alford, writing in the present tense suggests that the custom was still extant in Ruppin presumably after the Second World War, but further analysis implies this is a quote mentioned earlier from Adalbert Kuhn and therefore from the previous century.[38] Also, there seems to be a dearth of information that is somehow unconnected with Percy Maylam or his sources. The Goethe-Institut suggested that the custom might still be prevalent in some of the villages,[39] although Ben Jones, whose brother Adam (also a hoodener) works at the University of Leipzig, avers that the custom in Lower Saxony has lapsed.[40] An enclosure sent from the Goethe-Institut runs thus:

> …The overwhelming wealth of evidence from the 1932/33 Atlas of German Calendar Customs in answer to your question about Christmas processional types in existence is that, for the Germany of that time there were many such cases, less associated with legend, but rather more as a village prank. In this, the village youths were free to frighten and annoy girls or impressionable youngsters. Using various gestures, the youths transported themselves into a

---

[35]Maylam, p108 (citing Georg Rietschel, Weihnachten (Bielefeld und Leipzig, 1902)

[36]Inevitably, the URLs suggested in the first edition of this book no longer exist, but a good general article (with links to many other useful sites) by Robert Shea, which was mentioned, can currently be rediscovered at https://www.mrshea.com/germusa/customs/karneval.htm, while (equally inevitably) a lot of information can also now be found at https://en.wikipedia.org/wiki/Carnival_in_Germany,_Switzerland_and_Austria

[37]Johannes Künzig, Die alemannisch-schwäbische Fasnet (1950)

[38]Violet Alford, The Hobby Horse and other Animal Masks, p116 (London, 1978 Merlin Press); published after her death in 1972

[39]Gunhild Muschenheim (Goethe-Institut of London), letter to the author, 1 June 2001

[40]Ben Jones, email to the author, 21 June 2001

topsy-turvy world, and soon the feast night recalled something different to a holy Christian legend. The frightening and teasing that were acknowledged as customary practice in village tradition, said more of the nature of these customs as an interpretative effort rather than illustrating pagan culture. Disguise and improvisation set apart the individuality of those participating, and everything that went with it. Today you can find documented Christmas customs written indeed by older men who did the same thing themselves. Have we not travelled full circle?

(The custom comprises…) 1. Men were heard, naturally all in disguise. First was a policeman (ein Gendarm), then came the Schimmelreiter riding on the back with a horse's head in front; 2. Legs with white sheets on them hung down; 3. The stork with a long beak fixed by a long needle; 4. A chimney sweep; 5. A barber (ein Barbier); and 6. A Gipsy.

The policeman asked upon entering the house, if they were allowed to step inside. The schimmelreiter, who must be extra nimble and skilful, jumps up with its prospective rider over the tables and benches. When the tables had cups, plates and glassware upon it, this led naturally to breakages. The stork poked and prodded with his beak, whenever he got the opportunity. The chimney sweep in his black costume cuddled and kissed anyone who could not escape him. The barber squirted out bubble foam and soap on his victims, so that they had to snort out air. The gipsy had in her full ample bosom a weighty jug. From this s(he) poured strong schnapps and liqueurs, the pranksters were paid off, and had to remain sober. They had to make the entire village happy (in this way). They also moved off to neighbouring villages and, woe betide when they met up with other such performers outside their beat – this could result in a punch-up! This is how a party sometimes finishes up! There is the story that when two such schimmelreiter meet outside, that one of them dies during the course of the next year. When the procession has finished, the participants naturally empty the jug. Thus, the entire amusement was described.[41]

One is apt to put the custom of 'schimmelreiter' on a pedestal – Maylam even appeared to even give this character a predominance in popular culture which the German texts stay clear of. Whilst the reverse may have been true in Usedom where the white horse was key to the festival, this was obviously not the case in 1928 in Meckelburg-Pomerania where the schimmel was more of a bit player in a far greater pageant.

---

[41] Ingeborg Weber-Kellermann, Das Weihnachtsfest (1978, Bucher) – citing Lina Kellermann (born 1890) from Maleiken (now Nelidovo) in Masuria, East Prussia (probably around 1900) – translation of text sent to me from the Goethe-Institut, pp28-29 (the original is held by the Vaughan Williams Memorial Library at Cecil Sharp House). Maleiken is around 22 km from Mikalbude (now Suchkovo), where Anneli Jones reported seeing the Schimmelreiter in 1933 (p62 of 'Reflections in an Oval Mirror', also published by Ōzaru Books – see p243 of this current book)

CHAPTER 3: HOODENING AND CHRISTMAS IN THE THANET TOWNS AND PENINSULA

As will be observed, the practice of hoodening was confined solely to East Kent. Rather fortuitously, for the sake of organizing the text, the earliest printed references to the custom are derived from the far northeastern tip of the kingdom. This enables us to take an anticlockwise ramble starting at Ramsgate, through west Thanet, circumnavigating Canterbury across the Stour, and continuing to Deal and Walmer as we finish our journey. There is a suspicion that what took place in the towns of Margate, Ramsgate and Broadstairs was different from that which went on in the villages. But as we shall see, at least in the case of Margate, the tendency was for the hoodeners to come from the villages to the south of the town rather than the town itself.

Early References to Hoodening

The earliest direct reference to the hooden horse itself comes from 1807, and gives an excellent description of what took place, without actually saying who its participants were.

> ...At Ramsgate, in Kent, I found they begin the festivities of Christmas by a curious procession: a party of young people procure the head of a dead horse, which is affixed to a pole about four feet in length; a string is affixed to the lower jaw; a horse-cloth is also attached to the whole, under which one of the party gets, and by frequently pulling the string, keeps up a loud snapping noise, and is accompanied by the rest of the party, grotesquely habited, with hand-bells. They thus proceed from house to house, ringing their bells, and singing carols and songs. They are commonly gratified with beer and cake, or perhaps with money. This is called, provincially, a hodening, and the figure above described a Hoden, or Woden horse...It is, I find, general in Thanet on Christmas Eve, and, as far as I can learn, nowhere else.[42]

Percy Maylam made the comment that the anonymous author of this piece was 'clearly not a native of Kent' and did not speak from personal knowledge, since the whole passage began with the preface 'in a journey through Kent, I saw...' possibly indicating that he was just a visitor. Maylam also queried matters of detail, and thus its reliability. Firstly, the 'head of a dead horse' is noted, whereas the penchant in the region is for a wooden effigy to be used which, admittedly, is surmounted on a four-feet long pole. Why not the 'head' or at least a skull of a horse? Assuming either, the trick would then have to be for the jaws to be manipulated and maintained to ensure the 'loud snapping noise' that would be heard. The head of a decapitated horse would

---

[42]European Magazine, vol. 51, p358 (May 1807)

be impractical, and the use of a skull would depend on how many times the hinge on the jaw could be worked to make the resonance stated with effect before it all fell apart. In an effigy, this can largely be improvised by using wood alone for both top and bottom jaws, even to the extent of using hob nails in the jaws to enhance the sound and appearance of this key character. There is no reason why any one template for a hooden horse should preclude others from this appellation. Perhaps skulls were used by some parties; perhaps effigies by others. Other examples of a decorated horse's skull are used in Britain such as the Mari Lwyd in Wales and Old Ball in Cheshire. This, however, would neutralize the notion that the 'hooden' horse derived its name from being wooden.

Maylam supposed that the earliest evidence for the use of a wooden horse head was 1824 from oral evidence and the suggestion in the book Relics for the Curious published that year naming it a 'Hoden' or 'Wooden' horse. The 1807 account from the European Magazine is repeated virtually verbatim in eight other passages cited by Maylam, although one piece of local oral evidence may be gauged in the next paragraph.

This next earliest reference would have to be derived from a comment made by Percy Maylam's aunt Mrs Ann Lacy, that his 'great-aunt' told her she could recall seeing the beast in her lifetime. It is impossible to be sure of the identity of this great-aunt. The comment was made after 1838 when Ann Lacy moved to Ramsgate from her native Wealden farmhouse home at Ulcombe, and would recall a time in the first quarter of the nineteenth century.

> There is no doubt that within living memory the custom was practised throughout…the large towns such as Ramsgate and Margate, as well as the country districts. The custom has now quite died out in Ramsgate, and it is, perhaps, not strictly accurate to say it has been actually practised there within living memory, but rather that the recollection of its being practised there has not died out. My aunt, Mrs Lacy, who is now in her ninety-seventh year and who has lived in Ramsgate since 1838, tells me the custom was never practised in that town within her recollection. But she remembers being told by a great-aunt of mine of an incident which happened to the latter in Ramsgate when a girl. One Christmas Eve (probably in the twenties of the nineteenth century), the hooden horse put its head in the door in the usual way and, on her thrusting it out, the horse seized with its wooden jaws the packet of spice which she had in her hand and went off in triumph with the plunder. Mr George Chapman, one of the Borough Magistrates at Ramsgate, who has known the town well for over sixty years, tells me, though he has never seen the hooden horse there, yet he remembers hearing of it and he always understood that the custom had been stopped in Ramsgate by the authorities, owing to a woman being so frightened that she died. The custom would therefore appear to have died out in Ramsgate itself some time between 1807, the date of the account in the 'European Magazine' (or perhaps the earlier twenties) and 1838.[43]

---

[43]Maylam, p47

The Broadstairs Incident

The next incident of note is accurately pinpointed as Christmas Eve 1828. This event seemed to cause repercussions for the entire custom in perpetuity in what can be referred to as the 'Broadstairs Incident'. George Chapman, the Ramsgate magistrate has already alluded to it in the previous passage. John Mockett reported in 1836, that

> A very ancient custom prevails of men and boys being dressed up in various ways to amuse people at Christmas. It unfortunately happened this year (in 1828), that a man dressed in a bear skin met a young woman named Crow, the wife of John Crow, Broadstairs, and alarmed her so much that she was obliged to go to a friend's house to recover herself; and in returning home, she met the same man again, which so dreadfully alarmed her that she died the next day. A coroner's inquest was held on the occasion, and hand-bills circulated to prohibit such practice in the future.[44]

The 'man dressed in a bear skin' may well have been a person hiding in the shroud holding a hooden horse, which would tally magnificently with a similar occurrence, also in Broadstairs from around that time. Further corroborative evidence appeared in the local newspaper of the day, again repeating the notion that a 'bear' and not a hooden horse was involved. Neither the Mockett reference nor the following newspaper account state at what hour this visit was made, except to add that this was a second and later sortie in the day. But it seems reasonable to suppose that in an age without street-lighting, to somebody unfamiliar with the custom, that the hooden horse borne by such Christmas visitors from outside the town may have been mistaken for a bear.

> An inquest was held on Monday at the Albion Hotel, Broadstairs, before Matthew Kennett, esq., Mayor and Coroner for Dover and its liberties, on view of the body of Susanna Crow, a young married woman about 21 years of age, who came by her death under the following circumstances:- It appeared that the deceased was in a very advanced state of pregnancy, and by the evidence of Mr Ketchley, the surgeon, who examined her head after death, that she had received a severe contusion from a fall, occasioned by a fit of apoplexy which, from the evidence, seemed to have been accelerated by fright, occasioned through a party from Margate who paraded Broadstairs on Christmas Eve with music, and one of whom was habited as a bear in a dress of the most hideous description. The Jury, after some deliberation, returned a verdict of died in the visitation of God, accompanied by a strong expression of their detestation of such practice; and the Coroner, who had the young men consisting chiefly of apprentices before him, caused the dress to be given up, and stated that if any repetition took place, the offenders would be prosecuted.[45]

---

[44]John Mockett, Mockett's Journal, p125 (Canterbury: 1836)
[45]Kentish Gazette, 29 December 1828, p4

Perhaps Mockett was citing the newspaper account in part. Further evidence is circumstantial or compelling depending on one's point of view, since any written record relating to any by-law being passed no longer exists, and has since passed into Broadstairs tradition. This was noted by Charles J.H. Saunders, writing in the Bromley Record in 1890 about a period before 1840:

> During my residence in the Isle of Thanet for some years, I have frequently conversed with old residents on the subject, and gather from them that the custom was discontinued some fifty years since, in consequence of a woman at Broadstairs being so scared by it that her death resulted…[in consequence of which, regarding the later custom at Minster]… 'after the Magistrates cried it down, they were afraid to go out with the 'hodenhouse' (sic) for fear they should fall into the hands of the 'patrols' and 'borsholders'. These were the officers of the 'Court Leet', and probably acted as assistant Constables'.[46]

Although obviously 'set up', when the Star Inn in Margate Road, Westwood, just outside Broadstairs was reopened and renamed the 'Poor Ole Hooden Horse' in June 1997, a police constable (who also happened to be an organizer of the August folk festival) turned up to 'arrest' the new landlord for the sake of publicity. The journalist for the local newspaper noted that the tradition banning the custom was well-known in the town.[47]

Christmas at Ramsgate

Focusing once more on Ramsgate, the newspapers of the day give some idea as to the competition with which any hoodening party had to compete at Christmas. A typical example is quoted in 1866:

> Early in the morning came the ever memorable 'carol singers' who doubtless thought it a duty of theirs to remind all persons with whom they came into contact that 'Christmas comes but once a year', is of the fact was well-known to everyone of no matter what age. Following close upon their heels came parties of men playing fifes and drums. One more conspicuous than the rest we could not help noticing. The leader of this party (which consisted of five men, one playing a fife, a second a side drum, a third the triangle, the leader the drum, while the fifth went round collecting all the loose cash which the bystanders had to spare) was an individual who rejoices in the somewhat extraordinary soubriquet of 'Harlequin Billy.' The whole of this group was dressed in a most fantastic and grotesque manner, the leader being attired in a most peculiar combination of Life Guard and Lancer uniform. None of them appeared to have any very great ear for music, for while the fife player was attempting to 'murder' some popular tune of the day, the two drummers seemed to have an idea that it was their duty to perform a quite independent duet upon their respective instruments. The result was, as anyone could easily

---

[46]Charles J.H. Saunders, in the Bromley Record, 1 January 1890, p15
[47]Thanet Extra, 8 August 1997, p1 – in 2001, the pub had changed its name back to 'the Star' (but see also p148)

imagine, a most dreadful discord. Later in the day, we met a number of 'trawler boys', half of who were armed with whistles, and the remainder with tambourines. When we came in contact with this troup of serenaders, one portion of the whistlers were trying to get through the air of 'When Johnny Comes Marching Home' while the remainder were evidently attempting to perform the bass accompaniment upon instruments of precisely the same pitch as those upon [which] the air itself was being played.[48]

From this, we can see that there was a wide variety of music and musicians of diverse skill on the streets, including people in costume. Harlequin Billy is still there seven years later as being the head of a less formal music group.

...On Christmas Eve, the streets were thronged with all sorts of persons to listen to the bands of music and singing, from the Artillery Volunteer band down to 'Old Harlequin Billy's' tin-whistle serenaders. The 'trawler boys', as usual, indulged in a little horse play, but on the whole, there was not much to complain of.[49]

The 'horse-play' involved should not be interpreted as anything to do with hoodening, although the author is sorely tempted! The trawler boys or smack boys were apprentices to the Ramsgate fishing fleet, and comprised a charitable institution living at the Smack Boys' Home which was opened in 1881. These were young high-spirited people in their early teens that went out during the season basically to make a nuisance of themselves. They have their own story to tell and, by the turn of the century, had been taken in hand by philanthropic bodies and treated to a more formal Christmas celebration. On New Year's Eve 1877, we hear of 'the music of the 'Waits', the hand-bell ringers, the Artillery Band, and the Band of Hope fifes and drums' and 'one troupe dressed in Chinese fashion',[50] whilst on Christmas Eve, Christmas Day, and Boxing Day the following year, 'the most discordant noises with tambourines, tin whistles, triangles, etc. that was ever attempted to be called music' was made.[51]

In 1881, only handbells and carollers were to be heard in the quieter neighbourhoods of Ramsgate.[52] There is a hint that hoodening is extant in the town in 1882 as will be seen in this passage:

In Ramsgate, Kent and the Isle of Thanet, the custom styled 'hodening' kept long in vogue. The 'hoden' which appears to be a cross between the 'white horse' and the Klapperbock of the Germans, is accompanied by a number of youths in fantastic dress, who go round from door to door ringing bells and singing Christmas carols.[53]

---

[48]Kent Coast Times, 27 December 1866, p3
[49]Thanet Advertiser, 27 December 1873, p2
[50]Kent Coast Times, 3 January 1878, p3
[51]Thanet Advertiser, 28 December 1878, p2
[52]Kent Coast Times, 29 December 1881, p3
[53]Deal Chronicle & Dover Gazette, 23 December 1882, p3

The reference to a comparable German custom has already been mentioned in an earlier chapter, and the journalist from the Deal Chronicle could be guilty of using the original text to compile his own. However, it is evident that there was some party of costumed entertainers in the town at Christmas in 1884.

> ...The drummers, the Mummers, and the pipers, as usual, made a considerable amount of noise on Christmas Eve. These together with the waits and the carol singers were to be seen from sundown almost to cockcrow in the morning.[54]

It is tempting to read this reference to 'Mummers' to mean a resurgence of hoodening long after it had been thought to have become extinct, but it seems to stand alone when analysed with reports on contiguous Christmas celebrations in the town. In 1886, there was no reference to it:

> Christmas this year passed off as usual in Ramsgate. The Town Band and the St Lawrence Drum and Fife Band made their annual round of the town and neighbourhood; and there was a variety of 'Christmas waits' the 'singing' of some of them was received with mingled feelings in the small hours of the morning.[55]

There is also one more spurious piece of evidence from perhaps the late 1920s, as witnessed by an anonymous 'former resident' visiting the library of the English Folk Dance and Song Society in 1957:

> You will be interested to hear that I had a visit the other day from a man whom I think is the publishing manager for a firm of stationers. In the course of our conversation, I discovered that when he was a very small boy, he remembered seeing the hooden horse come out at Ramsgate (where he was born and brought up). Whether or not it was the Ramsgate horse, he could not tell, and in Maylam's book, it is apparent that the Ramsgate horse ceased to appear some time in the last century. This man, Mr R. Penny, 103 Sunnybank Road, Potters Bar, Middlesex, cannot be more than about forty, so there was a hooden horse out and about more recently that I for one had certainly thought.[56]

---

[54]Kent Coast Times, 1 January 1885, p2

[55]Kent Coast Times, 30 December 1886, p2

[56]Letter to Barnett Field, 24 May 1957 from the librarian, Vaughan Williams Library collection, LIB COLL/GRQ 20 HORSE/33. A copy of this letter was also sent to Alex Helm and is lodged with his collection at University College, London (vol. 19a, p364). After examining electoral registers, and births, marriages and deaths indexes, the author is satisfied that the person presenting themselves at the library either gave a false identity and/or a misleading story, since no one under the name Robert A. Penny seems to match anyone from the Thanet area. (I am indebted to Gordon Ridgewell for carrying out a search of electoral registers at the Hertfordshire Record Office).

Percy Maylam's evidence is difficult to interpret since he requotes the 1807 European Magazine citation at Ramsgate time and again with little qualification. However, in 1859, there is one more passage that specifically states that a carved wooden horse's head was used rather than a skull or dead horse's head.

[Ramsgate.] A curious custom used to prevail called 'going a hodening,' which consisted in singing carols, while a horse's head (hoden) carved in wood was carried in procession; to the songs were added the ringing of hand-bells, and the snapping of the jaws of the hobby.[57]

A contributor to the Kentish Note Book, using the pseudonym 'Invicta' wrote to George Howell in 1888, and surmised after reviewing the 1807 account, that

From enquiries, I find that this old custom has died out, at least in Ramsgate. As will be observed, mention is made of hand-bell ringing in these grotesque processions, and it is interesting to note that, to this day, there are several families residing in Ramsgate who are clever hand-bell ringers, and who have been for some generations back.[58]

Charles J.H. Saunders, who worked as a chemist and druggist in the St Lawrence High Street in Ramsgate, tried to resolve the matter in 1890 as to the custom from within living memory.

During my residence in the Isle of Thanet for some years, I have frequently conversed with old residents on the subject, and gather from them that the custom was discontinued some fifty years since, in consequence of a woman at Broadstairs being so scared by it that her death resulted. I cannot find that it was practised at all beyond the Isle of Thanet, so conclude that it was peculiar to this portion of the county of Kent. A natural horse's head was rarely hired owing to the difficulty in procuring one, but one carved from a wooden block was generally used as a substitute. The Company consisted of a man carrying the horse's head upon a short pole, and attired as you describe, one called the 'Jockey', one dressed as, and called the 'old woman', with a broom, two singers, and two stalwart attendants, who were useful in the case of a 'row'. The Jockey placed himself upon the back of the man carrying the horse's head, and it was the sport of the bystanders to remove him, if possible, from his mount. This led to some rough play, and it was frequently necessary to call the services of the 'stalwarts' into requisition. Many a bloody battle, they tell me, has been fought out at a 'Hodening'. The 'old woman' swept with the broom the feet of those who answered the knock at the door, and well chasing the girls was only induced to desist by a gift of money or

---

[57]Mackenzie Walcott, Guide to the Coast of Kent, p110 (Edward Stanford: 1859)
[58]George O. Howell (ed.), The Kentish Note Book, vol. 1, p19 (22 December 1888)

refreshments. The singers indulged the whole time, in carols formerly, but in combination of carols and songs latterly.[59]

Margate and its Environs

We must return to Percy Maylam to find out what other examples there were of hoodening in the Thanet towns. The earliest we hear is in 1832 from an unnamed author who evidently lived on the fringes of Margate town rather than in the town itself.

> …As an old resident of Margate,…I remember the hoodening horse as far back as 1832. Your description of it (from an article in Keble's Gazette) is right, but added to the party was a man dressed as a woman – 'Molly' with a birch broom sweeping the kitchen floor where they all come inside, with several men who played the violin and fife. I do not remember what other instruments. I do not think they went about the town but mostly in country and farm houses. We lived a short distance from the town, and we children, being home for our Christmas holiday, were much amused by the performance. They were regaled afterwards with beer. After them, bellringers would come and play some old-fashioned tunes such as 'Auld Lang Syne', and then lastly, some psalm singers would come and sing some beautiful hymn – the last one I remember well:
>
> *'All hail the power of Jesu's name,*
> *Let angels prostrate fall,*
> *Bring forth the royal diadem,*
> *And crown him Lord of all.*[60]

The next instance occurred on the southwestern fringes of Margate in 1855, possibly in the Garlinge district.

> As regards Margate, the custom probably lingered to a later period, and by chance I am able to fix a date at which it was actually practised at that place or at any rate the outskirts of the town. The late J. Meadows Cowper, to whom all Kent antiquarians are so much indebted, once informed me that on Boxing Day 1855, he walked from Faversham to Margate, and on reaching Margate, being both tired and hungry – he went into an inn (the name of which he did not remember) on the outskirts of the town for rest and refreshment, and while there a party with a hooden horse visited the inn.[61]

Job Barrett writing in Keble's Gazette at around the time Percy Maylam was using it to elicit information, gave information from another anonymous contributor, in the same year as Cowper's visit to the town.

---

[59]Charles J.H. Saunders, in the Bromley Record, 1 January 1890, p15
[60]Maylam, p49
[61]Maylam, p48

'A friend of mine has asked me to give him any information that I may have gleaned with regard to the custom of what he termed 'Hooden horse.' He says that as far back as 1855, the custom of carrying round a horse's head, made of wood and with moveable jaws, existed in Margate. The horse was accompanied by various musicians, who passed round the hat...[62]

Barrett evidently knew of the custom, but very little about it and was thankful to his readers for enlightening him further:

'...From information I have received (that's good enough for the Police Court) the custom of 'Hoodening; or taking round the 'Hooden Horse', on Christmas Eve was an annual one in the villages in Thanet half a century ago...I have heard of three horses' heads which still survive the ravages of time; one in Acol, another at Mutrix, and a third at Northdown...[63]

Barrett fails to identify his sources, which would have been intriguing had he done so. Let us speculate on the nature of those at Mutrix and Northdown, since Acol is one of the villages in west Thanet I shall refer to in the next chapter. Mutrix Farm was a market garden situated at Garlinge, on the edge of the conurbation between Westgate-on-Sea and Margate itself. At the time of the hoodening, its owners were John Bushell and his mother. Northdown was owned by Margate magistrate James Taddy Friend, although his obituary fails to recall his feats as an agriculturist. The farm estate was situated on the southeastern perimeter of Margate on the road out towards Ramsgate, and its management delegated to his bailiff Edmund Sidney Linington. Linington was the son of a farming family from the Isle of Wight, and his successes led to being given the responsibility with other farms in the area, including that of the Quex Park Farm estate at Birchington. That said, it is to be supposed that Messrs Bushell and Linington were familiar with the goings-on practised by the hoodeners, although it is unlikely they took part themselves beyond that of being a sponsor by force of circumstance.

Maylam also extracted evidence from a Mrs Edward Tomlin of Cranbrook. As a young girl, she was Alice deVaynes and lived at Updown, just outside Margate in the mid-1850s. She could recall the hooden horse being brought by farm hands to the house at Christmas time. This occurred as far back in time as she could remember, the last visit made at that place being 1865. It appears that some words of introduction were used when the horse arrived, but what they were, she could not remember. It was also said that in the deVaynes household, the hooden horse was 'supposed to be keeping up the tradition of the wooden horse celebrated in the Siege of Troy.'[64] What is meant by this is unclear. Obviously, this cannot be a direct comparison with the concealment of a platoon of Grecian foot soldiers within a giant effigy. The operator is certainly hidden, but only in that way may any alignment to classical mythology be deduced.

---

[62]Job P. Barrett, in Keble's Margate & Ramsgate Gazette, 16 November 1907, p2
[63]Keble's Margate & Ramsgate Gazette, 7 December 1907, p2
[64]Maylam, p49

CHAPTER 4: HOODENING IN THE WEST THANET VILLAGES

One of the best descriptions of hoodening arose because Percy Maylam witnessed the event during his boyhood. Also, the fact that three one-time performers were identified when the custom was revived at St Nicholas-at-Wade in 1966. Most of the latter part of this chapter is given over to the consequences of this, although we shall then make comparisons with the custom elsewhere in the Thanet villages (especially Minster), then preface it with Maylam's observations in general.

Percy Maylam at Monkton

What better place is there to start when looking for an eyewitness account of the hooden horse and its practitioners, than with Percy Maylam himself, who stayed with his uncle Francis de Berckem Collard at Gore Street Farm, Monkton, during the Christmas period from 1888 to 1892. Gore Street Farm today is situated on the main road between Ramsgate and Canterbury to the west of Monkton village itself which has itself been by-passed. On standing beside this road waiting to cross, you are taken with the sight of the flat landscape and open plan cauliflower fields littering it, across which you can see the prominent church tower and self-contained village of St Nicholas-at-Wade itself under a mile away. Maylam comments:

Anyone who has spent a Christmas in a farmhouse in Thanet – it has been my good fortune to spend five – will not forget Christmas Eve. When seated round the fire, one hears the banging of gates and trampling of feet on the gravel paths outside (or, if the weather be unseasonable, the more cheerful crunching of crisp snow), and the sound of loud clapping. Everyone springs up, saying, "The hoodeners have come, let us go and see the fun." The front door is flung open, and there they all are outside: the 'Wagoner' cracking his whip and leading the Horse (the man who plays this part is called the 'Hoodener'), which assumes a most restive manner, champing his teeth, and rearing and plunging, and doing his best to unseat the 'Rider', who tries to mount him, while the 'Wagoner' shouts out 'Whoa!' and snatches at the bridle. 'Mollie' is also there! 'She' is a lad dressed up in woman's clothes and vigorously sweeps the ground behind the horse with a birch broom. There are generally two or three other performers besides, who play the concertina, tambourine or instruments of that kind. This performance goes on for some time, and such of the spectators as wish to do so, try to mount and ride the horse, but with poor success. All sorts of antics take place: Mollie has been known to stand on her head, exhibiting nothing more alarming in the way of lingerie than a pair of hobnail boots with the appropriate setting or corduroy trousers. Beer and largesse are dispensed and the performers go further. Singing of carols is not usually a part of the performance and no set words are spoken. In Thanet, occasionally, but not always, the performers, or some of them, blacken their faces. Years ago, smock frocks were the regulation dress of the party.

In a house which possesses a large hall, the performers are often invited inside. At times the horse uses little ceremony, and opening the door, walks in uninvited. In the bright light indoors, the performance, though the cause of much amusement, is deprived of all illusions. The crude make-up of the horse is glaringly apparent and we recognize the performers plainly, as the Bill and or Tom of everyday life, who look after the horses. Without doubt, the hooders are seen at their best outdoors – in the court or on the lawn of some old farmhouse. For the eyes of the spectators coming fresh from the light inside, take in only an impressionist picture of the scene. And the horse in the dim winter's night, made even more distinct by occasional cross rays of flickering light from the windows, becomes a monster of weird and awesome possibilities. And the stranger to the custom, who sees it thus for the first time, may well feel he is beholding the mutilated remnant of some pageant of the past – lost to us save so far as these few relics have remained fixed in the traditions of the countryside.

Good old hooden horse, the possible frightener of children and to those no longer children the bringer-back of memories of happy frights when once they were. "Is the hooden horse coming round?" is the first enquiry of the exile on his return home for Christmas after years of absence.[65]

How much of that text is taken from memory without further embellishment is open to conjecture. Maylam leaves little to the imagination. He has only mentioned in passing who the hooders actually were and where they worked. We could surmise who the audience might have been at this impromptu performance: Percy Maylam was 24 years old at the time. One assumes that his mother and father were present, and certainly his aunt and uncle with whom they were staying, There is every chance that his cousins Ambrose and Frank might have been staying, his sister Elizabeth and brother Clark, although we are not considering young families in either case. To round the Collard household off, there were also two servants: the sisters Ann and Mary Bennett.

Intriguingly, we have an independent account of what took place from the standpoint of the local vicar, although Maylam takes him to task on not exploring further.

The Rev. H. Bennett Smith, vicar of St Nicholas-at-Wade, the adjoining parish to Monkton, wrote as follows in 1876: "I made enquiry of an old retired farmer in my parish, as to the custom called Hoodning (sic). He tells me that formerly, the farmer used to send annually round the neighbourhood the best horse under the charge of the wagoner, and that afterwards instead, a man used to represent the horse, being supplied with a tail, and with a wooden [pronounced ooden or hooden] figure of a horse's head, and plenty of horse hair for a mane. The horse's head was fitted with hobnails for teeth;

---

[65]Maylam, p2

the mouth being made to open by means of a string, and in closing made a loud crack. The custom has long since ceased."[66]

Of course, the custom hadn't ceased, and Maylam is scathing in the imbumbent's lack of scholarship in not pursuing this further than the one possible expert in the matter, to whit, the unidentified retired farmer mentioned.

'Sometimes it is difficult to comment on inaccuracies in a courteous manner. There is a hooden horse at St Nicholas-at-Wade to this present day, it went round this very last Christmas (1908), and there is ample evidence that the custom has been regularly carried on in that district as far back as living memory goes. I have spoken to men who can speak from personal knowledge of the early forties of the last century and of tradition behind that. I saw it myself at Monkton, the very year the Dictionary was published. Perhaps the 'old retired farmer' was a curmudgeon (though there are not many in the Island) and the hoodeners may have feared a pail of cold water from the first floor window in return for their performance, instead of the customary oblation, and on that account they may never have visited him…'[67]

The names of any of the team members seen by Maylam are unknown. However, it is interesting to note that Collard's neighbours were the Sladden family. Circumstantial evidence, as we shall see, directs us to believe that George Goodson took Edwin Sladden with him when he moved from Cleve Court Farm in Acol to Felderland in Worth. Could it be that the Sladden family were part of Maylam's first hoodening party? Coincidence, or what?

The Hale Farm Hoodeners, 1905

But, Percy Maylam's interest was on a purely qualitative level, and with the technology available to him in the first decade of the twentieth century, he also wanted to illustrate his work amply. As we shall see in this next passage, his eye for detail was such, that when the time came for taking photographs using ambient lighting with an appropriate rural backdrop (at Bolingbroke Farm, Sarre), he couldn't find a besom broom for the character known as Mollie.

I had for some years been wishing to have a group of hoodeners photographed, but the difficulty of doing so at Christmas time…was very great. The company (to be photographed) ultimately appeared, they were men employed with the horses on Hale Farm, St Nicholas-at-Wade. (There was) nothing so ancient as a birch broom (in the yard where the photographing took place, and) it was impossible for Mollie to sweep with a bass broom. One of the musicians is armed with a tambourine, next comes Mollie, unfortunately without her broom (which was even in course of manufacture), then the Horse with the Rider standing behind, while the Wagoner is holding

---

[66]Parish & Shaw's Dictionary of the Kentish Dialect (1888) citing the Rev. Bennett Smith's treatise
[67]Maylam, p23

the halter in his left hand and the whip in his right. The group was completed by the concertina player.'

Maylam further noted that the 'rider' wore a military outfit of khaki that clearly belonged to the post-Boer War period, and 'certainly had nothing to do with our pagan ancestors.'[68] In fact, in Maylam's photographs, all but the musician are costumed. The wagoner is wearing a black top hat and long dark coat. The rig of the rider has already been noted, omitting only the detail that he is also wearing some kind of peaked cap. Moll is wearing a long dark dress and bonnet and, for the purposes of the photo-shoot as holding a triangle. The character on the left-hand side holds a tambourine, and is wearing a black top hat. He is further clothed in a patterned suit that may be best described as some kind of floral design – although Ben Jones prefers to interpret this as pyjamas!

The Hale Farm party posing for Percy Maylam at Sarre in 1905

Olive Brockman (then aged 11) guessed some 73 years later that the wagoner might be a Trice, the Hoodener or the Musician with the top hat might be Walt Patterson, and the Boy might be Gibbs. Edmund Trice told Tristan Jones that the horse was made by Arthur 'Chuck' or 'Chip' Bolton, who might also be one of those pictured.

Thanks to the memories of elderly people living in St Nicholas-at-Wade following the revival of the custom in 1966, we can identify three of the people photographed by Maylam, but sadly not the identities of the hoodening gangs he saw during his

---

[68]Maylam, p2

Monkton Christmases. We cannot definitely say whether they came from Monkton itself, over the fields from St Nicholas, down the road from Minster, or even served on the same farm, nor even whether they were hired hands or permanent workers there.

There is no proof of any kind of unbroken tradition between the hoodeners regularly seen at Monkton, the newspaper reports at Minster, the Hale Farm group photographed by Maylam in 1905, or the extant team who did their rounds before and after the First World War. The best-known example of hoodening in the Thanet villages comes from St Nicholas-at-Wade, of course, thanks to the intervention of Maylam. It might have been thought that he might conduct an interview with one or more of the team he met at Bolingbroke Farm, Sarre, around the time of the photo session. What evidence he gathered seems to be minimal. He deduced that the team assembled was the one and only 'hooden horse party in the Isle of Thanet, that it to say, the one belonging to Hale Farm, St Nicholas-at-Wade...This horse still does Sarre, Birchington and St Nicholas at Christmas.'[69] In identifying the members of the team from the first three plates in *The Hooden Horse*, elderly villagers from St Nicholas recalled some of the people posing in the photographs. One elder statesman was Mr Bert Smith (1882-1979), who could remember hoodeners coming to Nether Hale when he was a boy in the eighties or and/or nineties, but not who they were. In 1978, Tristan Jones interviewed Olive Brockman (1894-1979) who was 11 years of age when the photographs were taken, who was able to identify two of the people pictured in Maylam's plates, thus:

> Plate A, the man on the extreme left was Walt Patterson of Hale farm; the youngster behind the horse was Gibbs. Plate B, the man of the extreme right might be a Trice. Man in Plate C was Walt Patterson.[70]

Edmund Trice said once that his horse (used in the 1966 revival) was made by Arthur Bolton, and this specimen is quite clearly that used in 1905. Bolton is listed in the 1891 Census as a single labourer living at Upper Hale farm and it is thus possible, but by no means definite that he was one of the other hoodeners in the photograph. Without further adjudication, we shall never know.

An independent account of the St Nicholas hoodeners is reported by Maylam from an account written in 1907 by Alfred Loft, the publican at the Crown at Sarre:

> Mr Alfred Loft of the Crown Inn, Sarre, Thanet, writes: "...With regard to your allusion to the old Christmas custom of Hodening, I am able to inform you that it is still carried out in its entirety at this old-world village of Sarre. I had several visitors from London staying here last Christmas, and very much to their surprise and amusement, the 'Hodeners' made their appearance, and

---

[69]Maylam, p43
[70]Anneli Jones,'The Changing Face of St Nicholas-at-Wade', p58 (St Nicholas: 1978)

regaled us with a selection of old country songs. The general 'get-up' of the troupe was much as you have described."[71]

Minster and other Thanet Villages

At least Maylam went to lengths to broaden the geographical locus of the custom from literary and oral sources. So far as the Isle of Thanet villages are concerned, this note was included from a letter by Charles Saunders of St Lawrence, dated 16 December 1889 and published in the Kentish Note Book:

'In Hone's Every Day Book, published in 1827, is mentioned the custom as appertaining to Ramsgate chiefly, but also in the Isle of Thanet. All the neighbouring villages, St Peter's, St Lawrence, Minster, St Nicholas, Acol, Monkton, and Birchington, I find observed it, but an old resident informed me that Minster was the 'headest and toppingest' for it.'[72]

Saunders lived in the St Lawrence High Street in Ramsgate, working as a chemist and druggist, and was described as an antiquary in his obituary.[73] He obviously knew a thing or two about local customs, having tentatively identified eight possibly different groups of hooteners from his own knowledge. It must be commented that Minster, St Nicholas, Acol, Monkton, Birchington and Minster are clustered together sufficiently for the author possibly to misidentify one party seen on different occasions as a separate group without knowing better. He also knew of the 1828 incident at Broadstairs when Susanna Crow was literally frightened to death upon seeing the bear (or hooden horse) described in the previous chapter (see p40). Certainly, there are more independent accounts of the custom in the Birchington area late in the nineteenth century, as we hear from the journalist Job Barrett, who rejoiced in the pen-name of John Pharos for Keble's Gazette.

…All that I know of it (the hooden horse custom) is that at Christmas 1881, I saw the custom carried out at Birchington. I am under the impression that the performers came from the 'shires', that is from outside Thanet, and I have never seen it since.[74]

The same author acted as a medium for Maylam in gathering information after a request made in this newspaper. Evidently, Barrett became familiar as to the nature of the custom very quickly – thanks to his readers who enlightened him further.

Barrett then went on to give an excellent account contributed by Thomas Bush Whitehead (1840-1936) who, thanks to his longevity was given an extended obituary upon his death, providing a few more clues as to his credentials as a witness. He was born at a farmhouse in Canterbury Road, the son of a farm labourer who worked for

---

[71]J. Harris Stone, Common Objects of the Seashore at Ramsgate in Health Resort, p20 (1907)

[72]George O. Howell (ed.), The Kentish Note Book, vol. 1, p320 (26 April 1890), quoting a letter from Charles J.H. Saunders of St Lawrence, 16 December 1889

[73]East Kent Times, 16 August 1905, p5

[74]Job P. Barrett, in Keble's Margate & Ramsgate Gazette, 16 November 1907, p2

Edward Neame. After receiving an elementary education, he became 'an assistant to a farm labourer, it being the practice of labourers to employ boys on 'piece-work'. Before he was 15 years old, he went in a full-time capacity to a Birchington farm and was afterwards at Chamber's Wall Farm, St Nicholas.' He didn't stay long in the job, and shortly afterwards went away to sea.[75] From this we learn that before leaving Birchington, he became familiar with the 'extramural' practices of a farm labourer in the mid-1850s. It is nowhere suggested that he took part in hoodening himself, although it is known from later evidence that Chamber's Wall Farm was one venue visited by local parties in pursuit of largesse. Barrett writes:

> I am indebted to Mr Whitehead of Margate (a native of Birchington) for a very clear description of the 'Hooden horse' party. About the year 1855, he recollects having seen as many as three parties on a Christmas Eve in Birchington. Each party came from one of the neighbouring farmhouses, where farm servants were hired for the year and lodged on the premises. Five men formed a party, and they had no musical instruments. One man was the groom, who held the bridle. The second was the horse, he was in a stooping position, covered with a cloth, and he wore then horse's head, with a stick attached; and third was slim youth, to represent the jockey. The fourth was dressed as an old woman, who carried a broom; and the fifth collected the 'oof, sometimes in a tinder box. The party sang a country song, and then knocked at the door. On opening the door, the scene that presented itself was a prancing horse, opening and closing its jaws with a loud snapping noise, the groom shouting 'whoa,' the jockey attempting to mount, the old lady busy sweeping and the collector looking on. If invited into the kitchen, the acting would be continued there, when, of course, the success depended much upon the ability of the various performers, who, at least, amused the little folks.'

Not surprisingly perhaps, all the Thanet newspapers focused more on Ramsgate and Margate news, with only occasional comment from a reporter in one of the villages. The largest of these was Minster in Thanet (to distinguish it from its Sheppey namesake). In fact, Percy Maylam commented on the custom at Minster during the 1860s in his discourse, omitting to cite how the practice developed over the years, not having the full scope of newspapers of the day available to him at the time. A typical account would describe Christmas Day at the workhouse, or the distributions from the Mary Belsey charity (from 1861 onwards, now seemingly defunct) which gave one guinea each to four of the oldest men and four of the oldest women in Thanet. Anything else reported (e.g. that of a hoodening) was a bonus in the parish news of the day. The earliest useful account to illustrate this goes back to a Deal newspaper describing Christmas Day 1862 in the village, presumably to portray the musical progress of the church choir in pursuit of the high ideals sponsored by church improvement groups (such as the Oxford Movement) in the provinces.

> Our usual quiet village was enlivened at a very early hour on Christmas morning. Mr Barnes, the organist, with the men and the boys of our choir,

---

[75]Isle of Thanet Gazette, 2 January 1938, p8

gave the inhabitants such a treat that they could not easily forget. So unlike the carol singing which is prevalent nowadays throughout this country, the pieces (Eldon's 'Nunc Dimittis' and Kent's 'Song O Heavens', and several others equally appropriate) were such as plainly showed that Mr Barnes must have no ordinary skill and perseverance to have enabled the choir to perform them with such accuracy and taste as we heard them. This is the first attempt of anything of the kind, and as the only object was to give the people a little musical treat while they were enjoying a comfortable snooze, we hope that having gained their object so creditably, that the choir will feel their services appreciated, and for the future pursue the course they have now begun.[76]

The first mention of a hooden horse at Minster in the local newspapers came two years later, although by then, the custom was evidently well-established:

…On Christmas Eve, we had the merry old church bells pealing forth the glad tidings. The band enlivened the streets; hooded horses not hooded quite up to the old style, perambulated the streets, and the carol singers 'in' tune and others 'out' of tune were very numerous.[77]

The fact that the appearance of the hooden horse was not guaranteed is evident two years later, when we hear

Christmas Eve, or rather Saturday night, was as usual enlivened by the numerous troupes of carol-singers, hand-bell ringers, &c. The church bells tolled out their joyful sounds and the place was quite alive, but we missed the 'wooden horse' for the first time; probably this animal is now among the extinct species. The juvenile band, directed by Master Swinerd was out on Tuesday, and was much admired.[78]

Perhaps the clause that the journalist had 'missed the wooden horse' could be reinterpreted that the hooden horse wasn't seen by the reporter because he was out elsewhere on his rounds. If this horse was parochial to Minster itself, there is no reason to suppose that its supporters and performers had not yet arrived in the village centre to enrich his experience. 'Hoodeners' of sorts were there in 1866, but not apparently with the horse.

…Our 'Hoodeners' on Christmas Eve did not infuse much new music into their 'waits'. The old hooden horse seems now lost among other extinct animals. The hand, or rather horse bells were more out of tune and contained

[76]Deal, Walmer & Sandwich Telegram, 3 January 1863, p4
[77]Thanet Advertiser, 31 December 1864, p3
[78]Kentish Observer, 4 January 1866, p6

larger cracks than usual, excepting one set who performed their ringing very well...[79]

In 1867, the horse is definitely present and, judging by the comments made, sounded as though he had never been away!

Christmas has been and gone again, with its varied pleasures and happy meetings. Our merry old church bells, which have probably never failed to give out the good tidings since their tongues were placed in them, about the year 1620 – that Christmas was at hand, have not failed in pouring forth their homely sounds, only fully appreciated by sensitive minds. Hoodening was also the order of the evening on Christmas Eve, and although there are but few things without exceptions, we fear carolling does not improve and the jingling noise called hand-bell ringing was fearful. The hooden horse we thought, was as extinct as the megatherium, but there was one that came again to see how the world was jogging on. The darkies performed their parts very well, and one or two sets of carol singers put one in mind of the days of yore...[80]

The 'darkies' here, in our politically-correct age, are buskers who blacked their faces using burnt cork, who went out rendering the Christy Minstrel songs which were very popular at that time. In any case, this is the penultimate citation, for the hooden horse that did the rounds at Minster in 1868 evidently did not meet with the approval of the writer, although one wonders what he expected on the occasion. Perhaps the hoodener had no shroud or cover with which to disguise himself, shedding himself of any air of mystery, or perhaps the horse wasn't adorned with brasses or ribbons that the journalist had come to expect. He commented:

The Christmas of 1868 with its pleasures has come and gone as other Christmasses have....Carolling has become very lean, even the 'darkies' grow smaller by degrees. There was an apology for a hooden horse going his rounds, but the singers and actors attending him must have affected his constitution, as he was but a skeleton. The handbells have lost their tone of old, and the singers go out without much practice.[81]

Beyond this date, there is a change in the way 'hoodening' at Minster was reported. The horse is never cited. There is even a hint that the practice is confused with the 'waits' or carolling – although some authorities deem hoodening and carolling synonymous, with or without the use of a horse. In 1871, we hear that

[79]Thanet Advertiser, 29 December 1866, p3
[80]Kentish Gazette, 7 January 1868, p4
[81]Thanet Advertiser, 2 January 1869, p3

...The old customs have been adhered to this Christmas, but 'hoodening' has degenerated, and the carol singing also, so that Christmas Eve serenading is not a thing to be enjoyed...[82]

The above notion is reinforced by the report of Christmas in Minster during the following year.

...There is not much to record in the keeping of Christmas here, only the carol singing, or what was by some called 'hoodening' by others the 'waits' becomes worse every year...[83]

The very last citation for the Minster hooden horse was during Christmas 1875, where the words 'almost extinct' are ample evidence of his survival, however tenuous.

Christmas has been and passed away again without affecting much change in our village customs. The hooden horse, almost extinct here, but still in existence in the neighbouring villages, was trotted out...[84]

It is a pity, of course, that we are not told which of these 'neighbouring villages' had the custom at this time. However, something could be said to be taking place the following year although what the terms 'discordant comicals' exactly meant is confusing – was some kind of dramatic performance involved, or was it a reference to their singing?

Christmas was kept as of yore...The waits or 'hoodeners' fell short of days gone by when serenaders with their Christmas carols sung appropriate songs for the season; it is now degenerated into discordant comicals.[85]

Reiterating the possible confusion in terminology between that of hoodening and the 'waits', one is left wondering whether singing was somehow expected in the role of the hoodener and any other addendum to performance was a bonus, as we hear for the report in Christmas 1877.

The customs of Christmas Eve have been adhered to pretty much in the old fashion, except the 'Hoodeners' or 'Waits', the charms of which deteriorated yearly. The singers don't give any sounds to indicate any rehearsals of their places...[86]

*...And that was it for the tradition. Nothing is heard for another two years, and then the custom or customs are placed in some kind of retrospective.

---

[82]Thanet Advertiser, 30 December 1871, p3
[83]Thanet Advertiser, 28 December 1872, p3
[84]Thanet Advertiser, 1 January 1876, p3
[85]Thanet Advertiser, 30 December 1876, p3
[86]Thanet Advertiser, 28 December 1877, p3

The Christmas customs are gradually dying out. Carol singing and the hooden horse must be placed as extinct...[87]

There is nothing like the demise of a perished calendar custom to make the journalist long for the good old days. When hoodening was revived in 1882, only three years later, there was almost a whiff of nostalgia in the air.

A novel and highly commendable way of 'Hoodening' was started here on Christmas Eve. Three young men took a turn of singing at the principal houses in the village and were rewarded for their talents by getting paid 18s. 6d. which they handed over to a respectable man here, who has for some time past been very ill, and consequently in straitened circumstances. The wife of the sick man received the amount very gratefully. The success of the young men, we hope, will induce them to some day make a similar effort.[88]

There is one other account that was written retrospectively in 1959 by a Mildred Ellen 'aged 86' in a letter to the Kent Messenger:

...Now living at Orchard Bungalow, Littlebourne, she remembers that her father had a hooden horse of his own when living in Minster, Isle of Thanet. Later he moved to Bekesbourne, "and...he kept his horse in a shed, but it was never used in my time. I have never forgotten how terrified I was of the terrible looking animal with its great clapper jaws and head all decked with gay ribbons, etc....My father used to love to tell us tales of how he and his friends used to go around on festive occasions with it, dancing and singing and getting quite a big sum of money to share out" – especially, it seems, at Christmas time.[89]

The father spoken of was Richard Kemp who was born in Bridge in 1847. None of the census returns between 1851 and 1871 list him as resident in Minster, and by 1881 he took up his residence at Bekesbourne. His eldest child was born in Sheerness in 1873, so it can be assumed that he was in his twenties when he went a-hoodening at Minster at some time in the 1860s: well within the timespan suggested by the local newspapers.

The only other Thanet village that Percy Maylam mentioned at any great length was Acol, which is barely two miles north of Minster itself on the road out towards Birchington. One tantalizing newspaper snippet of the custom at Minster itself could be extrapolated from a report emanating from Christmas 1890:

---

[87]Thanet Advertiser, 3 January 1880, p3
[88]Pullen's Kent Argus, 30 December 1882, p3
[89]Mildred Ellen, letter to the Kent Messenger (Canterbury Telegraph edition), 18 September 1959, p11

On Christmas Eve, the village was enlivened by a peal of bells, by tunes on the handbells, and by one amusing party from Acol and adjoining places, who paraded the streets in quaint costumes…[90]

So, who were their quaintly-dressed performers? Let us hear what Maylam himself had to say:

The men on George Goodson's farm at Fenland (Felderland), Worth near Sandwich, have a horse which, at the proper season now goes round the district. This horse is, however, not a native of Worth, but as Mr Goodson explains, it was 'bred at Cleve.' That is to say, it was originally made by one of the farm men who were with him at Cleve (Monkton, Thanet). Mr Goodson went to Worth at Michaelmas 1899, and about four years ago, this horse came into the possession of one of his men who had gone with him from Cleve to Worth, and since then it has been brought out regularly every Christmas. To survive such a transplanting shows the old custom still has vitality, the vigour of this particular beast was shown to me by accident; the presence of a hooden horse at Woodnesborough was reported to me shortly after Christmas 1908. I knew of none in that parish and enquiries proved that it was the Worth horse which had taken in Woodnesborough on its round. So far as I can ascertain, this horse, when at Acol, used to visit Minster and was the last one to do so.[91]

In fact, the location concerned was Cleve Court Farm on the road between Acol and Minster. Circumstantially, George Goodson, who originally came from Preston-next-Wingham, took up residence at Cleve Court during the 1890s before moving on to Felderland Farm near Worth in 1899. The implication is that he took the horsemen who oversaw the hooden horse custom with him, and they continued it in the vicinity. As we may see in the next chapter, there was latitude for confusion between them and Elbridge Bowles's team from Deal if Sandwich or Eastry were to be included on the Felderland horse's rounds. The fact that Maylam fails to cite Sandwich and Eastry as venues for the Felderland horse, would seem to indicate that territory may have been observed should the local teams be aware of one another's presence. Beyond speculation, we shall never know.

It is tempting to speculate who these horsemen were that Goodson brought to Felderland with him. One clue may be supplied in his obituary that lists the mourners and their floral tributes. Two 'old employees' are thus credited. One of these was a Mr Sladden, namely Edwin Sladden who, at the time of the 1881 Census, worked as an agricultural labourer for Francis de Berckem Collard of Gore Street Farm, Monkton, i.e. Maylam's uncle. Edwin Sladden's name also appears on Electoral Registers for Acol in 1900 and for Worth in 1906, as does a John Smith who, one assumes, also went to Felderland with Goodson.

That might be all to be said on the matter, but for the fact that when Ben Jones placed an advertisement in the Birchington Forum newsletter in November 2001

---

[90]Pullen's Kent Argus, 27 December 1890, p8
[91]Maylam, p44

asking whether anyone had memories or knew of hoodening during the early twentieth century, he had two replies. One of these came from the musician Phil Martin of Minster who recalled stories of Steve 'Mouser' Terry of Birchington, who earned his nickname by biting the heads off mice for a dare! He had the reputation of being a local hell-raiser, and was said to have fronted a gang calling themselves the Birchington Hoodeners most likely during the 1890s. Little more is known of the gang, and the story seems to derive from the barber's shop banter of local hairdresser Vic Holton.

Another came from Mrs Violet Phillpott, the daughter of William Castle who once lived in Acol and worked at Quex Park Farm. She recalled her father describing the custom to her in the context of the 1954 revival by the Evening Townswomen's Guild of which she was a member. Fortunately, the Thanet Advertiser described the whole event in full under the heading 'Old Custom Revived' relating to a revival that took place in 1922:

> The Yuletide amenities at Birchington were added to this year by the revival on Christmas Eve of the old English custom of trotting out the hooding horse. The equine role was filled by Mr C. Denne, jun., Mr Doddington Port acted as captain of the party, and he was accompanied by Messrs. Leonard Harris and W. Castle, who were the necessary musicians. After perambulating the village and giving delight to the juvenile population especially, the horse paid a state visit to the Beresford Hotel in the evening, doing a round of the tables. The diners entered thoroughly into the spirit of the occasion. On Boxing Day, the horse and its attendants performed in the Square, and made a collection on behalf of the Fire Brigade funds.[92]

No further report is made for any successive year, except in 1925 which repeats the entire paragraph appended to a report about hoodening in Ramsgate throughout the nineteenth century which has already been outlined. Mrs Phillpott further recalled that a Mr Burton also took part, although this claim is refuted by Len Harris's granddaughter, Mrs Mary Chidwick. John Downes Port (1847-1929) worked variously as miller's carter at the time of the 1881 Census and later as a gardener at Quex Park. William Frederick Castle (1875-1942) also worked at Quex, as did Harris's next-door neighbour William Edward Burton (1875-1956). The junior member of the team was Charles Denne (1904-1988) whose father worked at the mill.

Seemingly, the leader of the troupe was Len Harris (1883-1958). He worked at Quex Park as a driver, taking skins to London for taxidermy as part of the Powell-Cotton collection for which the house is a visitor attraction. It is known that he kept the horse 'in the cupboard under the stairs' at his house in Park View because a young Mary Chidwick (born 1933) was 'really scared' to go there. The horse, pictured in photographs, is rather ornate in its carving compared to the archetypal horse, being reminiscent of a fairground galloper, although it was made so that its bottom jaw could open and shut in the traditional manner. Whilst most of the team could be described as Birchington born and bred, this does not appear to have been the case with Burton who moved to the district in 1908 from the East End of London.

---

[92]Thanet Advertiser, 30 December 1922, p2

Len Harris's Acol horse and party, September 1945

Another account to be considered came from the pen of local archaeologist Miss Mary Abbott (1859-1931) writing from her home in Canterbury:

In reading the article in last month's Occult Review on Radnorshire legends, I was reminded of…the old custom of the Hodening or Hooden Horse in Thanet. The 'hooden horse' is a model of a horse's head, with a movable lower jaw studded with large brass-headed nails. The one I saw was black, decorated with brass trappings and red ribbons, the man carrying it being covered by a black cloth. The lower jaw was worked by a string, so that the teeth clap together. It was taken round at Christmas time, accompanied by several men dressed in different costumes, but one was always dressed up as a woman with a broom, who would sweep the steps of the houses they were singing at.[93]

Miss Abbott was no more definite in defining either location or timespan when this occurred. In 1881, she lived at Harbledown, and there is no evidence that she was ever anything more than just a Christmas visitor to (presumably) western Thanet. The description of the horse is consistent with that of the Trice brothers' horse, of which more later. Today, a hessian shroud is used, as opposed to the black cloth described. Interesting too is the mention of singing as part of their mode of performance.

But the story continues with two more interesting discoveries made in 2002. The first was that of a rustically-hewn hooden horse when clearing out the estate of a Mr Hope in Lincolnshire – significant in that the sackcloth hood bore the stencilling

---

[93]Mary Abbott, letter to Occult Review, vol. 34, no. 4 (October 1921) p234

'William Gardner, Birchington' upon it. Gardner operated an agricultural and corn merchant's business between 1908 until his death in 1956, and the vintage of this horse could come from the same period as Len Harris's Acol horse – which is clearly different. We cannot explain its migration over a hundred miles northward, and there is a disclaimer by Mr Hope's daughter that it 'might have been made' by her father, who was 'interested in folklore'.

Mary Chidwick on Len Harris's Acol horse, 1953

The photographs of Mrs Chidwick's grandfather's horse used at the V-J (Victory in Japan) celebrations in September 1945 show a completely different horse to that discovered in Lincolnshire, so we are certain the two are not one and the same. This latter event was not a 'hoodening' as such; rather the case that a party led by a pseudonymous 'Mr Ralph with his 'houdling horse' who took part in a fancy-dress parade. The photograph shown is misleading since it comprises many of those competing in the inevitable competition. In fact, only Len Harris (second from the left), the man in the horse, and the anonymous bearded gentleman smoking a pipe were confirmed as taking part – although Mary Chidwick thought that the accordion player, 11-year-old John Swannack from Hackthorn Farm at nearby Woodchurch, was also part of the gang. The horse was later used again in a fancy-dress competition at the 1953 Coronation celebrations when Mary Chidwick played the part of Roy Rogers mounting 'Trigger'.[94]

The Trice Family of St Nicholas-at-Wade

What could be construed as surprising is the thought that there may have been no relation between Maylam's Hale Farm team in 1905, and that led by the Trice brothers that had established itself shortly after Maylam's photographic expedition. Remarkable, inasmuch as the team seen by Alfred Loft as noted earlier at Sarre performed in much the same way with respect to the performance of 'old country songs' by the Trices' team in the district five years later. When Edmund Trice's wife moved to St Nicholas, she recalled her future husband taking part as the rider, with his brothers, and brother in law William West also participating. In an interview with Tristan Jones, it was noted that:

> Talking to the Trice brothers and Edmund's wife prior to their leaving St Nicholas for Chatham, Edmund (then 89), his wife (then 88), Frank (79). Mrs Trice [the former Emily Gertrude Stevenson, born in Holborn in 1889] came to the village in 1910 and claimed that she remembered the Trice boys performing in that year. Both brothers aver they have no recollection of any earlier hooden horse performance in the village. At the same time, they were unable to explain how it came about, and initiated the custom. The horse had been given to them by Arthur 'Chip' or 'Chuck' Bolton who was the groom to old William Broadley, the then owner of St Nicholas Court, later bought by Col. A.G. Tapp. The object of the horse was to have some fun, to make some beer money at Christmas. They thought they'd sometimes make as much as two to three pounds each, although this seems doubtful. Hoodening was a 'great walk'. Farms and homes included the Powell-Cotton house at Quex Park; the Champions at Bolingbroke Farm, Sarre; the Steddys at Sarre Farm; Gore Street Farm, two or three years ago the home of the Willetts; Monkton Court; St Nicholas Court. They remembered singing a song 'All Along the Rails' (concerned with finding your way home along the railings)…At Gore Street, they were given whisky. There was no set pattern in the performance. The 'knocker up' had the job of gaining entry to the house, if necessary keeping his feet in the door to keep it ajar. At the shout of 'whoa', the hooden ers would rush in. After the horse, a sing-song followed. The horse indulged in horse play. Drink was dispensed, the wagoner collecting any cash contributions. At the time they lived on 13 shillings a week, being paid two pence an hour working on the fields. Edmund used to catch moles, selling the skins to Grantham, his wife buying a sewing machine with the proceeds.[95]

---

[94]Violet Phillpott, letters to the author 18 October 2002, 11 November 2002; Mary Chidwick, letter to the author 3 November 2002; Isle of Thanet Gazette, 5 October 1945, p3; Ben Jones, various emails received between 14 November 2002 and 5 December 2002

[95]Tristan Jones, draft of an interview with the Trice brothers and Tom West, 19 January 1977

A similar but separate note jotted down by Tristan Jones again, presumably from one or more of the Trice brothers, added that:

This quintet collected for Margate Hospital (and other places) at Christmas, singing old songs rather than carols, one of which was 'All Along the Rails'. The horse would visit all the houses in the village. The horse would stick his front leg in the door before it was slammed (i.e. using the pole).

The Trice family's hoodening party, c.1919

From left to right: George Trice as the Moll, George Holliday as the musician (note his costume, justification for Ben Jones's 'pyjamas' in the modern revival), Frank Trice inside the horse, Tom West as the jockey, Ern Trice holding the tambourine, and Walt Trice as the wagoner.

It is assumed that no performances were given during the First World War, but were revived again at Christmas in 1918 or 1919. Walter Trice's wife volunteered two more photographs of hooders from this revival to Anneli Jones who edited the booklet The Changing Face of St Nicholas-at-Wade in May 1978. The first of the two, which was thought to been taken in 1919, shows a gang of six; five men and a boy, who were positively identified as (from left to right) George Trice as Mollie, George Holliday holding an accordion, Tom West as the boy, Frank Trice in the horse, Ernest Trice, and Walter Trice as the wagoner. The other one said to have been taken in 1921 shows a gang of five: four men and a boy, and comprise (from left to right) Walter Trice holding an accordion, Tom West as the boy, George Trice as Mollie, Edmund Trice holding the horse, and Steve Howland as the wagoner. Two more photographs of this group appear and are included in the St Nicholas hooders' website. These were also taken in 1921: one included the fivesome noted beforehand plus Tom West's

63

father William West dressed as some kind of clown wearing a curly-haired wig under a top hat. The other had wagoner Steve Howland standing behind the horse (presumably played by Edmund Trice).[96]

Caricature of the St Nicholas team of 1919

This design by Lawrence Heath, originally for a Christmas Card, was used for the cover of the first edition of Discordant Comicals

When compared with Maylam's photographs taken in 1905, the photograph assumed to have been taken in 1919, shows similar costumes almost fourteen years later. Moll is still wearing a long dark dress, plays a triangle, and has some sort of flat hat. The accordion player is wearing the floral trouser suit, and a trilby type of hat. The boy is dressed remarkably similarly to the corresponding character in 1905 with a khaki uniform and peaked cap. The wagoner again is seen wearing a black top hat and dark long coat. The other character is also wearing a top hat, holds a tambourine, and some kind of coat with light sleeves. Two years later, the accordion player is seen wearing a top hat, with a light-coloured coat with dark sleeves and collar. The rider is dressed quite differently from that of 1905 or 1919, wearing a pillbox cap at a jaunty angle, a coloured tunic with rosettes pinned to it, and light-coloured trousers. There is a character that one may assume to be a clown (namely Will West in his curly-haired wig) further wearing a similar floral trouser suit and ridiculously large bow tie. The man bearing the horse is in ordinary farm worker's clothes of flat cap, open-necked

---

[96]Ben Jones's website, hoodening.org.uk

64

dark shirt, and light jacket. The wagoner, as before, wears his black top hat and long coat, and holds what appears to be a whip in his right hand. Moll still holds a triangle, and appears to be a younger person than previously (thus suggesting that the natural age of the actor is not meant to reflect the intended age of the character portrayed), and on this occasion is wearing a flattish hat, and long skirt beneath a thigh length coat. (This is at odds with evidence that Moll is George Trice on both occasions – perhaps the camera angle and lighting serve to flatter on the later occasion.) Clearly, there is some 'tradition' in what was worn, although apart from the wagoner who invariably wears top hat and long coat, the remaining costumes are improvised about what is to hand – clearly, the floral suit idea remained constant over the sixteen years in question, but its wearer varied. Tom West as the rider had clearly grown in height in the years between, and presumably would no longer fit into the khaki uniform of previous years. One assumes that any costume used had a shelf-life, depending where it was kept and how it was maintained in the fifty-one weeks it wasn't being worn! Despite what we shall hear later, nor was it the case that 'blacking up' was evident in the photographs taken, which were, of course, in daylight and not 'on their rounds' during their calls.

The Trice family's hoodening party, c.1921

From left to right: Walter Trice as the musician, Tom West as the jockey, Will West as the fool (note ridiculous wig and outsize bow tie!), Edmund Trice holding the horse, Steve Howland as the wagoner, and George Trice as the Moll.

The boy taking part, Tom West lived to a ripe old age, and gave several interviews to various people recalling his experiences as a hoodener – not always consistent ones – but painting a very graphic picture of the way things were. Putting the more significant interviews into chronological order, Tristan Jones spoke to him on the same day he saw the Trices in January 1977 although, with time, more facts were brought to mind.

Born in 1907, he thought he was at least 14 when, in 1921 he participated in the hoodening. Tom West added to the places they visited: Cherry Brandy House, the King's Head at Sarre, Val Smith's at Hale (where Maylam said the St Nicholas hoodeners came from), the big house at Brook's End, Ropeyard Farm, Wall End Farm at Upstreet. Hoodening took place on two nights in Christmas week, one night being devoted to shops, pubs and big houses in St Nicholas. On the second night was the 'great walk'. Their turn took place using popular songs on sheets published by Felix McGlennon, including such old favourites as 'the Farmer's Boy', 'Sussex by the Sea', 'Teach me how to Fly'. The jockey had to attempt to ride the horse who, in turn, tried to throw him. He, Tom, was too young to drink – he usually had to direct the others home. Their faces were blacked with burnt cork, and money was collected on the tambourine. That, the triangle and the accordion were the instruments used.[97]

A closer view of the Wagoner and horse in 1921 (Jones collection)

Despite prompting later in his life, Tom West seldom repeated the names of the songs performed in this recollection, recalling only 'Teach Me How to Fly' and 'The Tree in the Wood' – the latter of which he didn't name previously. McGlennon was a composer and publisher active during the era of music hall and variety. The song 'Farmer's Boy' was also sung by Len Harris of Acol. The lengths taken by Tom West's seniors to learn other songs seem remarkable. The quest for the sheet music for 'Teach Me How to Fly' – which can only be identified today from a British Library source –

---

[97]Tristan Jones, draft of an interview with Tom West, 19 January 1977

is testimony to this. The singing doesn't seem to have comprised any choral affair. According to Tristan Jones's gardener Frank Stickells, this was led by Edmund Trice, although since most of the songs listed had choruses, one is left with the impression that the remainder sang any reprises.

In an interview with members of the hoodening team revived in 1966, he adds to his earlier story, correcting himself in the assertion that he first took part in 1921, and adding that he took part three times in all. It is evident from his costume alone in the photographs, that he took part on more than one occasion. All interviewees seem to concur that the team folded in 1921. The words that follow used in parentheses, serve to paraphrase the question used in the interview and/or put the answer into context.

(I became a hoodener) just after the First World War – probably 1919. I remember watching them when I was a tiny child, and before the war my father (William West) had played the accordion for them. My uncle Walter Trice was then the jockey; but after the war my father dropped out, my uncle who was three years older than me became the wagoner, and I took his place as the jockey. (There was) George Trice as Molly, the old woman; George Holliday, me, Frank Trice as the horse, Ernie Trice, and Walter Trice. We performed every night for a week before Christmas. We spent one night at Monkton, where we visited Gore Street (Willetts), Monkton Court, Monkton Parsonage, the White Stag (then called the New Inn), Vinson's (Walter's Hall, where the oast house is), Sherrif's Court, and Hoo Farm. At Sarre, we visited Pocock Farm, Bolingbroke, the Elms, The King's Head, the Crown, Sarre House (then a private house), We went to three farms at Brook's End, as well as Crispe Farm, Road Farm, and Hale. Then at St Nicholas, we went to Shuart, Chamber's Wall, Down Barton, St Nicholas Court, the Bell, Walter Packham's draper's shop, and Albert Packham's bakery. I remember the horse throwing me into a pile of biscuit tins at the bakery. He also threw me over the counter at the King's Head. (We didn't really enjoy it.) We did it because we needed the money for Christmas, just as the carol singers did. Molly collected the money in the tambourine. I got the least out of it, as I wasn't supposed to drink and was given a smaller share of the money. The only advantage I had over the others was that I didn't have to smear my face with burnt cork: the Horse and I were the only ones who didn't black up. (Not all the hoodeners worked on the same farm): The Trices worked for Broadley's (St Nicholas Court), my father worked at Smith's farm in Birchington, George Holliday worked for William Smith at Chamber's Wall, (and he) was a cowman. (We didn't know of any other villages where hoodening took place), but then one didn't know much about what was going on in other villages. We used to knock on the door (of a house) and start singing right away. Then we would go inside and the others would continue singing while the Horse capered around with me. He used to keep on throwing me off. I held on to his reins and did my best to stay on. Then we were given drinks, mince pies, and so on. The people gave us quite a lot to eat and drink. (We didn't rehearse beforehand), but the singers did. They used to buy the words of a song (McGlennon's song sheets; you could buy them in Woolworth's) and listen to a record of it over and over again, till they knew the tune. I remember then singing 'The Tree in the Wood' (with the chorus 'and the green grass growing all around'), and a song which began 'Teach me how to fly, dear, in your aeroplane'. (No carols were sung, nor any rehearsed words spoken). Frank (Trice) was an ex-navy man (and must have been very strong. He, inside the horse set out to frighten people) by snapping his teeth together. (All performances were indoors, but no furniture was damaged. We walked everywhere) that is why it took so long. We'd set out each evening straight after tea (about 5.30 p.m.) We sang a lot more on the way home than at the houses. My grandmother had to get a lot of hot water ready for when we returned, to wash off the burnt cork. (No one was forewarned regarding their visit so they could invite guests:) they knew we'd be round some time that week, but not which day. (The audience were unable to join in with the songs, because) they usually didn't know them. (The wagoner) probably waved it (his whip) around a bit (rather than crack it or use it to beat the horse as) there wasn't room to do more than that. (Tom, as the rider wore) khaki trousers and tunic and some sort of cap. (Nobody was in charge, as) most of them were brothers, anyway. (When asked why the hoodening stopped, he commented:) I did it three times, so it probably stopped in 1921. Perhaps it stopped because it was a changing period, and because of competition from other forms of entertainment, including radio. But I think one of the reasons was that it was so closely tied to one family (the Trices), and when they didn't want to do it, it stopped.[98]

There is one more excellent lengthy interview that Tom West gave in existence, that being one conducted by Martin Beale in November 1983 which was passed on to BBC Radio Kent presenter Simon Evans.[99] Much of what is said repeats the above information, so extracts are taken to present anything novel, or counter or enhance that already said.

(The hoodeners were) in my mother's family, the Trice family. They used to do it on their own – it was a family affair then. They used to go round just before Christmas. I suppose there wasn't so much money about in those days, and it was one way of having a good time doing it. They used to go to Monkton: all the farms were expecting them to go, and they had a good time. Most of my uncles were horsemen at St Nicholas Court, my father went with them – he was a wagoner, and so most of them were. (We started) a couple of weeks before Christmas, and we used to walk round, but it used to be worse Christmases than they are now – used to be snow on the ground and that. And walking back from Minster or Monkton wasn't a joke really.

It is difficult to dissect what was said over-critically, since cross-examination is no longer possible. In this account, Tom West has extended the hoodening seasoning

---

[98]Tom West, interview conducted by David Gray, Adam Jones, and Ross & Connie Bentley, and published in the St Nicholas-at-Wade Parish Magazine, January 1981

[99]Tom West, interview conducted by Martin Beale, 30 November 1983 (Simon Evans collection)

beyond the 'week before Christmas' stated, and it is endearing to note that within his lifetime that the weather was more inclement at Christmas compared to today. He then went on to describe the horse, his own costume, and mode of performance:

> (The horse was made up of) a wooden head on a pole with a loose jaw that used to clap and frighten kiddies, and bells and all the brasses on it. Then there would be a sack over, the chap used to bend down and the sack used to cover him up and the tail was the hind part. And the jockey was dressed up like a little Scots boy and used to jump on his back and get thrown off. ...I used to wear a tam o'shanter and scotch trousers, and a scotch – like an army jacket. And the old Woman, she dressed up like an old Irish lady, I suppose, funny old hat, long skirt and that. The wagoner would have corduroy trousers and string round his trousers, and top hat.

In describing the costumes used from the black and white photographs seen, it is difficult to gain any feel for what colour might have been used. The comment that the rider that Tom West played wore a tam o'shanter should brook no quarrel, but there would seem to be a complete absence of tartan in three of the four photographs where he is present, although he is standing behind the horse in two of them.

Tom also went on to describe the mode of performance thus:

> It used to be frightening: the horse suddenly appearing and sticking its head through a window, and this sort of thing. If they went to a place where there were maids, the horse used to leave the jockey and get after the maids, but it was really hilarious. ...There was no programme...nothing pre-planned. It was just a matter of singing these songs and danced and mucked around. Actually, the biggest attraction was the horse and the jockey, I think, being thrown around. (In public bars) they used to make room for us, actually. But as you say, there wasn't much room because they were expecting us on that certain night, and there were more people there. (Out of season, the horse was never kept in the stable with the other horses) they used to keep it at home, always kept it in the bedroom, actually!

The ethos of the custom was never quite understood, in contrast to what was said earlier about collecting for charities such as Margate Hospital. Perhaps village tradition had it wrong: the hooteners did go out during the First World War years, and the fundraising concerned did go to the hospital for the war effort in the days long before the National Health Service. In any case, the reverse was said on this occasion:

> I had no idea why I was doing it – just that it was something that had been going on for years and years. Just that it was an ancient thing that they done to get money – a little extra for Christmas. They kept the money – not like today, when it goes to charity or some special function. They used to share out the money. I used to come worse off, I think, because I was the littlest. I wasn't allowed to drink, and I don't suppose I got my fair share of the money.

(It was a rough affair) from my point of view. The others, they were all right. But I was the one who was getting all the buffeting about and sprawling around. The horse always used to be someone pretty hefty, and once he'd had two or three drinks…well, that was it. It was just unbearable. I went home with more knocks and bruises than was healthy, I think. It was nice though. I used to enjoy it.

The neo-masochistic comment that he 'used to enjoy it' is in contrast to the earlier one that 'we didn't really enjoy it' noted three years earlier. Certainly, nostalgia played its part in looking back at an event that took place over sixty years earlier at the age of fourteen.

CHAPTER 5: HOODENING AND CHRISTMAS NORTH OF THE STOUR

The compartmentalization of East Kent in relating our story is purely arbitrary. In Chapter Three, it seemed natural to take the peninsula towns and villages as a unit; and in the following chapter, consider the west Thanet villages as a token entity. There is an expanse called Manston in between them where there is a paucity of information on hoodening which seems to justify this, yielding an imaginary line drawn between Westgate-on-Sea and Ramsgate separating east from west. In this section, the lands north of the Great Stour and west of the Wantsum Channel have been notionally segregated. As one drives along the Thanet Way from Faversham to the Gate Inn at Boyden Gate, on approaching Marshside, you are aware of a steep incline down to this appropriately named village. In travelling eastwards from the roundabout at St Nicholas, then approach Marshside from the north, you will see the wide waterway that is the Wantsum Channel to your left. Indeed, this was navigable up until 1485 as a passage between Reculver and Richborough, but now silted over and impassable, making the notion of Thanet as an island fanciful rather than real.

It has already been noted that hoodeners from the St Nicholas area during the first part of the twentieth century had a wide circuit that took in Hoath, Chislet and Upstreet that fall in this region. However, the hunt is on to find teams that were indigenous to this area, and for help in this, we must turn once more to Percy Maylam. In quoting Peter Lombard's 'Varia' column in the Church Times published in 1891, an anonymous correspondent wrote how:

> When I was a lad about 45 years since, it was always the custom on Christmas Eve with the male farm-servants from every farm in our parish of Hoath (Borough of Reculver) and neighbouring parishes of Herne and Chislet, to go round in the evening from house to house with the hoodining horse, which consisted of the imitation of a horse's head made of wood, life-size, fixed on a stick, the length of a broom handle. The lower jaw of the head was made to open with hinges. A hole was made through the roof of the mouth, then another through the forehead coming out by the throat. Through this was passed a cord attached to the lower jaw, which when pulled by the cord at the throat caused it to open and close and open. On the lower jaw, large headed hob-nails were driven in to form the teeth. The strongest of the lads was selected for the horse. He stooped and made as long a back as he could, supporting himself with the stick carrying the head. Then he covered with a horse cloth, and one of his companions mounted his back. The horse had a bridle and reins. Then commenced the kicking, rearing, jumping, etc., and the banging together of his teeth. As soon as the doors were opened, the 'horse' would pull his string incessantly, and the noise can be better imagined than described. I confess that in my very young days I was horrified at the approach of the hoodining horse but as I grew older I used to go round with

them. I was at Hoath on Thursday last, and asked if the custom was still kept up. It appears it is now three or four years since it has taken place…There was no singing going on with the hoodining horse, and the party was strictly confined to the young men who went with the horses on the farms. I have seen some of the wooden heads carved out quite hollow in the throat part, and two holes bored through the forehead top form his eyes. The lad who played the horse would hold a lighted candle in the hollow, and you can imagine how horrible it was to one who opened the door to see such a thing close to his eyes. Carollers in those days were called hoodiners in the parishes I have named.[100]

There is little new that we have not yet encountered relative to the horses of Thanet, but for the spelling of 'hoodining' and the hollowing out of the head so that a lighted candle could be held to give an eerie effect as it shone out of its eyes. This raises visions of a health risk should the candle tip to dislodge its hot wax upon the face of the hoodener, not to mention the fire hazard involved and the problems with keeping a candle alight out of doors on a windy winter's evening.

Percy Maylam also spoke to several interviewees in the block of land north of the Stour bounded by the Whitstable-Canterbury road in the west that also had the custom. Since such a wide area is under discussion, the block of text concerned will be broken down into composite districts. Forgiving the geographical error of placing Hawe Farm in Sturry rather than Herne, he starts by saying:

The remainder of Kent permits of being treated in sections. In the first place, let us consider that portion of Kent which is bounded on the west by the main road from Sturry to Herne Bay, on the west by the main road from Sturry to Sarre, on the east by the Isle of Thanet, and on the north by the sea. There is no question that the custom was generally practised throughout this district down to a period of about twenty years ago. Reculver, Chislet, Upstreet, Hoath, all had the hooden horse, Rushbourne also, and Mr Edward Fleet well recollects it at Hawe Farm, Sturry, in fact until forty or fifty years ago. Sturry village itself was visited. I was at first of the opinion that the main road from Sturry to Herne Bay was the westernmost boundary of this district, but Mr Edward Cladish of Blean, who himself has a faint recollection of the custom here some fifty years ago, made enquiries and was informed by an old inhabitant that boys used formerly to come round the parish of Blean on Christmas Eve singing the following song, though they had no hooden horse:

Three jolly hoodening boys
Lately come from town,
Apples or for money
We search the country round;
Hats full, caps full,
Half bushel baskets full –
What you please to give us

[100]Maylam, pp27-28, citing Peter Lombard in the Church Times, 23 January 1891, p78

Happy we shall be.
God bless every poor man
Who's got an apple tree.

I was afterwards able to connect this song directly with the hoodeners from information obtained from Mr Thomas Culver of Broad Oak, a hamlet in the parish of Sturry. He can remember the hooden horse at Broad Oak, and that this was the stock song of the party, but he states that the custom has been discontinued there for quite forty years.[101]

Perhaps we should not take the adjectives in this song too seriously as definitive proof that, in the Blean and the Sturry neighbourhood, hoodening parties consisted uniquely of three people of a merry disposition! This would pose the unanswerable question: what roles did they perform? Even Maylam comments on the idiosyncracy of the custom here, and how it appeared more similar in character to that of wassailing the apple trees, which is well-known throughout the south and west of England. Curiously, the only comparable examples in Kent occurred at Rogationtide, at neighbouring Keston and West Wickham, which today comprise dormitory villages in the Bromley area – and not remotely close to Canterbury! Maylam uses one instance elsewhere as a case study, continuing thus:

It would be of interest to know the manner in which this song became associated with the hooden horse, for these verses appear to show an influence of the custom of wassailing the orchards…as being present at Chailey in Sussex. It is called Apple-howling. A troop of boys visit the orchards, and encircling the apple trees, they repeat the following words:

Stand fast root, bear well top;
Pray the God send us a good howling crop:
Every twig, apples big,
Every bough, apples enow.
Hats full, caps full,
Full quarters, sacks full.[102]

Remaining in the district north of the Great Stour, we may now consider a singular text written by Christina Hole in 1941. This includes several novelties compared to Percy Maylam's findings, and specifically relate to Reculver.

The Hodening Horse did not invade the local houses in quite so free a manner, but he went round the village with a band of men and boys and leapt and pranced very spiritedly before the open doors. He wore a white sheet which covered most of his body, and a horse's head whose jaws opened and shut on hinges and could be made to snap in a very ferocious way. Hodening,

---

[101]Maylam, pp50-53
[102]Notes and Queries, series I, vol. 5, p293 (1852)

which has not long died out, and which is still remembered by many people not far beyond middle age, was a winter custom, taking place at Christmas in some districts, and on All Souls' Day or Eve in others. At Reculver only, men who worked with horses during the year were allowed to take part. The strongest man of the party represented the horse and carried a wooden head, with large nails for teeth, on a pole. He was covered by a horse cloth, wore reins and a bridle, and carried one of his companions on his back. The horse-man and his followers visited the farms in the neighbourhood and were given ale and other gifts.[103]

The references to the hoodener wearing a white sheet, and the custom taking place 'on All Souls' Day or Eve' in other districts is mentioned nowhere else. Maylam refers to the custom taking place during or around the Christmas season, rather than an autumnal one. What else Christina Hole knew on the subject is, alas, unrecorded.

It is evident that Percy Maylam's own interest triggered off revivals in parts of Kent that he visited. He partly acknowledged that when he said in *The Hooden Horse*:

> At Hoath, after a discontinuance of twenty years, I understand there has been a revival of the custom during the last three Christmas seasons.[104]

What Percy Maylam was unaware of was the history behind the Hoath hooden horse discovered in 1974. He commissioned the local builder H.H. Miles to find a hoodening gang. This turned out to be the Hale Farm team, and photographs were duly taken at Bolingbroke Farm, Sarre, as mentioned earlier. It seemed that Miles then went away and mused as to the feasibility of emulating the Hale Farm team. The horse was found in a barn at Millbank Farm, Hoath in 1974, although how it fitted in with the story wasn't quite appreciated at the time.

Chris Smith with the Hoath horse at the Gate Inn

---

[103]Christina Hole, English Custom and Usage (Batsford, London: 1941) p10
[104]Maylam, p45

The horse came from Millbank in Hoath. We bought an old house which had lots of barns. In the corner of one of these barns, we found what we thought was a child's hobby horse – we didn't take much note of it. We went to Machin's just before Christmas, and the St Nicholas hoodeners arrived. When they started doing their play, I thought: "We've got one of those!" When the play had finished, I said to the chap, "We've got one of those (hooden horses)." (He replied) "Have you got it?" So, I said "yes" and went back up and got it."

The informant concerned is Chris Smith, who with his wife Carole ran the Gate Inn at Marshside until 2011, and was inspired by the St Nicholas hoodeners to found the Marshside Mummers. In telling this, he added that he

...used to live next door to an elderly lady called Miss Miles who reckoned it was her grandfather who made it, who was a carpenter. She could remember as a child the hoodeners arriving and would hide in her mother's skirts. Miles the builders. This was at the turn of the century, so the horse is at least 100 years old.

Miss Miles was then well into her eighties, and Chris was insistent that this was in 1972. He couldn't recall her Christian name.

"You didn't. The lady who ran the village hall was called 'Mrs Johnson'. It wasn't until her funeral I found out that her name was Ethel."

Carole told me afterwards while she was clearing up the glasses, that she believed 'Miss' Miles was a 'Mrs' Miles.

"My mother has a better memory. She married into the family, a Miss Camborne was her sister who lived in the same cottage. She came from Acol."[105]

Whilst acknowledging the deference that Chris Smith had to the elder generation as a young man, further information was forthcoming in her obituary.

The funeral of Mrs Ethel Miles of Homeleigh, Millbank, Hoath took place at Holy Cross Church, Hoath, on Monday. Mrs Miles was the widow of Mr Bert Miles, well-known in villages around Hoath for his family building business. Born in Thorpe, Norfolk, Mrs Miles came to Kent after meeting her husband, and they were married at Chislet. Their first home was at Upstreet where Mrs

---

[105]Notes from an interview with Chris and Carole Smith of the Gate Inn, Marshside, Tuesday 21 December 1999 (George Frampton collection)

Miles was a member of the Women's Institute, and they moved to Hoath in 1942. During World War Two, she played an active part in the WRVS...[106]

Unfortunately, no such obituary was forthcoming in any local newspaper when her husband, the builder Bert Miles died in 1972. However, it does seem to confirm the notion that Herbert Henry Miles was the H.H. Miles that had Maylam's commission earlier that century, and also dates the hooden horse once kept behind the bar at the Gate Inn as being made around 1906.

It is interesting that the horse had a 'second lease of life' when it was adopted by the trustees of the Broadstairs Folk Festival. Jack Hamilton, who we will meet in connection with the 'revival' at Folkestone in a later chapter, recalled:

...In the early years of the Broadstairs Folk Show, we used to make an excursion to outlying villages on the Thursday. On a visit to the Gate Inn, we took a hooden horse. The next year, Chris Smith told me that the horse had triggered his memory: he had played many times in a nearby barn when very young, where there was what he took to be a toy horse's head in the corner. Having seen our horse, he revisited the barn and found the 'toy' still there. He then produced it. I volunteered to take it in hand, revive it for use, etc. This horse returned to the Gate Inn alone and made a most dramatic entrance. In a few following years, the Folk Show borrowed the horse and used it throughout the week's activities – it was the horse's seaside holiday.[107]

Another account of possibly the same horse in this district before the First World War came from the pen of Miss Mary Abbott who we have met in the last chapter.

In reading the article in last month's Occult Review on Radnorshire legends...I was reminded of...the old custom of the Hodening or Hooden Horse in Thanet...One was taken round at Whitstable about sixteen years ago, but was brought from some other town...[108]

Although open to interpretation, she doesn't appear to have acted as an eye-witness here, but in dating the custom as around 1904 suggests this might have been Bert Miles's horse taking a wider circuit, or a completely separate example.

Continuing our tour north of the Stour, we come to the next village north of Hoath towards the coast.

From Mr Henry William Christian of Herne Common, who was born in 1839, I find that the custom was formerly practised in the parishes of Herne and

---

[106]Herne Bay Press, 22 July 1977, p2

[107]Jack Hamilton, letter to the author, 11 April 2000. The 'early years' would refer to 1965 onwards, and the hooden horse they 'took' is presumably one built by Jack himself as a 'dancing horse' for the Broadstairs festival. It is worth noting the discrepancies between Jack's account and my own interview with Chris Smith a few months earlier (see p75 above). Sadly, there is little objective evidence on either side now.

[108]Mary Abbott, letter to Occult Review, vol. 34, no. 4 (October 1921) p234

Swalecliff. He himself as a lad had many times formed one of the party, but it appears to have been discontinued in that district for years. The last time he went round with the hooden horse was when he was wagoner's mate at Chestfield, Swalecliffe, this was that indefinite period 'donkeys' years ago.' He cannot remember the date except to this extent. That the last time he went out with the hooden horse party was the same year that he saw a policeman for the first time. Since then he has not so much as seen the horse. Among the useful purposes served by the introduction of the rural police one must therefore include that of fixing doubtful chronological points of folklore, one not anticipated by Sir Robert Peel. According to Mr Christian, the party consisted of the Hoodener, the Driver, the Jockey, Mollie, and three or four more who played the concertina etc. and, as he says, 'bones.' He confirms the use by the hoodeners of the song furnished me by Mr Cladish, which he repeated of his own recollection, with, however, the addition of the words given by Mr A. Moore.

The doggerel that was chanted, as quoted in Moore's newspaper article, ran thus:

We wish ye a murry Chri'mus
An' a 'appy New Year,
A pocketful a money, an'
A cellarful o' beer"[109]

As Maylam noted in the text, there was the opportunity to identify almost exactly when William Christian was a hoodener as the year when 'he first saw a policeman', without chasing this further. In fact, the Kent County Constabulary was formed in 1857, although this doesn't confirm this as the year concerned. John Land suggests that a petty constable system was still operating in St Nicholas-at-Wade ten years later manned by village artisans on a part-time basis – the same was probably true for other villages.[110]

Moving to the coast, a conundrum is found in 1888, that suggests another outing for a hooden horse in a curious parallel to the central character in the Broadstairs Incident of sixty years earlier (q.v. page 40).

On the night before the festival (Christmas), round many a bright seasonal fire, friends were beginning to gather, the advance guard of the morrow's jocund party – and when the lamps were lit and the curtains drawn. Inside many an old memory was revived only to be interrupted by sounds, outside, appropriate to the season. All day long, the Herne Bay Town Band had been playing old tunes with creditable skill, children sang their plaintive carols, and the 'Mummers' had performed the old tragedy of the defeat of the dragon by St George. This last revival, capable of great extension and of being made an attractive and instructive exhibition, is the relic of a custom which has existed

---

[109]Maylam, pp50-53
[110]John Land, A Parish History of St Nicholas-at-Wade and Sarre(1990: Thanet District Council) p41

So, who were these 'Mummers'? What was this 'defeat of the dragon by St George?' The archetypal Christmas Mummers' play elsewhere in southern England comprises a central character called St George (or King George) who challenges various 'champions' from sundry dominions to battle – notably a Turkish Knight (Turkey Snipe), Bold Slasher, and/or Prince of Egypt – and despatches them accordingly. A doctor is summoned, who revives them using quack medicine. George is lastly vanquished by the feeblest of the party 'Johnny Jack, with his wife and family on his back' – end of story. In Kent, the custom was known as 'championing' and the play as 'the Seven Champions of Christendom'. The custom was found along the Darent valley, villages in the Maidstone area, and also at Milton Regis north of Sittingbourne.[112] At this latter location, a second guisers' play was also found, mainly lampooning local personalities.[113] As we shall see shortly, there is evidence of a play at Harbledown, and the suggestion of one at Dover. However, none of these plays mention any slaughter of a dragon, despite the association of St George killing one in legend. Even allowing that the light may have been poor in 1888, it is a fact that street lighting had arrived in Herne Bay. It seems that the journalist concerned had no previous idea of the nature of the 'beast' that tagged along with these 'Mummers'. This tempts one to draw the conclusion that a hooden horse had been seen taking part in some rustic – the wordsmith uses the word 'ludicrous' – play.

It is now to the cathedral city that we next turn for evidence of the custom, as Percy Maylam once more reports.

There appears to be some recollection of the custom having been observed in this district as far westward as Harbledown. Mr James Browning, who is a woodreeve at Blean, tells me that about fifty years ago, for several seasons he dried hops for Mr James Hearn at Wingate Farm, Wingate Hill. (The older people pronounce the name 'Winkit'.) In the parish of Harbledown, and at Christmas time he was accustomed to go to Wingate Farm House for a Christmas box (which in those prosperous times was of a substantial character) and to share the Christmas festivities, of which a visit from the hooden horse party formed part. Although he could not remember details, the snapping jaws of the horse he had never forgotten.[114]

Modern-day Harbledown is barely a suburb of Canterbury itself on the London Road out towards Faversham. Yet it seemed to be a 'hot bed' for Yuletide calendar custom. The collection of alms for the elderly and needy known as 'goodening' has already been noted – which may or may not have had similar etymological roots to

---

[111]Herne Bay Press, 29 December 1888, p5
[112]E.C. Cawte, Alex Helm and N. Peacock, English Ritual Drama, p48 (Folklore Society: 1967)
[113]Denham Jordan, Annals of a Fishing Village (Bath: 1969) pp239-244
[114]Maylam, pp50-53

that of hoodening. There was also that of 'championing' which we have just mentioned, recalled thus:

> ...The writer remembers when, as a small boy, seeing the Mummers on their rounds. The band consisted of about ten youths and men dressed in paper hats, coats and trousers, who would call at the various houses and go through their speeches and performance. Unfortunately, there is only one survivor of the last band, who went out in about 1897, but from the memory of his short speech, it would appear that the whole could be constructed from that which is still performed in other parts of the country. He was the youngest and last of the troop, and his part was as follows:

> *Up Comes I, Beelzebub,*
> *In one hand I carry a club,*
> *In the other a dripping pan,*
> *Don't you call me a jolly old man?*

> This is practically identical with what is known as the soul-caking play of Cheshire. In our village, however, and no doubt in other parts of East Kent, the party were called 'Champions', and the round was called 'championing.' This is no doubt a allusion, as our dialect dictionary points out to one of the scenes in which St George the Champion fought the Black Prince (not the great one, but a representation of a negro or moor). Our friend remembers these two characters, but cannot recall their speeches...Our Dictionary of Kentish Dialect defines championing as 'the lads and men who go round as Mummers at Christmastide singing carols and songs.' Our recollection is that the performance took place in the summer and without the carols and songs.[115]

We are now at the western limits of where hoodening was once practised. There is a suggestion that it was a feature of Christmas at Sittingbourne some 15 miles northwest of the cathedral city, according to writer Sarah Tooley:

> Kent was a county noted for 'hodening' or going round with the 'hodening' horse, a fearsome creature made of wood with great jaws studded with hobnails for teeth. A boy carried the head having his own person concealed by a horsecloth. He held a cord which worked the hinges attached to the hideous jaws and made them open in a ferocious manner; at the same time he kept up as much kicking and plunging as possible. Young men from the farm stables usually went round with the horse, to the terror of small children.

---

[115]Walter Norris, Some Notes on the History of Harbledown (1965: typed manuscript held at the Centre of Kentish Studies, Maidstone)

The custom was kept up at Walmer and Hoath until comparatively recent times at Christmas, and also at Sittingbourne.[116]

This short paragraph appears in a ten-page article on Christmas customs in the counties. Its illustrations include images of the Plough Monday custom at Haxey in Lincolnshire, and the Abbots Bromley horn dance. Mrs Tooley is more noted for her books on and about the Royal Family, also Florence Nightingale and the nursing profession. She was the wife of the Rev. George Tooley of Kensington, and it is plausible that her quote was derived in part from the Church Times article cited earlier. No other mention of a Sittingbourne hoodening is present in literature, nor was there a man-beast used in the Milton Regis champions play last performed in 1904, although the possibility of one being used beforehand cannot be dismissed.

There are two more examples north of the Stour. One comprises the note by Rev. Pegge in his dictionary of Kenticisms between 1731 and 1751 when vicar at Godmersham. He defines a 'country masquerade' without elaborating further, but proffers no evidence that the custom was extant itself in the village of his stipend.[117] Let us then climb the North Downs to Challock on top of the hill that stands three miles to the north of Godmersham Park. A hooden horse was said to have been used as an effigy there, but involved in what was known as 'tin-canning' – a custom known elsewhere as 'rough music', bringing to mind the skimmerty riding episode in Thomas Hardy's The Mayor of Casterbridge. Owen Hams related the custom to his son Fred, who recalled thus:

My father (Owen Hams) was very vague (about the hooden horse usage in Challock). It had become discredited and it was almost swept under the carpet. People got it out or were said to have done in the 1880s or 1890s. It was used at the time for shaming people, like if somebody was living with someone they shouldn't – this thing was paraded. It had become like that, with a thing they called 'tin-canning'…It had become like a thing that people didn't want to know about or weren't allowed to know about. It had come to the hands of a few (people)…If it got its blood, they both disappeared a bit…[118]

Although little is recorded of 'rough music' in Kent, John Land refers to it in his booklet on St Nicholas-at-Wade, where it was known as 'sweeping out'.

The late Olive Brockman had a vivid early recollection: just before the turn of the century, she witnessed what she called a 'sweeping out'. The setting was the bottom of Court Road. Amidst the commotion of people, an old man was 'swept out' of the village with a besom broom. A violin and an accordion provided a musical accompaniment. The present writer has heard of 'drumming out' with dustbin lids, but not a 'sweeping out'. This may simply have been a Hoodening rehearsal. But given the Court Road location with its

---

[116] Sarah A. Tooley, 'Old Christmas Customs in the Counties' in The English Illustrated Magazine, vol. 30, p270 (December 1903)

[117] Maylam, p12

[118] Fred Hams, notes from an interview, 1 August 2000

workhouse associations, one wonders whether this was the time-honoured mode of ejecting vagrants or disreputables.[119]

Two allusions cited to hoodening also being an aid to 'rough music' doesn't imply that the practice had a second general usage beyond that of a Christmas calendar custom. The best article on the subject was written by the historian E.P. Thompson, but his references to the custom in Kent are limited to its London environs, without acknowledging any use of an equine effigy.[120]

With that, let us now cross the main road between Canterbury and Ashford, so we can progress south and east of the Stour.

---

[119] John Land, A Parish History of St Nicholas-at-Wade and Sarre(1990: Thanet District Council), p54

[120] E.P. Thomson, Customs in Common (Penguin: 1993), chapter 8, p467

CHAPTER 6: HOODENING AND CHRISTMAS SOUTH OF THE STOUR

For reasons that will become apparent, let us progress a short distance from Chartham which lies alongside the Great Stour, and start with this most colourful of descriptions in the whole of hoodening history.

Lower Hardres

There was formerly a party of hooteners at Lower Hardres under the leadership of a man named Henry Brazier, who died about sixteen years ago at the age of eighty-six. I have seen his son John, now living at Lower Hardres, who tells me that he first went round with his father's party in the year 1857, he would not say how long before that this father had done so, but it would be for great number of years. He could give me no information as to how or when his father had become acquainted with the custom. Henry Brazier was a famous player on the bells (not handbells, but bells on a stand), which were always struck with a stick in time and tune: these bells were always a great feature of their performances. The performers were Henry Brazier, his son John, Fairbrass, and two men named Noble. The original horse head of this party was of great antiquity; its ultimate fate was curious, as will be seen by the following tale:- One afternoon, forty-nine years ago last Christmas (i.e. Christmas 1859), they visited Lower Hardres Rectory on their round. A German gentleman and his wife were spending Christmas with the then Rector. The German lady was an invalid and had not walked for seven years. She was wheeled out in her chair on to the lawn to see the hooteners perform. Henry Brazier, who was the horse, in the course of his customary antics, made a feigned jump at her. The lady's fright was so great that she, who had not put her foot to the ground for seven years, promptly sprang out of her chair, ran indoors, and walked all right for ever afterwards. I tell the story as it was told to me, and I do not question the truthfulness of my informant, John Brazier, who saw the occurrence; but the story is not ended. The German gentleman clapped Henry Brazier on the shoulder, and said, "Well done, daddy! You have done more for my wife than all the doctors. You must sell me this horse as a remembrance." This, Henry Brazier promised to do, when the season was over. There was a party at Lower Hardres Rectory on the New Year's Eve, at which they gave a performance, and then the German gentleman bought the horse and took it with him back to Germany. In 1860, a fresh horse was made by 'old George Noble' who appears to have been the only man in that district able to do so.[121]

Let us now draw breath and look at a few implications from Maylam's text. He has elicited the names of the entire hoodening party, and their addresses, ages, birthplaces and occupations can be deduced from the 1861 Census, on the assumption that they still lived in the district less than two years further on. Not surprisingly, it is learned that each person named was an agricultural labourer. What may be more surprising, is that not all of them remained in the immediate district ten or even thirty years later at the time of public release of the 1891 Census. The 'two men named Noble' were the brothers William and Henry, sons of William and Mary Noble. Henry was working as a Canterbury carpenter at the time of the 1881 Census, and brother William as a miller at Sellindge. William Henry Fairbrass too, had moved out of Lower Hardres (pronounced 'hards'), but was still within a five-mile radius of the Bridge registration district at the time of his death. George Noble lived at Upper Hardres in 1871. Henry Brazier himself did actually live at Lower Hardres at the time of his death, but originally, he came from Elmsted about six miles away. Let us now explore the 'beat' of the Lower Hardres hoodeners. Maylam continues:

This horse, some years afterwards, was bought by Squire Thomson of Kenfield, in the parish of Petham, and another one made in its place. John Brazier kept the custom up till about 1892, his father having discontinued a year or two before, but he found the absence of the bell playing a great disadvantage.

The Lower Hardres party appears to have been an important feature at the Christmas balls or parties of the country gentlemen in the district. John Brazier recollects visiting Mystole, in the parish of Chartham, in the days of old Sir John Fagge, on the occasion of a ball or party there. This happened in 1859, the same year as the incident of the German lady. They went round for a week or ten days at Christmas time and must have covered a wide district, Petham and Waltham, Upper and Lower Hardres, and Nackington, even going into Canterbury itself, where they entertained parties of soldiers in the public houses. But this was not altogether a success, the soldiers being too vigorous with their horseplay, quarrels and black eyes were the frequent result. Mr Edward Mount Collard recollects this party visiting Sextries in the parish of Nackington, from 1870 to 1890. Mr Thomas Collard tells me that in the early sixties (of the last century), the hooden horse used to come at Christmas to St Lawrence Farm House, Canterbury, which was then his home. He also tells me that the Lower Hardres horse visited Winter's Farm, Nackington, until a year or two before he left that farm, which confirms the date of discontinuance, so far as concerns the company in question, as being about 1892.

---

[121]Maylam, pp53-57

...I was at first of the opinion that Stelling had at one time possessed its own horse, as so many people there were acquainted with the custom, but it appears that the one which visited Stelling and Stelling Minnis was that belonging to Brazier's Lower Hardres party; my authority being Mr Edward Mantle, who is nearly ninety years of age and has lived in Lower Hardres and Stelling all his life – he says he was well-acquainted with Brazier's horse, but never knew of any other.

Brazier's testimony tells us a little about some of the 'big houses' that were visited. Squire Thomson was Richard Edward Thomson J.P. (1807-1892) who lived at Kenfield House, just over a mile northwest of Petham village. The house itself is a large Georgian mansion that is today used as a residential home for the elderly, and commemorated in the nineteenth-century painting 'the Cricket Match at Kenfield Hall'. Today, Mystole is also a retirement home, but in Brazier's day was the residence of the 'squarson' the Rev. John Fagge – a keen sportsman and ardent supporter of the turf. The family name is commemorated in the pub on the southern edge of the village on the ridge linking Chartham to Petham and Lower Hardres: the Fagge Arms. The rectory at Lower Hardres was occupied by Maria and the Rev. George Rashleigh who was also vicar at Horton Kirby near Swanley in Kent. The story of the German lady invalid does not appear in any Canterbury-based newspaper, despite its proximity to the cathedral city, nor, alas, is it recalled in any diary or journal of the day. Having already mentioned that the hoodening gang were prepared to tour the Chartham Downs in search of largesse, let is now speculate as to their further involvement in Chartham village itself. Maylam continues:

...There is also some doubtful trace of the custom having been practised at Chartham. I had a conversation in April 1909 with Mr William Jacob Hubbard who lives at Puddledock, which is close to Chartham Hatch in the parish of Chartham. He was seventy-four years of age and had been there all his life, and of his own knowledge knew nothing of the custom. But he recollected a story which used to be told by his father, William Hubbard, who died about fifteen years ago, aged eighty-one, to the effect that once, at Christmas, he (that is, the father) was at Mystole, when some of the Chartham village men came with a wooden horse's head which moved its jaws with a man underneath. His father explained that he was at Mystole in connection with his duty as one of the patrols, who were banded to protect property at the time of the stack-firing troubles in Kent. We have seen that the Lower Hardres horse certainly visited Mystole, and I think that in all probability it was the horse of that party which Hubbard saw, but my informant was certain his father said they were Chartham village men. The time of the stack-firing troubles would fix the date between 1838 and 1848.

This date 'between' is ambiguous in its wording. Why not 1830, the year of the Captain Swing riots with its rampant incendiarism?[122] The Poor Law of 1834 was

---

[122]Philip G. Rogers, Battle in Bossenden Wood – the Strange Story of Sir William Courtenay (Oxford University Press: 1961)

sufficient to raise the ire of parish councils and those less well-off incited to riot. If Maylam specifically meant 1848 – this could refer to the march on Parliament led by Feargus O'Connor of the Chartist movement in an attempt to force an extension of political power to the working classes (including universal suffrage). The Kentish Gazette notes one incendiary incident during the late Summer and early Autumn of that year, but not at Chartham. If 1838, perhaps the event was the uprising led by John Nichols Tom, otherwise Sir William Courtenay, convicted madman, self-styled peoples' champion and religious zealot. His march on Canterbury with his followers culminated in the 'Battle of Bossenden Wood' near Herne on 31 May that year, followed by his attempted arrest and the subsequent murder of Nicholas Mears, whose brother was charged with the duty of serving Courtenay's arrest warrant. The local newspapers were full of this news item well into the Autumn, and seem the most likely evidence referred to by Hubbard senior.

Lastly, Maylam gave a full description of the Lower Hardres horse, comparing them to those he had seen or had described to him elsewhere. One implication from this is that the jaw of the beast had no hobnail teeth and/or that the mode of performance made no mention of snapping the mouth. Why bite the hand that feeds it when money is offered? What happened to the coin placed in the horse's jaws went unrecorded. Was there a slot for it to roll into? Did the wagoner extricate and pocket the money before the horse dropped it and be lost in the dark?

> The Lower Hardres horse is described to me as being 'more like a horse' than either the Thanet or Walmer horses, having a distinct neck with a white streak down the forehead and the eyes painted in; the covering sheet being of a shiny dark material. The characters in this group of performers did not include Mollie, and they have no tradition or recollection of her. The proper mode of bestowing the gratuity was, as at Walmer, to put the coin in the horses's jaws; though sometimes a cap would be placed between the jaws and carried round amongst the spectators by the horses itself. The called the horse the 'hooden horse', but it also appears to have been known as the 'Christmas horse.'[123]

The Wye Downs, Elham, Eythorne and Hythe

The circuit of Henry Brazier's hoodeners took in a wide swathe of the countryside. Petham is three miles southwest of Lower Hardres, and Chartham four miles due west crossing over the downs themselves into the Stour valley. It was obviously difficult for Maylam to tease out what might have been separate hoodening parties, therefore coming to the conclusion that what was witnessed at Chartham and Lower Hardres were, in fact, the same team seen at different times. Further out on the Wye Downs, the custom was not recalled at Hastingleigh, but it was at Evington from hearsay evidence.

> Mr Thomas Vickers, of Evington, informs me that he remembers his father (Mr Thomas Vickers, senior) telling him there used to be a hooden horse at

---

[123]Maylam, p56

Evington, in the parish of Elmsted, but from his own knowledge this must have been discontinued there before 1860.[124]

Maylam then speculates as to other possible hoodening gangs in the vicinity, having already visited nearby Stelling Minnis and Upper Hardres without success. He then tried asking elderly people at Elham.

I next called on a Mrs Clayson who was then eighty-eight years old. She had always lived in Elham and there had been no hooden horse there in her recollection, but she had heard her father say that when he was quite a young man, they used to go round at Christmas time at Elham with a wooden horse's head. Her father's name was File, and he died some thirty years ago over eighty years of age, which of course, takes us back nearly one hundred years.[125]

It is not easy to identify the gentleman who accompanied this horse's head. From the information supplied by Maylam, we know that Mrs Clayson was born around 1819 and died in 1908, while her father, Mr File, was born before 1797 and died before 1877. Census records and online family trees indicate that she may have been an Eliza File, born between 1818-1820, who married Mark Clayson on Christmas Day, 1837. If so, her father would have been one Thomas File (1776-1859). However, his years are twenty years earlier than expected, whereas there is a Stephen File whose dates are significantly closer (1784-1873), and who also had a daughter called Elizabeth... yet she appears to have married one Alfred Harvey. The huge number of people with almost identical names in Elham at this time makes it practically impossible to be sure which individuals are being referred to. Either way, the dates imply that the incident recalled must have been at the start of the Napoleonic Wars at the turn of that century. One must add that Maylam's enquiry of Mrs Clayson must have resounded with her to have triggered such a seemingly trivial memory associated with her father's involvement in the custom – perhaps she was aware of Henry Brazier's team's activities?

In the now redundant Kent coalfield north of Dover, the word hoodening was recognized at Eythorne, but with a different meaning, as we have already heard from Alfred Moore's testimony.

...I have just had a visit from some lads (presumably at Eythorne) who tell me they are 'out hoodenin' and who have shouted loudly

We wish ye a murry Chri'mus
An'a 'appy New Year,
A pocketful a money, an'
A cellarful o' beer'!

---

[124]Maylam, p56
[125]Maylam, p56

Geographically, Eythorne is only a few miles west of the circuit taken by Elbridge Bowles's Deal hoodeners, as we shall see in the next chapter, and but a few miles south of Wingham and Goodnestone. However, apart from the mysterious Guston horse cited shortly, the Dover district at the 'Hellfire Corner' associated with the Second World War did not have the hooden horse as part of its annual circuit.

Before we move on to consider the custom at Deal, there is one further piece of uncorroborated evidence to relate following an appeal for information in the newsletter of the East Kent Federation of Women's Institutes. Hythe had a hooden horse that did its rounds in the mid-1930s according to John Ludlow who, at the time of writing, lives there. The horse was the property of workers at C.R. Thomas's building works based in Bartholomew Street in Hythe, and Mrs Annie Ludlow's house in Hillside Street backed onto its yard where it was seen by her son. Charles Russell Thomas himself was a Londoner who lived at nearby Blackhouse Hill, Hythe until his retirement in 1932, leaving his son Harold to continue the business using his name. John Ludlow's father, Dan worked as a baker in Sandgate before he opened up his Hythe branch in the High Street in 1934, and this would date any outing of the horse from this information, however sceptical. No report of this was included in the newspaper the Hythe Reporter whose focus was on things more of interest to the middle classes, so one assumes that our hoodeners never got into any trouble, and/or that the custom was short-lived. Incidentally, the author's informant was Mrs Joy Ludlow (*née* Roberts) whose father once ran the Rose and Crown public house in Deal and recalled carol singers visiting the pub in Deal in the 1930s, but not the hooden horse – although she was familiar with the names of Bob Skardon's colleagues that we shall meet in the next chapter.[127]

The 'Wingham' Horses

One is hard-pressed to re-appraise a custom such as the 'hooden horse' without merely repeating Percy Maylam's eponymous work, infiltrating it with a smattering of newspaper texts. However, at Wingham, we have a conundrum – or rather two conundrums – whose exact origins remain unresolved. We shall set the scene with a newspaper extract.

On the eve of Christmas was 'Hodening or Hoodening', which many of our readers can remember – the party of young men with the head of a dead horse, that they affixed to a pole about four feet long. A string was tied to the lower jaw, and a horse cloth attached, which covered one of the party, who, by pulling the string, kept up a loud snapping noise, while the rest of the party were grotesquely arrayed. From house to house they went, singing carols and songs, receiving in return cakes and ale or money. Some forty years ago, this

---

[126] Alfred Moore, in the Kentish Express, 5 January 1895, p3

[127] Joy Ludlow, phone conversation with the author 14 January 2001. This was followed up by searches in street directories and electoral registers at Hythe and Folkestone public libraries (with thanks to Joy Adamson of the latter for assistance)

practice was common in Thanet, and about twenty-five years ago was last seen in Wingham...[128]

The plain fact is that two horses' heads were found 'in the Wingham district' by members of Wye Agricultural College, presumably in the early 1950s. They were then donated to Maidstone Museum in 1956.[129] The college itself (now a department of Imperial College, London) has no further detail as to where exactly the heads were found, who found them, or what activities were being pursued at that time – only to add that there was no college annexe or research station in the area.[130] The museum still has the heads in storage rather than on public display, but is willing to allow anyone to see them upon request. On occasions, it has allowed them to be photographed privately and by the local press in support of related news stories. Other information is that the heads were 'voted into' the museum on 1 May 1956, but this does not guarantee that the heads were found recently in that year, and no newspaper item reports their discovery or transfer. One irony is that Wye College now has its own agricultural museum of rural bygones at Brook near Ashford.

There have been several descriptions of the horses to extend their stories. One came when Tristan Jones wrote to Graham Hunter, the curator of Maidstone Museum, and received a reply dated 20 December 1977.

...as far as I can be judge of the two horses, the more elaborate dates from 1900 to 1910. The plain one dates from about 30 years earlier.[131]

Geoff and Fran Doel describe the horses accordingly:

Maidstone Museum has two hooden horses which were found in a barn at Wingham. These are most interesting but are in poor condition. One is quite small (perhaps 3 feet 6 inches) with wooden pole (fixed) and could be for a child. The horse has leather ears, and nostrils are cut out and the eyes indented and is painted black, red and white, with a blanket covering and jaw that is pulled open and shut with a string, stones being fixed in the jaw to create the snapping noise.

The second head seems to be full-sized, but lacks its pole and its string is broken. It also has stones for teeth and a horse brass on its forehead and a rosette. It has a studded belt.[132]

The author visited the museum in October 1983 and later in February 2001 to make notes. The 'stones fixed in the jaw' referred to are definitely hobnails. The note that the heads were 'found in a barn' can be taken to be an assumption based on the

[128]Kentish Gazette, 26 December 1896, p6

[129]L.R.A. Grove, in Archaeologia Cantiana, 1956

[130]Tom Hill (Brook Agricultural Museum), email to the author, 27 November 2001

[131]Graham Hunter, letter to Tristan Jones, 20 December 1977

[132]Geoff & Fran Doel, Mumming, Howling and Hoodening: Midwinter Rituals in Sussex, Kent & Surrey(Rainham: 1992) p17

possible circumstance surrounding their discovery. Barnett Field recalled that the heads were 'discovered by Wye College students' which is again plausible as to circumstance – more so, because of his extended association with the custom.[133] The former horse is the one that has been photographed upon request for publication, such as in Robert Goodsall's book A Third Kentish Patchwork. Its canopy comprises a red chequered cloth on a faded green background, rather than hessian or anything so obviously agricultural. There are also rosettes on either side of its head, with a streamer depending from its centre. The only thing to add about the second horse is that, despite not having its pole, one can quite clearly see the socket inside the head into which one might fit. There is also a circular brass surmounted upon the crown with a vertical mirror-like disc hanging down from an annular frame – a distinctive brass matched by other hooden horses in the region.[134]

Lastly, there is speculation of what was meant when Maidstone Museum's curator Allan Grove said that the horses' heads were found in the Wingham district. As already stated, Wye College denies that they had any research station there.[135] Percy Maylam notes that

> There is also evidence that the hooden horse, up till about twenty years ago, visited Preston-next-Wingham, but in regard to both Stourmouth and Preston, I have not been able to ascertain whether these places possessed horses of their own or were only visited by wanderers from Thanet.[136]

One further hypothesis is constructed as to the origin of the 'Wingham' horses. In 1967, Barnett Field prepared a paper for a symposium of the Folklore Society and, in passing, noted that a horse's head had turned up at Guston at 'sometime in the early fifties'.[137] Nowhere else in Barnett Field's notes prepared for lectures, dissertations, and the like, does he repeat this, and one muses who might have told him, and why he refrained from reciting this. After correspondence with the Guston local history society, coupled with a newspaper search in the Dover area, it seems no knowledge of any hooden horse discovery exists within living memory. It could be that Barnett Field had met a business client or some other contact (e.g. through an East Kent morris outing) who told him about the 'Guston' find – such loose talk often happens. The Kentish dialect being what it is, it could follow that what he heard was 'Goodnestone' (pronounced Goon-stun, with the 'oo' pronounced as in 'hood') not 'Guston'. This would imply that the heads were discovered four miles from Wingham village itself, rather than the Dover suburb. Sadly, whilst there are copious records of the Brook Bridges family of Goodnestone deposited at the Canterbury Cathedral Archives and the East Kent Records Office, payments in them to any Christmas visitors such as hoodeners are absent. However, such disbursements are seldom recorded in material deposited at such places.

---

[133]Barnett Field, in Folklore, vol. 78 (1967) p203
[134]Notes made following a visit to Maidstone Museum, 28 February 2000 (George Frampton collection)
[135]E.M. Lucas, Imperial College at Wye, letter to the author, 30 March 2001
[136]Maylam, p50
[137]Barnett Field, in Folklore, vol. 78 (1967) p203

The Lower Stour Valley

Continuing with our tour to the east of Canterbury, Percy Maylam takes us to Ash-next-Wingham and to Stourmouth, and once more avails us of information from an earlier source.

> Mr Thomas Vickers of Evington, tells me that his mother used to speak of the hooden horse at her home at Ash-next-Sandwich when she was a girl.

Also,

> …Mrs Edward Collard tells me that during the time her late husband lived at Dean Farm in the parish of Stourmouth (1872 to 1882), the hooden horse came every Christmas. A man dressed up in woman's clothes was one of the party, but whether known as 'Mollie' she cannot say.[138]

Lastly, whilst listing his findings in *The Hooden Horse*, he kept his analysis into what hoodening comprises to a minimum. Obviously, there was the horse, people in costume (including a 'Mollie'), one or more musician, and largesse involved. There might be some interplay between the horse and one or more of the performers and/or audience. Whilst minor differences occur between types relative to timespan or geographical locus, only the following extraordinary case study deserved singling out from its peers.

> Wishing to ascertain if there were any tradition of the hooden horse in the Sandwich district, I made enquiries on that point of Mr G.C. Solley of Richborough, Ash-next-Sandwich, and the information which was the result of my enquiry, I will set out in Mr Solley's own words as follows:
>
> 'My father, George Solley, was born at Richborough Castle Farm on St Thomas's Day in 1814. He lived there nearly all his life and died at Sandwich in 1899. He has told me that when he was very young (about ten years old he thought), a party of hoodeners from Ash used to come round on the day before Christmas Day. Some of the party were dressed as fools and there was with them a Maid Marian (this was his own term and he explained it as being a man dressed up in woman's clothes). One of the party has a kind of black rug thrown over him, and carried a horse's head, which kept nodding about. He remembered seeing the hoodeners knocking one another about with sticks and bladders on the green at the back of our house. I myself was born at Richborough, and I recollect that about 1872, for some years, two old men used to come on Christmas Eve singing songs. We always called them the 'hoodeners' though they had no hooden horse.'[139]

---

[138]Maylam, p50
[139]Maylam, p92

This was sufficient evidence for Maylam to postulate a Robin Hood theory based on this Maid Marian character. But is there anything else within Solley senior's experience which might embellish or distort this tale? Fools with bladders, a horse, a man-woman character? Modern-day research would find a mate with the May pageantry taking place at St Mary Cray in the period 1889-1895 – it was in all the newspapers, including the Illustrated London News of the day. But this is hardly 1824, and the season is wrong. 'Robin Hood' and 'Maid Marian' characters are pictured dancing in front of a jack in the green character at Whitstable in 1895. However, neither theorem is near to providing an alternative hypothesis as to what George Solley had actually seen over seventy years earlier. A story which he related to his son who, in turn, reported the same to Maylam.

CHAPTER 7: HOODENING AND OTHER CHRISTMAS CUSTOMS IN DEAL AND WALMER

Introduction

In considering the Christmas custom of the Hooden Horse in Deal, and to a lesser extent Walmer, one is struck by the occupational differences between its participants relative to St Nicholas-at-Wade and elsewhere. The contrasts couldn't be more marked. Although one is never quite certain where Deal ends and Walmer begins, what is assured is that whereas the custom at Walmer was mainly the preserve of the farm worker, that at North Deal belonged to the boatmen and allied trades. More than that: in Deal, this was a town-based custom that had to vie with other Christmas buskers to survive. This rivalry could be expressed either on the professional or amateur front. For example, until recently, Deal was home to the Corps of the Royal Marines and its bandsmen. There was also a town band and, of course, the church choirs. The musicians and actors who comprised the hoodening troupe would have had to compete with these – for attention, if not money.

The Deal and Walmer picture about to be painted is difficult to envisage writing a century after the event, but it seems natural to appraise the custom in what could today be conceived as a nascent conurbation. In fact, when arriving at Walmer railway station from Dover, you are still a mile inland and have literally barely left the cabbage fields and a windmill on the Ripple road behind before encountering streets full of bungalows after walking down the station approach. Contrast this to your arrival at Deal railway station, with the hustle and bustle of a town centre only a few minutes' walk from the sea front.

The Custom at Deal

In the nineteenth century, entertainment was provided every year at the annual Christmas festivities in Deal barracks, but that did not prevent sundry visits by certain buskers there in an effort to elicit largesse – as seen in this account from 1858 headed 'Christmas in the Royal Navy':

> …We dined at our usual hour of six, and while over our wine after dinner, we heard two or three taps at the door, which then opened and displayed one little banjee attended by sundry grotesque-looking figures, attired as clowns, &c. Permission was requested to sing us a song, which was of course afforded: they sang 'the Old Folks at Home' very well, accompanied by the music. This drew a toast from our president for 'Our Absent Friends' which was drunk with great applause…[140]

---

[140]Deal, Walmer & Sandwich Telegram, 5 January 1859, p4

In the town itself in the run up to Christmas, the local newspapers in the week beforehand invariably gave a discourse about the fayre and other merchandise that the local tradespeople had on offer, as well as to list train timetables. There might even be a short account in the next issue after Christmas itself as to the atmosphere created by ad hoc groups, although one senses the adjectives chosen by the journalist concerned may be tinged with irony indicating that such was not entirely approved of. In 1866, we hear that:

> On Christmas Eve, our town presented a very lively and animated appearance. In the early part of the evening, a band paraded the streets and discoursed 'sweet' music, and the houses and shops in every street and lane were besieged by bellringers, carollists, &c. Our most active shopkeepers with their nimble and sprightly assistances were hardly able to keep pace with the almost unlimited demands made upon the resources of their establishments...[141]

No mention of the hooden horse is made by the local press until 1877, when the Deal, Walmer & Sandwich Mercury described at length the events prefacing the season.

> ...On Christmas Eve, the band of the 5th Cinque Ports Artillery Volunteers perpetuated the reputation of departed 'waits' by blowing midnight strains outside the residences of certain unhappily-privileged persons in various parts of the town, while earlier in the evening skirmishing detachment of young Deal Uhlans, varying from five up to fifteen, with considerably more of lungs than harmony, perambulated the principal streets and terraces, pouncing on every other door and bestowing a reminder of the holy season by vehemently carolling the inmates in a species of rhyme as guiltless of metre as of tune. This again was supplemented by the bearing round of a stupid piece of foolery with a hideous head, and which is known as the horse, though what connection it bore to Christmas we failed to see. It was decidedly wooden-headed – we mean, of course, the horse, not the bearers – and its exhibition appeared to be confined to the principal shops in Lower Street and elsewhere. These annual customs, however, disappeared as the eve wore away, and Christmas Day was left free of all such tolerations.[142]

We now need to put these celebrations into context with what Percy Maylam had to say on the subject. Rather belatedly in his research, he finally made the acquaintance of local fishmonger Bob Skardon of 104 Sandown Road, whom he treated as the authority on the subject. Robert John Skardon was born in 1857 and told Maylam that he had

> ...lived at Deal all the fifty-three years of his life and had always known of the custom. When he was a lad, his father used to have a hooden horse party: he carried the head, his father played the drum, his uncle John Beney the fiddle, and old Harry Chawner the piccolo. For many years, there has been

---

[141]Deal, Walmer & Sandwich Mercury, 29 December 1866, p4
[142]Deal, Walmer & Sandwich Mercury, 29 December 1877, p2

no 'Mollie', but formerly the party included a man dressed up in woman's clothes who was known as 'Daisy.' I could find no recollection of any beginning. Skardon's Uncle Beney, who died about two years ago, aged seventy-five, had been at it all his life and his father before him. Skardon himself, it appears, about twenty years ago started a Christmas band and discontinued the horse…(but on)…discontinuing it, the custom was and is kept up by Mr Elbridge Bowles of 5 Fairfield Cottages, Great Mongeham. He is one of Skardon's band, but after Christmas, he and one other man go round with the horse. He plays the tin whistle while the other man represents the horse. They do Deal, but finding the country districts welcome them more, of late years they have visited Finglesham, Ripple, Tilmanstone, Eastry and Betteshanger. At the time of the South African War the horse was, with great success, got up with full military equipment.[143]

Let us now analyse some of what Maylam discovered upon meeting Bob Skardon and put it into greater context, with some minor details appended after publication of *The Hooden Horse*. If John Beney's father had been a hoodener in his time, we are talking about a period possibly as early as the 1820s if we could accept he took part as a younger man. John Ashley Beney (1810-1856) of 120 Lower Street, Deal, was described as a mariner in the 1851 census returns. His son, John James Beney (1832-1907) – Skardon's uncle alluded to earlier – had various addresses in North Deal noted in the censuses for 1871 through to 1891, but each list him as a boatman. Harry Chawner (1854-1906) was listed as a general labourer and son of carter Henry Chawner, according to the 1881 Census. Bob Skardon's father was Charles Ramsay Skardon (1824-1878) who was a labourer in the employ of the carrier Richard Prescott. Elbridge Bowles (1871-1940) was a painter and decorator, learning his trade from his father, William Bowles.

The 'horse' they led about the streets was described by Maylam as having a forehead covered with black plush in representation of a horse's coat, the ears made of the same material and the eyes painted in. There is a rosette between the ears rather than a swinging disc or bells. The covering is a dark green material, a kind of box-cloth, which at one time may very well have been the lining to a billiard table or bagatelle board. The horse used by the modern-day Deal Hoodeners is modelled on this – the original being lost, presumed destroyed in the 1950s. We have no idea how the hoodeners were costumed. Plate G in Percy Maylam's book depicts Bob Skardon as musician playing what looks like a hexagonal-ended English concertina, although it is difficult to judge this accurately by the way his hands mask the buttons in the keyboard[144]. At his right hip is a bugle. He wears a dark top hat and trousers. He is also sporting a patchwork jacket, which could possibly be a tailcoat. The newly-formed Deal Hoodeners base their costume on this, but as I have already noted in an earlier

---

[143]Maylam, p45

[144] Two aficionados on the www.concertina.net forums agree that it appears to be an "Anglo with at least a partial third row of keys", and also comment that "[Maylam] refers to 'concertinas' several times in the text but uses the word indiscriminately for the instrument in the Deal photograph and for the melodeons in the photographs of the Sarre and Walmer horses"

chapter, it seemed a feature at St Nicholas-at-Wade for the musician to dress up individually, and one is left to speculate how anyone else might have been attired.

A costumed Bob Skardon with Elbridge Bowles inside the Deal horse

The story thus far throws into confusion the activities of hoodening in Deal town itself relative to a perceived timeline. We are assured that something went on from the 1820s to around 1889 when Skardon gave up hoodening in favour of his band. The question arises: how exactly did Bowles continue the custom in the town itself, or just in the satellite villages around Deal that Maylam noted earlier? To put Bob Skardon's band into greater context, we may compare Maylam's account with that cited in the Deal, Walmer & Sandwich Telegram which reported the Christmas celebrations of 1886:

> …On Christmas Eve…there were hand-bell ringers about – one set, we are bound in honesty to say, of a very out of tune arrangement, evidently not hailing from a near radius of Deal. Murray Larkins, although looking far from well, brought out his fiddle and gave his usual selections, of course, not omitting 'Tar the Rain Butt'; we did not recognize any fresh tunes; from this, we must gather, that nothing worth Murray's notice has been brought out this year. There is one little annoyance that might perhaps be put a stop to – young children under the guise of carol singing, going about really begging. A couple of youngsters pitch up some music hall ditty, and after a verse or so knock and ask for pence. If anything was calculated to take all the poetry out the idea of carol singing it is this. To hear the old carols sung in the stillness

of night is very pleasing, but to drag the old custom down to this low depth is worse than degrading…[145]

Whilst Murray Larkins is nowhere listed as a member of any hoodening party, he was obviously noted as an amateur musician and local character. His signature tune 'Tar the Rain Butt' was either a tune well-known locally to him, or a self-penned composition, since its title appears nowhere in national collections – or is, at best, obscure. The same newspaper describes his activities the following Christmas, together with a name we have already recognized from earlier.

…On Christmas Eve…there were the usual number of little urchins going from door to door singing 'Once in Royal David's City' to various tunes, 'Alleluias' in very minor keys, snatches of hymns and selections from Christy Minstrel Songs. Hand-bells were jingled not over musically, and Hodening horses were patiently led about, but did not seem to meet with much favour (by the way, no one seems to know much about the origin of this Christmas exhibit). Murray Larkins, following the traditions of his father, perambulated the town with his fiddle, accompanied by some youthful players on the drum, tambourine, etc., and scraped away at 'Tar the Rain Butt' and other ancient terpsichorean tunes with a vigour that must have told on his muscular powers, while his brother 'Cock' Larkins, with White as fiddler, and Harry Chawner as piccolo, formed another band, which if not particularly harmonious as to music were very friendly, for when Harry finished a piccolo solo with drum and violin obligato, he was rewarded by the encouraging approval of the drum beater, who shouted out "Well done, 'enery." The Deal brass band were out and played selections of popular airs at the houses of the principal inhabitants…[146]

This, indirectly, appears to be the source of Bob Skardon's band, although he is not named amongst the musicians here. The supposition that Larkins's band was the forerunner to Bob Skardon's is admitted as such in a retrospective published in the East Kent Mercury at Christmas 1938, which suggests that the band was formed in 1871.[147] Another newspaper retrospective of 1926, reports that 'the 'hoodening horse' is associated in the minds of many Dealites with the days when, at Christmas time, 'Lardy Dooks band', a fiddle, a fife, and a drum, and Murray Larkins, similarly equipped went round the streets, and the Upper Deal handbell ringers made mirthful music in the town.[148] 'Lardy Dooks' appears to have been somebody's nickname – possibly a corpulent band leader with the surname Duke, not that the Censuses of the time support the notion of anyone of that name living in the town. Without leaping to further conclusions, it seems obvious that musicians such as Harry Chawner and John Beney were prepared to play anywhere where they could get a few bob and perhaps a good meal. The Kentish Telegram, in describing a public dinner given for

[145]Deal, Walmer & Sandwich Telegram, 1 January 1887, p5
[146]Deal, Walmer, Dover & Kentish Telegram, 31 December 1887, p5
[147]East Kent Mercury, 10 December 1938, p4
[148]Deal, Walmer & Sandwich Mercury, 2 January 1926, p8

the North Deal boatmen in January 1896 showed how Beney and Skardon were pressed into action:

> On the evening of New Year's Day, the North Deal boatmen, to the number of about 125, assembled in St Andrew's Parish Room to partake of a substantial dinner…The room…had been gaily decorated by Jack Adams, who was assisted by several ladies.
>
> …The tables having been cleared, the Chairman (the Rev. J.H. Champion McGill) who was supported by Mr W. Chapman and Mr Cruickshank, called upon Fiddler Beney and R. Skardon to entertain the company. These amateur musicians, who did their best to accompany the songs throughout the evening, played a lively air on their violins…[149]

Bob Skardon's North Deal band

Top row 3rd from left is Dickie Lill, bottom right is Robert Skardon

For the record, the songs sung during the evening for which Beney and his nephew might have been expected to provide accompaniment, included 'When Shall

[149]Kentish Telegram, 8 January 1896, p5

We Meet Again', 'We're Bound for England's Shore', 'Poor Old Joe', 'Good Old Saturday', 'For They are Jolly Good Fellows', 'Auld Lang Syne' and 'Angel Mother's Dream'. The same story was reported by a different journalist in the Deal Paper, who added 'Sister Mary' was another song performed, saying that 'generally speaking, sailors' songs are remarkable for the same characteristics as his yarns – length. This, however, appeared to be greatly appreciated on Wednesday evening, and the greater the length of the song, the more loudly it was applauded. The most essential part of all nautical sings – the chorus – in every case, was highly appreciated, and vigorously sung by everyone.[150] Judging by issues of the Telegram and Paper in preceding and successive years, this feast appeared to have been a 'one-off', namely, if it did take place early or on New Year, it was never reported. A similar feast was held for the Walmer boatmen the following week, but the names of the participants cited fail to match any of Maylam's hooeners or other musicians known to have been active at Christmas time.

Bob Skardon's band: peace celebrations outside the Saracen's Head in Albert Square

---

[150]Deal Paper, 4 January 1896, p5

Bob Skardon's great-grandson David with the band's instruments (now on display at Deal Museum)

Little is known of the make-up of Bob Skardon's North Deal Band. We know that their instruments comprised at least a bass drum, two side-drums, triangle, tambourine, bones, fife,violin, mandolin, six-string banjo, and diatonic accordion (a.k.a. melodeon), as depicted in their 1919 photograph and two later photographs of Jim Skardon's four-year-old son, David sitting down surrounded by these musical devices. Of course, the instruments used are likely to have changed over time. The museum exhibits further include a zither-type of instrument and a whip! Skardon's obituary says that he was 'deeply interested in music, he founded a band that became known as Skardon's North Deal Band, which was engaged for various social functions, also playing in the streets of the Borough and the villages.' The museum guide concurs claiming that they went around at Christmas. However, one wonders why (or if) they restricted themselves to this one time of the year. There is another photograph taken during the Peace Celebrations in May 1919, of an informal group of people including musicians dressed in sailors' and soldiers' uniforms, together with a pierrot and a circus ringmaster standing outside the Saracen's Head Inn in Alfred Square, some holding instruments that one wouldn't necessarily associate with the standard brass band. These include a banjo, bass drum, snare drums, accordion, triangles, and tambourines. The 1938 retrospective referred to earlier speaks of the Skardon Band dying out 'sometime before the Great War' but added that 'some members of it appeared in the North Deal Jazz Band which enlivened Peace Day festivities' which is obviously the subject of the photograph.

Among the newspaper and magazine accounts that Percy Maylam accumulated in his research was that of Peter Lombard who wrote his 'Varia' column in the Church Times. In late 1890, Lombard was appealing for information on hoodening, and elicited a number of replies. Although difficult to date, one was received from a parson's wife who once lived at Deal, perhaps from the 1850s or even 1860s:

When we lived at Deal, our children used to be half frightened and half amused by a performance which took place annually on the day you mention (i.e. Christmas Eve) We were warned of the arrival of this creature by a very loud clapping noise, and on rushing to the street door, saw a horse's head, supported on a pole by a man in a crawling position so as to resemble an animal, and covered in front by a coarse cloth. Nothing was done or sung by the small crowd around; and the clapping caused by the opening and shutting of the mouth continued, till the creature having been satisfied with the money was driven away...[151]

So far as the scope of the visits by Skardon's or Bowles's hooteners is concerned, for the most part, we have to rely on the evidence given to Maylam. However, in newspaper retrospectives, some clues are given to the journeying these performers undertook.

In reference to our paragraph in last week's issue (based on Hone's Everyday Book)...a correspondent very kindly sends us the following particulars: "Hodening, or Hooden or Hoden Horse goes on in Deal at Christmas, I believe, to this present day. One man is dressed up in an artificial horse's head, the underjaw is a clapper, and he is attended by three or four men, generally farm labourers, who go from house to house getting what they can." Another correspondent informs us that at Mongeham and the neighbouring villages, the custom still prevails at Christmas and the New Year. The farm labourers who attend the Hoden Horse are armed with bells. They generally call on their employers and, when the door is opened thrust in the head of the wooden horse and keep it open. Then, by keeping up an incessant clapping of its jaws and ringing their handbells, they generally succeed in getting something from the inmates of the houses.[152]

This report of 1893 could be interpreted as indicating the presence of two separate parties, rather than the same party witnessed by two separate spectators. We know that Elbridge Bowles took the horse around Great Mongeham and the villages, and if the 'belief' of the newspaper reporter could be ratified as fact, this would answer the question of whether the horse was paraded around Deal town centre at that time. The only query would be the identity of the 'three or four men' said to be farm labourers, since the custom in Deal tended to be the preserve of the boatmen and their support industries.

In one eyewitness account, under the heading 'How Many Can Still Remember the Carolling Wagoners?' we hear of circumstantial evidence of one perambulation of Bowles's hooteners, in that:

There must be few people who can still remember the original 'ooteners – those carters and wagoners who used to trail around the darkened streets and villages in East Kent carolling and handbell ringing. But Mrs O. Field of the

---

[151]Peter Lombard, in The Church Times, 2 January 1891, p20
[152]Kent Coast Times, 12 January 1893, p2

Folkestone National Dance Group tells me she has discovered two people with such memories. One of them is Lady Tuff, widow of Sir Charles Tuff of Godwyn Road, Folkestone. She recalls that the clapping jaws of the hooden horse used to frighten her as a child.[153]

Lady Tuff was Helen Constance Denne (1885-1965), the daughter of Thomas Tuff Denne of Homeside, Walmer – she acquired her title by marrying her second cousin, i.e. her father's mother Mary Ann Tuff was the sister of Henry Tuff, father of the M.P. Mr Charles Tuff and thus Sir Charles Tuff's grandfather. The Tuffs were well-known lime-burners from Rochester. The comment about being frightened as a child, would date the visit to Homeside as some time in the 1890s. The Walmer address quoted in Lady Tuff's wedding announcement in the local paper, together with Thomas Denne's address cited in Kelly's Directory is confusing until the layout of the parish boundaries is realized. Denne was also listed as the proprietor of a limeworks and brickmakers at Walmer. Contemporary maps show Homeside Farm on the southwestern perimeter of nearby Ripple village – which included gravel works in its vicinity – and is the most likely domicile of Field's interviewee. Recognizing that hoodening parties were likely to visit the homes of their employers to solicit alms, this notion is further reinforced in Elbridge Bowles's obituary, which noted that he was employed by Messrs T.T. Denne of Walmer, and afterwards of Messrs G.H. Denne & Sons Ltd. of Deal.[154] That so, it is more likely that the future Lady Tuff must have witnessed Bowles's horse rather than Laming's Walmer horse that was also doing the rounds at the time.

Or, what can we make of this incident from the Deal, Walmer, Dover & Kentish Telegram in 1892 in Mr Francis's draper's shop. In this case, there

…was to be seen a couple of negroes, one apparently playing his violin and singing, while the other very cleverly manipulated an eye-glass with his left hand, and a cigar with his right causing much amusement, as he proved himself an accustomed smoker by placing the cigar in his mouth and puffing the smoke out after each draw.[155]

This doesn't sound like the normal, run-of-the-mill Christy Minstrel mentioned earlier at Minster – but was he a violinist known to any hoodening party of the day? And who comprised the 'groups of players in grotesque costumes with instruments of every kind, who were on every hand, and there after the two days of quiet, made their appearance again on Boxing-day, and paraded the otherwise almost deserted streets…' as reported in the Deal, Walmer & Sandwich Mercury in describing the scenes of Christmas 1893?[156] Ten years later, the same newspaper notes the absence on the streets of any musicians save the odd group of waits without any great enthusiasm and obvious indifference.

---

[153]Kent Messenger, 1 January 1963, p10
[154]Deal, Walmer, Sandwich & East Kent Mercury, 27 July 1940, p1
[155]Deal, Walmer, Dover & Kentish Telegram, 28 December 1892, p4
[156]Deal, Walmer & Sandwich Mercury, 2 January 1893, p5

Between the publication of Percy Maylam's book and the Second World War, there are a number of further eyewitness accounts to the continuation of hoodening. This note comes from Arthur Williams in 1952, a native of Canterbury and inveterate letter writer to the Kentish Gazette, when he reported:

> I see that you state in your current issue that the hooden horse was seen as recently as 1907. May I add that it was still a regular custom in 1920 in Deal...[157]

Another note of hoodening at Deal was suggested by the classical musician Beatrice Patterson (1873-1963) in a letter to the librarian of the Vaughan Williams Memorial Library in 1932:

> I was asked if I knew of any vestige of a Mummers' play in Kent, but am only able to give this very slight piece of information for what it is worth. I remember this when I lived at Deal, as a child, and am told is still 'continuous'. Probably at the 'North End' only among the boatmen's houses and for money...[158]

She then continued by quoting the passage on 'hodening' from W.D. Parish and W.F. Shaw's Dictionary of Kentish Dialect published in 1888 rather than describe the event she herself had witnessed, but appended: 'My recollection of the 'horse' calls up more of a hippopotamus and was definitely terrifying.'

When the Deal Maritime and Local History Museum opened in 1974, there was an account quoted relating to hooden horse among the exhibits, and Christmas in general from a Mrs Kate Parker (1895-1970) recalling her childhood:

> Then Xmas Eve was another happy time; after tea there would be two or three bands come to the door, a drum, concertinas, and violins (fiddles as they called them), we loved it all, but now when I think of it, I think there may have been plenty of drum and not much tune about it. These boatmen were collecting for the very poor children of Deal to give them a Xmas tea...Then there was the 'Oogling Horse', the hooded horse of Queen Elizabeth I's reign; a man under a sack with a wooden head something like a horse with two large clappers for a mouth, the man clapped them together, made a terrible noise, but that was part of Xmas.[159]

Circumstantially, the first sentence is a description of the sort of band that Bob Skardon might lead. All we lack are names by which to festoon the story.

---

[157]A.M. Williams, letter to the Kentish Gazette, 24 December 1952, p4

[158]Letter by Beatrice Patterson to Douglas Kennedy, dated 27 March 1932, Vaughan Williams Memorial Library Collection, GRQ20Horse/17-18

[159]Memories of Deal by the late Kate Parker, undated typewritten manuscript. I am indebted to Julie Deller for lending me her copy for the exact text. The original text was used anonymously by the Deal Maritime and Local History Museum at one time.

The horse is recalled by the Ramsgate newspaper the Thanet Journal in 1907 under the heading 'jottings' by a pseudonymous journalist called Scrutineer:

> What a fuss is being made about Hooden, or Hodden horses. They have, for years formed part of the outdoor Christmas festivities at Deal. It is only a polite way of drawing coppers from a kind-hearted public. A man is led about enveloped in a rag, and wears a horse's head, or mask, and he and his fellows make a good thing out of it. Evidently it is a remnant of the old Mummers.[160]

Another report that year suggests that the gang went as far north as to visit nearby Sandwich:

> A young friend tells me he has seen the 'Hooden horse' at Sandwich, and thinks the party came from Deal, where I am told it is often seen.[161]

The accuracy of this report depends on the age of the 'young friend' concerned, who had obviously seen the Deal horse before at some time in his life. Accepting that the party concerned did come from Deal, it suggests that not only were the townspeople fleeced for alms, but the horse also went further afield. It is hard to say from such circumstantial evidence.

In a communication from Mrs Naomi Wiffen (1902-2002) at Edenbridge, Geoff and Fran Doel noted her childhood experiences in Deal at around 1910 when,

> I remember as a child being taken out on Christmas Eve to the High Street in Deal where the shops would be open very late, and it was the only time Deal children would be allowed out in the evening, as parents were very strict. As we would be looking at the lighted shops, and listening to the people selling their wares, a horrible growl, and a long horse's face would appear, resting on our shoulder and when one looked round, there would be a long row of teeth snapping at us with its wooden jaws. It was frightening for a child. Usually, there would be a man leading the horse, with a rope, and another covered over with sacks or blankets as the horse.[162]

In fact, the Adams family, of which she was a member, must have been very familiar with the antics of the hooden horse. Naomi's father was Thomas Adams: a boat owner, channel pilot and lifeboatman, who lived in Castle Street. For the rest, one has to guess what the journalist may have meant in describing the Deal town scene just before Christmas in reports to the Deal Mercury. The presence was noted of the town band, various groups of waits and handbell ringers, but what did he mean when he described 'calls' by parties of 'vocalists' and 'instrumentalists' as party to the Christmas Eve celebrations in 1891?

---

[160] Isle of Thanet Journal, 18 December 1907, p5
[161] Keble's Gazette, 16 November 1907, p5
[162] Geoff & Fran Doel, Mumming, Howling and Hoodening, p14; also letter to the author from Donald Wiffen, 9 January 2003

After Doreen Benham's EFDSS revival at Aylesford in July 1939, she corresponded briefly with the folklorist Violet Alford the following year. The latter had contacts in Deal and confirms 1934 or 1935 as the last date of hoodening activity, as is evident from a letter saying:

> ...I believe you will find a traditional horse just outside Deal. I know they came into Deal quite lately, perhaps four years ago. The police wrote to me in reply to enquiries, and they ought to know.[163]

Elsewhere she stated that 'the Deal police, about four years ago, certainly knew where the Hoodeners came from. Of course, the sergeant may have changed by now' in a different tack from her original letter.[164]

At Deal, there are a number of accounts to suggest that the custom continued until around 1934, possibly because of Maylam's enthusiasm alone. After he had photographed Bob Skardon as the costumed concertina-player accompanying Elbridge Bowles who was hidden inside the horse, it is assumed that the former's interest was revived, and he continued taking round the horse as well as leading his band. One other member of the hoodening gang who introduced himself to Julia Small's team convened in 1974 was John Burton who claimed he had 'hoodened in his youth'. One other member of Bob Skardon's band was Dick Lill. At his death in 1951, the musical instruments were handed to his grandson Jim, who loaned them to the Deal Maritime and Local History Museum when it opened in 1974, and are currently on display there along with the Walmer horse and a 'colt' made by 'Jack' (Joseph Percy) Laming in 1956 (and formerly held at Folkestone Museum). The Deal horse was still in one piece in 1953 when George Revell, a Deal boatman, knocked on Mollie Skardon's door in Brewer Street. Upon opening it, she was confronted with 'this horse's head clapping its mouth. It was quite frightening at the time.'[165] Alas, the horse was 'got rid of' long before it was realized to have any greater extrinsic use. There was also a big drum that was damaged during the Second World War when Bob Skardon's premises were shelled. It was due to be repaired in London, but was burnt – again, before it was realized to be of any interest to anyone else.[166]

The last comments arose following the revival of the Deal Hoodeners in 1997, thanks to the efforts of Chris and Gill Nixon. After a feature had appeared on them in the East Kent Mercury, contact was made with Bob Skardon's grandson, Jim, who was able to furnish them with some more detail about the hoodeners' mode of performance. Three songs were specifically stated as being sung before 1934: 'The Moon Shines Bright', 'Phil the Fluter's Ball' and 'I Saw Three Ships Come Sailing In'. It was also commented by Jim that the hoodening 'season' began after Harvest and continued until Christmas. In an interview given to the 'East Kent Mercury' in January 1998, he claimed:

---

[163] Violet Alford, letter to Doreen Bennett, 22 January 1940 (George Frampton collection)

[164] Violet Alford, postcard to Doreen Bennett, 1 February 1940 (George Frampton collection)

[165] Mollie Skardon, letter to the author, 17 December 2001

[166] Jim Skardon, letter to the author, 3 May 1999

It was said a working horse needed one day rest a year – Christmas Day – and the band used to play at farms and take their 'horse' with them. Then it went on more than just Christmas Day, because it was so popular. In my early life I remember them playing in the town and the children used to follow the band. All the money collected was given to the poor of North Deal and I expect old people today remember seeing my grandfather playing at Deal Hospital and at Eastry, at the institution and at the village cross…the tradition died in the early 1930s when grandfather stopped playing…[167]

The Custom at Upper Walmer

But nowhere is there mentioned in newspaper text any hint of a hoodening or Christmas party from Walmer as opposed to Deal – unless the Walmer horse did the rounds of Deal's satellite villages as well. One reason for this, could be that Walmer was sufficiently peripheral over a century ago to preserve its own rural identity. Percy Maylam first visited the village in 1906, after a conversation with a fellow solicitor:

Shortly before Christmas, 1906, I had a conversation with Mr Vaughan Page, of Canterbury, as to the observance of the custom in Walmer. He told me that his father, Mr Henry Page (1826-1911) recollected the custom at Walmer back to, at any rate, 1849, in which year he became tenant at Walmer Court Farm, remaining there until 1896. During this period, the men on Walmer Court Farm always went round at Christmas with the hooden horse; the musicians who accompanied them relying to a large extent on sheep-bells – one in each hand. They had no Mollie.

Mr P.T. Greensted, who succeeded Mr Page, and was tenant of Walmer Court Farm until 1903, informs me the custom went on during the whole of his time. I subsequently ascertained that the leader at Walmer was Mr Robert Laming, May's Lane (sic), Walmer.

Accordingly, on Christmas Eve 1906, I went to Walmer, and having ascertained the time when the party would set out, I had a comfortable tea at the hotel near Walmer Station. Whilst at tea, a man in grotesque attire came into the room, and proceeded to blacken his face with burnt cork at the fire. I having had thoughts for nothing but hoodening, enquired of he were one of that party, "No," he said, and it appeared he was one of the Walmer Nigger Minstrels with no very great opinion of such obsolescent customs as hoodening.

---

[167]East Kent Mercury, 8 January 1998, p4. Jim Skardon told Chris and Gill Nixon that the songs that his grandfather told him about were as stated. It is interesting to note that 'I Saw Three Ships' and 'Phil the Fluter's Ball' were both used at various times in the annual Dover Christmas pageant 'Chrystmasse in the Olde Tyme' which might suggest a common origin. This also included a Christmas Mummers' play as part of its scenes (see Appendix A), 'The Moon Shines Bright' was originally assumed to be the carol, one version of which was noted by Cecil Sharp from James Beale at Hamstreet in Kent in 1908.

However, very shortly afterwards, the well-known clap! clap! Was heard from within the bar – the Hoodeners had come. I hastened to see them. The party consisted of four, the hoodener with the horse's head, the man whose duty it is to lead the horse, and when not doing so, to play the triangle, and two musicians, one playing the tambourine and the other the concertina. The wooden head is made on the same lines as the Thanet horse, but it is somewhat larger and the jaws open much further back and therefore wider. Here I found the practice was that the 'gratuity' had to be placed in the horse's jaws, and on this particular occasion the horse put his head on the counter of the bar while the landlord's little daughter was lifted up from the other side in order to carry out the proper form of giving the money, after conquering her fright, real or feigned, she accomplished her task. I had a short conversation with the leader, Mr Robert Laming, he told me that his horse was not the one which used to belong to the Walmer Court men, he did not know what become of that, that he had been out with his horse on Christmas Eve for this five and twenty years and missed doing so only one year. The Walmer party were in their ordinary clothes, but formerly I was told they wore smock frocks. At Walmer they had no Mollie, nor any recollection of her. I accompanied the party a little way on their rounds which I was told would not finish till about 11, it was then 6.30, and I found the hoodeners sure of their welcome, the horse gambolled into all the crowded shops, and at Christmas, they are crowded, and everyone was pleased except a collie dog who worked himself into a fearful rage but feared to try his teeth against the wooden jaws of the horse. On visiting the butcher, he, regardless of the graminiovorous habits of the animal, placed a mutton chop in the jaws besides the accustomed tribute, a piece of humour which met with great applause.[168]

Maylam arranged to meet the hoodeners again for the sake of taking photographs of them on 29 March 1907. The ploy was presumably so there would be less of a problem with light in relation to the camera technology available at the time. Ironically, he had difficulty finding a shady spot on the bright sunny day he chose to visit.

Maylam's only other reference to the practice at Walmer came from Peter Lombard's 'Varia' column in the Church Times. This comprised a letter from an unknown 'antiquary' who merely replied to an earlier query that: 'It was observed on Christmas Eve at Walmer in 1886, which was the last time I spent the festival there.'[169]

No distinct newspaper account exists to describe any of the Walmer hoodening parties of the day. Robert Laming did hint to Maylam that his was not the Walmer Court horse recalled by Vaughan Page, and it is notable that in the Walmer Court Farm team, "the musicians who accompanied them [relied] to a large extent on sheep-bells – one in each hand",[170] which seems to confirm that there was more than one hoodening party in the village. It is however unclear whether Laming's team was primarily based at Coldblow Farm, where his horse was later stabled, and whose owner

---

[168]Maylam, p7
[169]Peter Lombard, in The Church Times, 23 January 1891, p78
[170] Maylam, p7

106

Edward Mowll also ran Walmer Court Farm at one time (see p109) – or somewhere else. In December 1952, Jack Laming who was photographed with the tambourine by Maylam, was interviewed by the Kentish Express thus, in an article entitled 'He Can Tell You About Hoodening':

If you want to know anything about the old Kentish custom of hoodening, ask 66-year-old Joseph ('Jack') Laming of 54 Mayers Road, Walmer. He took part in the custom as a boy, and a Hooden horse, believed to have been made about 100 years ago, was once possessed by the family. His father parted with it just before the war. Present owner is Mr E.W. Mowll, of Coldblow Farm, Walmer. Jack's uncles usually operated the horse's jaw with its hobnail teeth, and 'Jack' accompanied the party playing a tambourine. His father played an accordion and a brother, Edward[171], now of Sandwich, a triangle. Visiting big houses around Walmer, they were often invited indoors and, on one occasion mixed with guests in evening dress at the ballroom of Liverpool House. The cook at one large house was so frightened that she bribed the company with sandwiches, to stop the horse chasing her.[172]

Hoodeners at Walmer posing for Percy Maylam

---

[171] It is worth noting that Caroline Bell (see p109) disputed this, and Maylam too indicates it was actually the father's brother, i.e. William Laming, who played the triangle. The Kentish Express reporter may have confused whose 'brother' was meant. "Jack's uncles" refers to this William and also to Harry Axon – the horse in the Maylam photographs – who was a brother of Robert Laming's wife Caroline Axon.

[172] Kentish Express, 26 December 1952, p4

Judging from these two accounts alone, it might appear that the gang that Maylam met up with were privy to Coldblow Farm rather than Walmer Court Farm, although the proximity of the two (less than half a mile apart) with Mayers Lane a short distance from either suggests they could have been one and the same – it is difficult to imagine on ground level today. Today, the buildings of Walmer Court Farm comprise a terrace of houses on the Dover Road, a barn given over to the sales of pine furniture and the like, and the windmill alluded to earlier. Coldblow Farm is much more secluded, being sited on the western side of the railway, and the farmhouse more grandiose. Obscurely, Kelly's Directory for 1903 fails to quote the resident at Coldblow Farm, citing one Charles James Roberts as a cowkeeper there, perhaps indicating that Coldblow was merely some kind of annexe to Walmer Court Farm, which seems unlikely. Liverpool House was the retirement home of the widower Charles Brogden Sperling, formerly of Dynes Hall near Halstead in Essex. Little is known of this gentleman upon his arrival in Kent beyond his penchant for throwing elaborate parties at Christmas, judging by Jack Laming's description. The site of Liverpool House on maps of the day, show it to have been on the western perimeter of the grounds occupied by Walmer Castle on its coastal edge, at the junction of Liverpool Road, St Clare's Road, and Castle Road. A nineteenth century photograph of the building concerned, depicts a mansion which befits the description of 'one of the big houses' that one imagines when describing places which alms-seeking Christmas groups might visit. All the shops in twenty-first century Walmer are concentrated on the crossroads formed by Dover Road, Grams Road and Station Road. The butcher's shop cited by Maylam could be one of three cited in Kelly's Directory: Richard Belsey of Crompton Terrace, Richard Walters of Dover Road, or John Webb whose address isn't listed. The public house where Maylam found himself was either 'the Drum' next to the railway station, or 'the Railway Hotel'. Today, only the latter exists as 'The Railway', on the corner of Station Road with Mayers Road.

It was Edward Mowll's daughter who knew where the horse could be found. Barnett Field, in his capacity as a bank manager, delivered a talk on 'money' to the members of the Great Mongeham and Ripple branch of the Women's Institute in October 1956. How this meeting related to the finding of the horse was never recorded, so we must guess as to what exactly happened. During question time, or after the formal business had been conducted, conversation must have turned to what he did in his spare time, and that led on to the hooden horse he had constructed for the 1953 Coronation.

Under the heading: 'The Hooden Horse will be up to his Antics Again', Barnett Field commented how he, as a result of this:

> ...recovered one of the ancient Hooden Horses from Great Mongeham (sic). After speaking to the Women's Institute there, he heard there was one at Coldblow Farm. He visited the farm, but the farmer did not know about it. His little girl, however, remembered there was one in the loft. It had apparently been put up there in 1912 and forgotten. It was in perfect condition, and is one of the original Hooden Horses of East Kent.[173]

---

[173]Kent Messenger(Maidstone edition), 19 December 1958, p10

An unidentified person must have referred him to Edward Mowll, and the following comprises a note made following a telephone conversion to 'the little girl' mentioned, namely his daughter:

> She is the daughter of Edward Mowll, formerly of Coldblow Farm, Walmer. It was he who kept the hooden horse in his attic at Walmer. He also had the running of Walmer Court Farm and Hawkshill Farm. He was a magistrate on the Wingham bench, whilst his wife was a magistrate on the Deal bench. The horse actually belonged to his cousin John Mowll. Caroline (born 1947) recalled that her father dressed up in the horse whilst she was a youngster 'mainly for amusement'. "He knew that he shouldn't because it was against local by-laws in some areas after a woman was frightened to death at Whitstable" (sic) – probably meaning the 1828 incident at Broadstairs (see p40). Percy *(i.e. Jack)* Laming's (pronounced Lamming) grandfather *(i.e. Edward David Laming)* made the old horse. He and Percy were both wagoners in charge of carthorses. She thinks the Kentish Express text stating that Edward *(James)* Laming took part in it is in error, and that the correct identification is *Robert's* brother, i.e. William Laming…Laming's 'foal' differed from the old horse in that 'its eyes glowed in the dark' being made of bottle glass…[174]

Upon his retirement, Barnett Field donated Laming's horses for display at the Folkestone Library, Museum and Art Gallery, although these have since been removed to the Deal Maritime and Local History Museum when the former location was redecorated in 1999. The Walmer /Coldblow Farm horse that one may view has no mane or tail, and has jaws that are hinged nearer the throat than the St Nicholas and Deal horses. No horse brasses are present, being replaced by three brass bells stapled to the top of its head between the ears and braiding rosettes on the side of its head. Its canopy comprises hessian sacking. A clue as to its mode of performance is given from Maylam's photographs with the comment that the 'horse was very fond of rearing', much as those morris teams who use such a beast do today. This feature of the Walmer horse was commented on as 'unusual' by the present-day St Nicholas team whose horse crouches down throughout its performance with but token animation by the person inside. Another function of the Walmer horse was to collect any money bestowed to the group, by a coin being placed in its jaws – as was the case at Lower Hardres.[175] Plates D and E in Percy Maylam's book show the four members who comprised the Walmer hoodening team. Whilst admitting they posed specifically for Maylam's benefit, it is interesting to note that none of the three outside the horse were costumed – not even the musician. All are wearing jacket, waistcoat and flat cap: Jack Laming even appears to be wearing a necktie! The musician, Robert Laming is pictured holding a one-row Saxony accordion.

Retrospectively, there must have been so many questions that ought to have found answers. Barnett Field met Jack Laming on two or three occasions before the

---

[174]Notes from a telephone conversation with Mrs Caroline Bell, Jacques Court, Elham, 1 March 2000
[175]Maylam, p55

latter's death in 1959, so fine detail was never forthcoming, apart from one snippet of information which the former declared publicly and usually quoted in his lectures to interested bodies concerning his contact with Mr Laming:

> ...Our expectations (in finding 'specific details of ancient hoodeners') therefore were not shattered when in 1955, in the back streets of Deal, my wife and I found Joseph *(i.e. Jack)* Laming – by then 82 (sic) – who appears far right in Maylam's 1907 photos. Old Joseph was so delighted by the revival and forthwith made a 'horse' for us – rather too small for use, but on show with the other original Walmer Horse in Folkestone Museum. With our handbell programme in mind, we asked Joseph what carols they had sung. He answered, 'We never sung no carols, we sung pop'lar South African War songs![176]

This tallies very nicely with the comment that the Deal hoodeners had something of a renaissance when 'at the time of the South African War the horse was, with great success, got up with full military equipment'. Sadly, no questions were asked of Laming as to the titles or nature of what these songs may have comprised, so one must resort to the local newspaper archives to establish the statistical likelihood of what these might have been. Topping this straw poll was the poem written especially for the war effort by Rudyard Kipling: 'The Absent-Minded Beggar' which was later set to music by Sir Arthur Sullivan. This was cited so many times as being sung at ad hoc concert parties and fundraising efforts, that one finds it difficult not to imagine it not having been used by the Walmer hoodeners in 1900 or 1901 whilst the War was on or still a recent memory – not that there's any definite proof in favour of this idea. Other items on the proverbial wish list by reason of concert hall popularity include 'Soldiers of the Queen', 'Take the Lion's Muzzle Off', 'Sons of the Sea', and 'Lads of the Red, White and Blue'. However, it must be stressed that, however scientific such a survey might appear, it is no substitute for hard evidence from an eyewitness.[177]

What became of the Walmer hoodeners after Maylam first contacted them can only be guessed at. Interviewed in October 2000, Olive Field described Laming's group as having a man-woman – a molly with a broom who swept the path clean when the horse came in, five or six characters, and a musician who played a six-sided concertina, but all of these details contradict Maylam's own reports from the time, so considering that she had never seen any of these teams herself, it is likely that she had confused Jack Laming's description of his own team with reports she had read of other groups. She qualified the South African War songs used as 'trooper songs' which, taken literally, might imply one of the party to have been a war veteran. In the same session, a written note was read out describing the same party as 'A small group of local farm hands touring round villages with their man-animal, a musical squeeze-box, and collecting box – commonplace by then at Christmas. Their repertoire was limited. Old Laming, who we met at (Great) Mongeham mentioned South African War songs.

---

[176]Folk in Kent, vol. 71, p15 (October 1989)

[177]Result of a sweep through the Deal, Walmer, Dover & Kentish Telegram for benefit concerts during the period October 1899 through to December 1900

It died out with the advent of the First World War, and mechanized age afterwards.'[178] There is precious little useful in the local newspaper to corroborate the stories already quoted, save a sentence from 1896 quoting past experiences in Thanet and Wingham with a guess at its currency in Walmer:

> ...On the eve of Christmas was 'Hodening or Hoodening,' which many of our readers can remember – the party of young men with the head of a dead horse, that they affixed to a pole about four feet long. A string was tied to the lower jaw, and a horse cloth attached, which covered one of the party who, by pulling the string, kept up a loud snapping noise, while the rest of the party were grotesquely arrayed. From house to house they went, singing carols and songs, receiving in return cakes and ale or money...In Old English Customs it is said to be still kept up at Walmer, where they use a rudely-cut wooden figure of the head of a horse, the teeth being represented by a row of hob-nails...'[179]

---

[178]Interview with Olive Field and Zonia Bateman, 12 October 2000
[179]Kentish Gazette, 26 December 1896, p6

CHAPTER 8: THE REVIVAL, 1939-1965

The division between 'tradition' and 'revival' owes much to one's own perception, and can, at worst, be viewed as merely pedantic. Indeed, the Christmas hoodening undertaken by Len Harris and his accomplices at Acol in the 1920s was viewed as a 'revival' by the local newspaper, despite agricultural workers being involved at the correct time of year. The horse was further used in village celebrations during the summers of 1945 and 1953 respectively in the manner earlier described. That said, when Bob Skardon discontinued his tradition at Deal in 1934, the hooden horse was shortly to take on new responsibilities, but not necessarily as part of a Christmas custom. As an aside, it should be commented that Percy Maylam died in March 1939, but few involved in the forthcoming revival seemed to be aware of his passing. The timing involved was sheer coincidence.

The Balgowan and Ravensbourne Morris Men's Horse

It has briefly been mentioned how a man-beast was associated with various forms of morris dancing. The use of Hob-Nob at Salisbury together with St Christopher, the giant, in a pageant comprising morris dancers as early as the sixteenth century has already been noted, which continued through till the twentieth. In the South Midlands, tourney horses were used to accompany various traditional dance teams, such as at Ilmington at Warwickshire. The incidence of so-called 'revival' dance teams during the 1930s was still patchy compared to today. One such team was the Balgowan Old Boys Morris and Sword Dance Club that was established in 1933 by Walter Faires, a science teacher at the Balgowan School in Beckenham. This team grew from the work of the English Folk Dance and Song Society that was formed in 1932 from the merger of the Folk Song Society and English Folk Dance Society, whose structure was on a county basis with salaried officers.

At the start of 1939, Kent found itself with a new Head Branch Teacher, Miss Doreen Florence Brittain ('Biddy') Bennett. She was born in Londonderry in 1914, and after attending school in North Yorkshire, came to live in Beckenham. She was aware of Balgowan dance team, and surmising a possible role for it when she decided to reinvigorate the county branch. At that time, the function of the Kent branch of the EFDSS included the organization of dance festivals at Chilham Castle, Orpington and the Friars at Aylesford respectively. Miss Bennett (later Mrs Benham) had many musical influences from her childhood in both Ireland and in Yorkshire, and was skilled on both violin and melodeon herself. She learnt of the hooden horse custom upon reading Violet Alford and Rodney Gallop's book The Traditional Dance published in 1935 together with an article the former had written for the EFDSS journal in 1939. But it was the Abbots Bromley hobby horse Miss Bennett had in mind when 'reviving' the custom, primarily because it fell within her experience. That said, her job was more as an enabler rather than organizer, and it was she who suggested to Walter Faires that the Balgowan men construct a hooden horse. Other sources used were Maylam's work obtained via Kent's libraries, and an article attributed to Sidney Bredgar and published in the Invicta Magazine in 1909.[180]

Walter Faires's Balgowan School team

Members of the Balgowan Old Boys Morris and Sword Dance Club from the school in Beckenham pose for the camera with their hooden horse in publicity for the folkdance festival held at the Friars at Aylesford in July 1939

So it was that Wally Faires set to work. It is not known for certain who actually made the horse. The best guess is that it was in the handwork department at Balgowan School, most likely by the woodwork master 'Nobby' Clear – and he was working to a tight schedule as it hadn't been finished with a week to go before the Aylesford festival! Doreen Bennett had written some notes, based on Percy Maylam's descriptions, detailing how it ought to be constructed based on the Walmer horse. 'Head – wood crudely carved and painted; cover – sacking glossy black material holland; mane – brightly coloured ribbon (caytis[181]); tail – horsehair and ribbons; bridle – leather studded', with a further note that brasses were to be used on the head and that bells could be used. A photographer was commissioned to take photographs of the beast on the day, although the feeling was that the team assembled was 'improvised'

---

[180]Notes from telephone conversations with Mrs Doreen Benham, Angmering (near Worthing), 4 and 8 February 2003; I am also indebted to her for passing on to me letters to Violet Alford dated 17 January 1940, and from Walter Faires dated 28 January 1940, detailing the history of the Balgowan hooden horse.

[181] Maylam wrote "brilliant coloured ribbon, in Kent called 'caytis'" but despite some research, no other example has been found of this word being used

rather than conceived. Faires committed himself, at this stage to 'provide (a) the 'insides' of the horse, (b) a 'leader' and asked Miss Bennett to 'manage the fool and (if wanted) the man-woman.'[182]

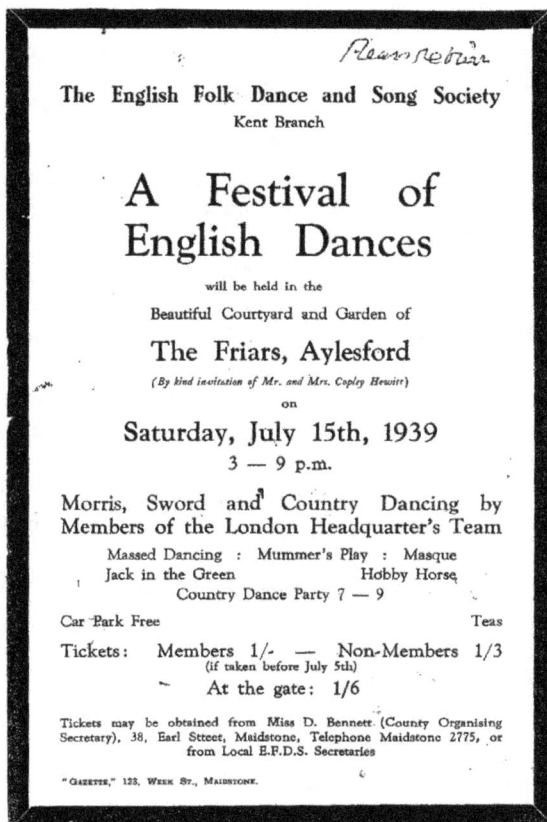

Pleaser return

The English Folk Dance and Song Society
Kent Branch

A Festival of English Dances

will be held in the

Beautiful Courtyard and Garden of

The Friars, Aylesford

(By kind invitation of Mr. and Mrs. Copley Hewitt)

on

Saturday, July 15th, 1939
3 — 9 p.m.

Morris, Sword and Country Dancing by Members of the London Headquarter's Team

Massed Dancing : Mummer's Play : Masque
Jack in the Green   Hobby Horse
Country Dance Party 7 — 9

Car Park Free   Teas

Tickets: Members 1/- — Non-Members 1/3
(if taken before July 5th)
At the gate: 1/6

Tickets may be obtained from Miss D. Bennett (County Organising Secretary), 38, Earl Street, Maidstone, Telephone Maidstone 2775, or from Local E.F.D.S. Secretaries

"GAZETTE," 123, WEEK ST., MAIDSTONE.

Handbill advertising the Aylesford dance festival of 1939

Note how the Hooden Horse is described as a hobby horse

A press release had already been published in late June 1939 advertising the Festival of English Dances to be held at the Friars at Aylesford on Saturday 15 July – then a private house, rather than the Carmelite priory it is today. Part of the entertainment was to feature the Hooden Horse who was to 'reappear in all his former glory', although the handbill described him as just a 'hobby horse'. The press release's justification in its use was that 'dancing from the Mummers' Play has continued to develop apart from the drama – in the sword and morris dances.' An appeal was made at the end of the article for people to come forward who could recall the horse performing since 1914. Coincidentally, the Kentish Express had already published an

---

[182]Eric Newman (Ravensbourne morris men), letter to the author, May 2000; Walter Faires, letter to Doreen Bennett, 8 July 1939

article on a Mr G.S. Martin who was photographed at about this time as being responsible for building a hooden horse for some other function – attempts to identify Mr Martin indicate no clue as to his location or envisaged performance.[183]

The hood of the horse itself appeared to have made by Miss Bennett or one of her colleagues, since it was sent separately to Walter Faires at Beckenham. The horse had its first outing on Thursday 13 July at Herne Hill at a pageant called 'the Symphony of Youth', and the performance repeated the following day. For the Aylesford event, the horse was photographed accompanied by 'his traditional followers – the Wagoner or leader, the Fool, and Bettie, the man-woman', and was described as making 'a dramatic entry with the Morris dancers'. Writing to Miss Bennett, Faires said that 'my fiddler is going to take the job of the 'horse insides' on Saturday and our fool will lead him. We can't manage any other characters owing to the transport difficulty.' Neither of the local newspapers described in any great detail the mode of performance, apart from saying the horse 'delighted the large audience by fully capturing the spirit of the old custom.'[184] Despite plaudits from the folk music world, and requests for further information and photographs, the school holidays denied any repetition. As it was, World War Two suspended further activity by the team, and the horse was given by Faires to Biddy Bennett for placement in storage.

All the members of the Balgowan team served in the War. However, it was found impossible to reconvene them afterwards, and its remaining members were absorbed into the new Ravensbourne club during the Winter of 1946-47. The hooden horse passed into their possession, and a new phase in its history was about to begin. The horse – christened 'Harold' – was used on many occasions, often to accompany EFDSS functions. Notable among these were newly-inaugurated May festivals held at Gravesend and Hythe in 1949 and 1950.

Barnett and Olive Field's Horse

Although they had lived in the Hythe area before the war, it seemed that Barnett and Olive Field didn't see their first hooden horse in action until they attended a Chilham Castle festival where the Ravensbourne morris men were performing. Olive was working as a physical education teacher who was particularly interested in National Dancing. In 1950, she was asked to start classes in international folk dancing at the Technical College, and soon the Folkestone District National Dance Group was formed. Barnett and Olive met Jack Hamilton at one of these Chilham meetings and, after reading Percy Maylam's book, the idea seemed to evolve to begin some kind of Christmas custom, possibly using the Beaux of London City Morris men of whom Jack was a member. Olive's dance team didn't quite appeal to Barnett. She claimed that Jack gave Barnett the idea of building his own hooden horse, and also suggested that he form his own morris team, which was later to become the East Kent morris men. Throughout Spring 1953, the nascent performers practised with the aim of dancing out for the first time on Coronation Day, as both the Ravensbourne and Beaux of London City teams were committed to celebrations of their own. Barnett Field had completed his horse, almost on time. Olive recalls:

---

[183]Kentish Express, 7 July 1939, p14

[184]Walter Faires, letter to Doreen Bennett, 13 July 1939; Kentish Express, 21 July 1939, p12; Kent Messenger, 22 July 1939, p7

Barnett was painting the head. I had got an awful cold. This was the day before Coronation Day. I had got a sacking for a cover. I dyed that to make it brown. Barnett was finishing the painting, but we got round it all right. It was a horrible day.[185]

Olive Field was referring to the weather. Originally, the plan was to have an open air public dance on Monday 1 June at the cricket ground in Cheriton Road, Folkestone, with Jack Hamilton calling and acting as master of ceremonies. In the end, this was moved to the East Cliff Pavilion, where the horse made his debut with Jack giving him a generous introduction. Three weeks later, the East Kent morris men made their first appearance at a party in the Dean's garden at Canterbury, and so it was that what was described as the 'brown horse' became their 'man-animal'. Its function as such was to collect money. To do this, Barnett Field had ingeniously designed the horse with a wooden mouth without hobnails, so money could be placed therein and slide into the bank moneybag located within its canopy – 'he was a bank manager, after all.' It was pointed out to potential contributors that:

If ye the Hooden Horse do feed,
Throughout the year, ye shall not need.

There was nothing actually traditional in this phrase even though Barnett Field mischievously dubbed it as 'Anon. Trad.' This was entirely of his own devising and included on East Kent Morris posters advertising future dance stands as early as 1954. However, because of its perceived anonymity and mystery, it has always been used to conclude the St Nicholas-at-Wade hooders' plays every year since their inception in 1966 – presumably because someone there saw this poster.

By the following Summer, the East Kent men had evolved their own programme of dance. The season was to start on Whit Monday at Charing parish church, where they were to dance atop its tower. There is supposition among some that the Morris is derived from pre-Christian ritual and thoroughly 'anti-establishment'. This notion certainly held sway in 1954, and since going into a church was involved, the symbolism of 'bridling the horse' to tame it was designed to enable its participation in the May Day festivities within permitted Christian acceptability. A tour around the villages would follow, ending with dancing in Folkestone and Hythe later in the day.

Handbell Hoodening

It should be stressed here that, whilst the East Kent men had the use of Barnett and Olive Field's 'brown' horse wherever it and they went, it belonged to the Field family, as can surmised from another use it acquired.

In the course of the year following, a small team of handbell ringers practised assiduously on bells which Olive Field had brought from her family home in Sussex. By Christmas Eve 1954, the 'Hooders' were ready to visit several of the large hotels in Folkestone where they presented for charity short programmes of carols. The Hooden Horse duly swallowed contributions of

[185]Olive Field and Zonia Bateman, interview held on 12 October 2000

money which the audiences had great delight in feeding to it. These unusual waites were very well received, and the revived annual custom has been maintained ever since.[186]

Barnett Field had read Percy Maylam's book and mused over ways of presenting a 'hoodening'. He was taken by the handbell ringing references. As we have seen previously, handbell ringing was very popular as Christmas entertainment in history at Minster, Deal and Ramsgate, to name but a few places in East Kent – although as a rival entertainment rather than component of any hoodening activity. The fact that Henry Brazier took out his bells which were 'hit with a stick' was the justification for selecting Olive Field's band of bell ringers as the kindred spirit involved – although it ought to be pointed out that, strictly speaking, the latter's bells were not the same as Brazier's.[187]

Barnett and Olive Field's handbell hoodeners

In Folkestone, with (from left to right) the 'brown' horse, Jack Laming's colt, and the Walmer horse

The leaflet detailing their history goes on to state that Barnett and Olive Field's band of 'handbell hoodeners' with their repertoire of folk and light classical music, took part in concerts, shows and special church services, at venues such as Canterbury Cathedral, and Leeds and Lympne castles where 'the acoustics are understandably fine.'

---

[186]Barnett& Olive Field, Midsummer Fire, (Folkestone: 1983) p28
[187]Barnett Field, in Folk in Kent, vol. 71 (October 1989) p15

They also toured separately and with Olive's dance group at home and abroad. They even recorded three sets of tunes, including the ubiquitous 'Winster Galop' on an album of folk music compiled from Kentish performers during the 1970s.

Barnett Field and his horse

In notes for the many lectures he was asked to deliver, Barnett made references to one incident that happened on one of these handbell hoodening tours at the Springfield and Westcliff hotels in Folkestone, whilst he was dressed up inside his brown horse. You can almost imagine this apparition sat on a bar stool next to the bar, disguised as a hooden horse, whose hand would occasionally reach out from under the canopy for his pint of beer – much to the amusement and bemusement of hotel guests and other visitors! Otherwise, you might have to sympathize with the person crouched down inside the horse for what seemed ages, waiting for his wife and the handbell ringers to arrive, oblivious to the knowledge that he or they were in the wrong place as we shall see:

> There are two hotels next to each other in Folkestone, and on Christmas Eve for many, many years, it was customary for the handbell Hoodeners to play carols and collect (via the Horse)…on that evening. They used to 'perform' at many venues leading up to Christmas. On this occasion, the horse (accidentally separated from the Bellringers) went into one hotel and 'sat' by the bar patiently awaiting the arrival of the ringers, whilst the ringers were in the other hotel, anxiously wondering where the horse was. They were finally

reunited, but not before a good many revellers were convinced they'd seen a horse, and just how merry they really were![188]

Hop Hoodening

On 21 July 1956, the pub formerly known as 'the Swan' at Wickhambreaux found itself with a new name: the 'Hooden Horse'. This came as a result of a competition by the brewer Whitbread in the days of 'tied houses' to rename some of its establishments to reflect local themes. This was attended with a great deal of pomp and ceremony. The dignitaries present were Sir Stephen Tallents (chairman of the conference for Local History), Anne Roper (Kent historian and president of the Association of the Men of Kent and Kentish Men), Robert Maylam (Percy's son), Douglas Kennedy (director of the EFDSS), and Donald Cassels (squire of the Morris Ring). A four-page leaflet was written for the occasion by Anne Roper, detailing the history and revival of the custom. Also present were the Ravensbourne and East Kent morris men with their hooden horses, and the handbell Hooders, together with Jack Hamilton.[189]

Hop-hoodening at Canterbury Cathedral Close, September 1988

Although intended as a 'one-off', the idea was nurtured to inaugurate a custom to involve the newly-named public house, and on 9 September 1957 the practice of 'hop-hoodening' began. The intention was to create some kind of 'carnival' as at the seaside to draw in visitors, and thus create interest. The existing Kentish morris dance teams with their horses would be key to this, using the hop harvest as a theme, the crops still being picked by hand in some parts of Kent, although the economic drive was for

---

[188]Zonia Bateman, letter to the author, 26 November 2000
[189]Barnett& Olive Field, 1983, Midsummer Fire, p11 and p32

machine picking. There would be a 'Hop Queen'. This was to emulate the well-publicized festival held at the Whitbread Hop Farm at Beltring in the Weald of Kent, but incorporating in spirit the May garland custom that once took place at nearby Yalding.[190] The result was a cage constructed as a bower swathed with hop leaves and berries, which was carried by the costumed 'queen'. She would lead a procession through the precincts of Canterbury Cathedral on the first or second Saturday in September. There would then be a display of dancing and handbell ringing after a blessing in the cathedral by the Dean of Canterbury. A tour was then organized which, in its first year, extended to the East Cliff bandstand at Ramsgate, the Oval bandstand at Cliftonville, and the Central bandstand at Herne Bay, before its conclusion at Wickhambreaux at a grand ceilidh or barn dance.

Hop-hoodening at Canterbury Cathedral Close, September 1988

Barnett Field was pivotal to its success. He had built up contacts in the financial community and knew the right people at Canterbury to grant access to the cathedral. The custom is still ongoing over sixty years after its creation. More recently, newly-inaugurated teams such as Kings Morris and the Wantsum Morris men have taken part, as well at sundry clog step-dancers. The finish of the tour at Wickhambreaux is also a constant feature, despite the fact that the 'Hooden Horse' pub closed its doors for the last time in 1979, leaving 'the Rose' as the sole hostelry in the village.

---

[190]Barnett Field, The Hooden Horse of East Kent, in Folklore, vol. 78 (1967) p203

Folkestone International Folklore Festival

In 1959, the East Kent men constructed a second horse which was christened 'Invicta' after the emblem of Kent. He was made by Arthur Hunt-Cook and carved by Derek Usher. He has a white, much more horse-like head than those photographed by Maylam, but has accompanied the East Kent men ever since. By choice, a much more upright gait was adopted in performance as it is used in the dance with the men, as well as for collecting. Up to this time, photographs of the Ravensbourne and Barnett Field's horses (i.e. his own 'brown horse' and the two from Jack Laming) in performance show them in the crouched down position, so the East Kent men perceived this as a new departure.

Throughout their early careers, both Olive, then Barnett Field's dance teams were invited to go abroad thanks to a sports link created between Folkestone and Middelburg on Walcheren Island in South Holland. The spirit of 'carnival' mentioned to the author by Olive Field had already been noted at Hythe which hosts its Venetian Fete on its Royal Military Canal every other August. The Nicolson Pipe Band of Folkestone was another body involved with this cultural exchange, and in 1959, the idea was floated for Folkestone to hold a folklore festival. The idea became a reality in June 1961, and the port held its International Folklore Festival every two years from then until the threat of the Gulf War in 1991 forced its cancellation. One popular group who first visited the festival was the Groupe Folklorique Boulonnais from Boulogne. They brought with them their two processional giants 'Batiste' and 'Zabelle' with them. Such entities are common today in the Nord-Pas de Calais region of northern France. In England, the sole survivor from history is St Christopher, the Salisbury Giant, as we have already seen in an earlier chapter. The French team were invited back to Folkestone two years later but, unfortunately, the giants were damaged on their return and were not allowed back in following years. Such was the impression left by these perambulating titans, it was decided that Folkestone should have its own 'giant.' So it was that in 1967, a giant hooden horse was made:

> This huge creature, fourteen feet high, was extremely cleverly constructed by Freddie Gosnold. The 'pram', with four pneumatic tyred Lambretta wheels, was very strongly made by Ray Strickland. The robust Horse, which has functioned impressively under the command of Don Paice in all subsequent festivals and at times in local carnivals, needs two occupants. These do not operate one behind the other, pantomime fashion, but one above the other. The upper one operates the head which, heavy though it is, has extreme mobility and jaws which open and clack like those of the smaller members of the family.[191]

At the 1967 Folkestone Festival, Barnett Field also read a paper at the symposium held which was published later that year by the Folklore Society. By that time, his portfolio on the subject of the hooden horse was very impressive. He had built his own horse based on a traditional design, used it to entertain spectators and as a mode of collecting money with his own morris team, adapted the practice noted at Lower Hardres to define a Christmas hoodening incorporating carolling and handbell ringing,

---

[191]Barnett & Olive Field, 1983, Midsummer Fire, p31 and p38

met with Jack Laming at Walmer who took part as a hoodener before the Great War, prompting the recovery and usage of the old Walmer horse used on this occasion, employed his own horse as a prop for one other function (i.e. hop-hoodening), made the acquaintance of Lady Constance Tuff who could recall a visit made to her by the Deal gang from over sixty years previously, and was pivotal in constructing a 'giant' horse that became emblematic of the biennial International Folklore Festival at Folkestone.

Edward Coomber's Hooden Horse

Another horse which was constructed and owned by an enthusiast rather than a group, belonged to Edward Coomber who was born in 1914 in the Tonbridge area. He worked in Canterbury as a school teacher, firstly at Kingsmead School, and later at St Stephen's School. He had a degree in folklore studies, and became interested in reviving hoodening in the early 1950s after being given a copy of Percy Maylam's book by the author's niece[192]. The horse was constructed by Arthur Clark in the crafts workshop at the Sir William Nottidge School in Whitstable, by the senior boys' woodwork class of which Mr Clark was the craft teacher. The design was based on the photographs taken by Percy Maylam over forty years previously.

The horse made its debut at St Stephen's Boys School on Tuesday 16 December 1952. The Kentish Gazette described the horse as consisting

'...of a horse's head rudely carved in wood which was fixed to the end of a staff. This was carried by a man (known as the hoodener), who was concealed under a cloth, this making a crude resemblance to a horse. The lower jaw of the head worked on a hinge, and could be made to open and shut by means of a string, making a loud clapping noise. The party was made up of the wagoner who led the horse, the rider, who was invariable thrown off, 'Mollie', a lad in woman's clothing, and two or three others with musical instruments. After various antics, the party would sing carols.[193]

One surmises that Edward Coomber stuck to the above formula by way of performance, and a photograph is shown of a bespectacled boy (John Carr) wearing a wide-brimmed hat as the wagoner, leading the horse (played by Brian Scamp) upon which Michael Clarke was seated as the rider. Sydney Oliver played the 'Mollie'. On the Friday of that week, it was reported that 'a party of hoodeners from St Stephen's School, with the choir of St Dunstan's church, will visit homes in the locality, singing carols, raising four pounds in aid of the Mayor's Chrismas Fund.'[194] The Canterbury edition of the Kent Messenger noted that Mr Coomber had intended to 'stage a show at Whitstable...but technical difficulties arising, he transferred the idea to his own school.'[195]

---

[192] Source uncertain; possibly Canterbury Journal

[193] Mark Lawson, notes from an interview conducted on 15 December 1999

[194] Kentish Gazette, 19 December 1952, p6 – the newspapers misleadingly refer to a St Dunstan's school in these accounts rather than or as well as St Stephen's school. It is assumed that the latter is correct.

[195] Kent Messenger (Canterbury Telegraph edition), 19 December 1952, p2

Pupils of the St Stephen's School under the tutelage of Edward Coomber on their rounds as hoodeners in 1954

The horse was kept in the Coombers' garden shed in Nelson Road, Whitstable, which was swept away during the floods of February 1953. The horse was rescued some weeks later from other debris and was cleaned up, although it still bore marks as a result. Edward Coomber decorated its forehead with oyster shells in imitation of horse brasses to commemorate its escape. During the Christmas season of that year, the hoodening once more took place, with the characters of two holly boys added for the occasion in commemoration of the separate Shrovetide custom of bygone West Kent whereby youngsters made figures of ivy and holly, with girls encouraged to possess themselves of the boys' ivy figure and boys likewise with the girls' holly figure. This done, each party would retire and ceremoniously burn the holly-boy and ivy-girl to the accompaniment of much shouting and merriment. The horse also went out with the carol singers of St Peter's church choir in and around Whitstable that year.[196]

With a formula established, Edward Coomber solicited parties to take round his horse in December 1954. A performance was given by Class IIIc of St Stephen's School, Canterbury on the Green during the afternoon of Tuesday 21 December. Once more he delegated out the roles of horse, rider, wagoner, Mollie, holly boys and musicians. The photograph in the Canterbury edition of the Kent Messenger outside Mrs Louisa Pay's almshouse at St Stephen's Green, together with another pictured in the Kentish Gazette, show the wagoner wearing a top hat, an attempt at a tail coat, and chequered trousers, a rider dressed like a Newmarket jockey, 'Mollie' wearing a

---

[196]Kentish Gazette, 25 December 1953, p4

123

sun bonnet, waistcoat, long skirt and holding a besom, and the 'holly boys' wearing dark jackets and short trousers with a cardboard crown and holding sprigs of holly with their arms extended. The musicians comprise a corps of percussionists and one boy holding an old-time accordion. Coomber also took his horse out again at St Peter's Church, Whitstable, and to Herne Bay Junior School, hoping that 'several 'horses' will be constructed in East Kent in time for next Christmas.' At Whitstable, the St Peter's church choir went round on Wednesday 22 December, singing 'the better known Christmas hymns', raising £1 8s. 6d. (£1 43p.) for the Whitstable Times Christmas Gift Fund. After beginning their tour at 6.30 p.m., they proceeded to Cromwell Street, Regent Street, Gladstone Road, High Street, Harbour Street, Victoria Street and Sydenham Street.[197, 198]

Edward Coomber's young Hoodeners, 1954

Note the improvised costumes, instruments, and 'holly boys' on each side

In 1955, Edward Coomber seems to have abandoned using school children as part of a pageant. The Kentish Gazette reported that:

On the afternoon of Wednesday, Thursday and Friday of the last week, parties were held for the Infant, Lower Juniors and Upper Juniors of St Stephen's County Primary School. During the proceedings, the children were visited by the Hooden Horse under the general direction of Mr E. Coomber. The Rev. and Mrs A.R. Barnes visited the children during the tea…'[199]

In 1956, performances were confined to Whitstable only, with an unspecified cast of actors. The event was organized by the Rev. R. Leeks of St Peter's Church, Whitstable and Edward Coomber. The Kentish Gazette says of this, that:

The gaily-caparisoned 'horse' with its wooden head and snappy mouth, frolicked midst the Christmas shopping crowds, accompanied by a witch sweeping her broom – a symbol of good luck – and the retinue of farm

---

[197]Kentish Gazette, 24 December 1954, p7
[198]Whitstable Times & Tankerton Press, 18 December 1954, p9
[199]Kentish Gazette, 23 December 1955, p8

workers in old time costumes. At intervals, performances were given in the side roads just off the main street out of the way of the traffic. This feature aroused a great deal of interest and the collection taken helped the funds of the Church of England's Children's Society.[200]

In previewing the same, the Whitstable Times correctly identified the witch as 'Mollie' who 'wields a besom to good purpose' thus demythologizing that aspect of the show. The report further stated that the performances lasted one hour in total between half-past three and half-past four, and comprised members of the choir, Youth Fellowship, and congregation of St Peter's Church.[201]

It is believed that Edward and Margaret Coomber continued taking round the horse at carol singing every year up until about the early- to mid-1970s – only ceasing because they were at retirement age. One eye-witness was a young Mark Lawson, who commented that in 1960 or 1961 when his grandmother took him from her home in Tankerton Road to see the custom:

> I must have been between four and a half and five and a half (years old at the time). My mother was able to supply me with dates when the street lighting was put in. I remember the dark crowd which I couldn't see the limits of, because it was all darkness and shadow with lanterns. I also remember being fascinated by the instruments they were playing. The horse went round frightening children by snapping at them, people went round collecting…I was watching this entranced, holding onto my grandmother's hand by the garden gate, then what I thought was a bush standing by the edge of the carol singers suddenly came towards me snapping its jaws. That sort of memory stays with you. I didn't know it was a hooden horse…until years later. I think I saw it at least once, possibly three or four more times.[202]

Mark added that Mr and Mrs Coomber took it in turns to be in the horse or to lead it. He recalled that the taut strings that operate the jaws, were manipulated by the horse holder, not the man inside. The orange reins were no more than just that. Also, the mouth was unable to swallow money (unlike Barnett Field's horse). In these latter days, neither of the Coombers wore any special costume, nor included any additional characters such as Mollie in their retinue. Nor did they recite lines or sing songs.

The horse was recovered comparatively recently, although as often happens with oral traditions, stories conflict – one version has it that it was in Dixie Lee's loft and passed to Mark by her, another maintains it was discovered in a rubbish skip awaiting disposal! More plausible is the alternative that when the Coombers' house was being sold, Mark was rung up and asked if he wanted an old Hooden Horse. And there it

---

[200]Kentish Gazette, 28 December 1956, p7

[201]Whitstable Times & Tankerton Press, 22 December 1956, p9

[202]Mark Lawson, notes from an interview conducted on 15 December 1999; also communication to the author, 19 February 1999

was, in the corner of the garage. Mark still has it and brings it out to the Hoodening moot – it has already celebrated its own golden anniversary.[203]

Birchington

The Townswomen's Guilds of East Kent were and still are a body concerned with the education of women, much in the manner of the more familiar Women's Institute. Birchington had two separate bodies: one that met in the afternoon, and another in the evening. In 1954, the Social Studies Committee of the Birchington Evening Townswomen's Guild were studying local customs, and came across that of the hooden horse.

> Led by Mrs Turnbull, we were able to revive this custom and the Guild made their first performance in Birchington Square, at the beginning of Christmas week 1954, and subsequent evenings ending on Christmas Eve. The result was quite a useful sum handed to the local Village Centre Fund…Our horse is a faithful reproduction of the original one which toured Birchington and other Thanet villages. It was designed for use by an elderly man who was one of the Hoodeners. (The custom) fell into abeyance in 1911…[204]

Where this date 1911 came from is unknown, unless it related to a perceived last known incidence of the custom in Birchington. The Isle of Thanet Gazette believed the 'last known hoodening party in Thanet was at Hale Farm, St Nicholas, about 1905'. In any case, the event was well-previewed and reviewed by East Kent's newspapers – even as far away as Ashford's Kentish Express. The Isle of Thanet Gazette reported:

> '…Accompanied by carol-singing members of the guild carrying coloured lanterns, the hoodeners created great interest as they toured different roads each evening, and at a number of houses children were brought from their beds to see the 'horse'. On Christmas Eve, the party was given a rousing welcome at the licensed premises in The Square, the antics of the 'horse' enlivening the pre-Christmas celebrations, and customers joining in heartily in the singing of carols. As a result of the week's tour, the party collected £14 3s. 10d. for the Village Centre Fund.'[205]

The report ended by listing the cast. Mrs Frances Venables took the part of Mollie, wielding her besom broom, and dressed in headscarf and shawl. Mrs Fanny Reed took the part of the wagoner, with long coat, hat, and whip. Mrs Jessie Payne is seen carrying a bucket, presumably to collect money, and Mrs Ruth Roach stands behind the horse. Under the horse was Mrs Dorothy Farebrother. Barnett Field, presumably based on correspondence he had had with the group, noted that the horse was made by 'Mr

---

[203]Mark Lawson, notes from an interview conducted on 15 December 1999; also communication to the author, 19 February 1999

[204]Birchington Evening Townswomen's Guild, typed note headed 'Social Studies: The Hooden Horse and Hoodeners' (Ben Jones collection).

[205]Isle of Thanet Gazette, 17 December 1954, p1

Wood of Birchington' and 'copied from the old Walmer horse.'[206] In a retrospective, the East Kent Times reported that the horse was made by 'the husband of one of their members.' It has proved impossible positively to identify Mr Wood, but a namesake indicated that the carol singers 'would have performed at the plush Beresford and Bungalow Hotels (both of which have since been demolished)' and that the hoodeners did the same.[207], [208]

Birchington Evening Townswomen's Guild in 1954

There is some evidence that the horse was taken round again in 1955 and 1956, but without the aplomb of its inaugural year. The decision to parade it had to be taken

---

[206]Barnett Field, 'The Kentish Hooden Horse Today' in English Dance & Song, vol. 21, no. 5 (May 1957) p173 – it is evident from Field's letter dated 10 October 1956 to Harriett Buck of the Birchington Guild, thanking her for lending her photo and details of her revival, that there was some correspondence between Field and the Townswomen's Guild. The latter visited Wickhambreaux to see the East Kent morris men perform, and still have a letter from Barnett Field congratulating them on their revival. The identity of the creator of the horse seems insoluble, since the three references cited provide something of a mismatch. Barnett Field's 'Mr Wood' is most likely to have been an Alfred Wood (1897-1989) but, if he was the 'elderly man who was one of the Hoodeners', this would indicate he participated just before or around the time of the Great War. The best interpretation was that Mr Wood was indeed its creator and the correlated reference is journalistic shorthand and misleading.

[207]Isle of Thanet Gazette, 31 December 1954, p1
[208]East Kent Times, 18 January 1967, p9

at a monthly meeting in October. In each case, it was resolved to have it accompanying carol singers, and in 1956, the proceeds went to the Spastics Society (nowadays called 'Scope'). Collective memory of the Guild today has it that the horse definitely went out in 1957, although no mention of this was reported in the local press.[209]

The horse was also used in a pageant 'Once They Lived in our Town' at the Granville Theatre in Ramsgate on Wednesday 9 May 1956, enacted by members of the East Kent Federation of Townswomen's Guilds. Scene 13 belonged to Birchington, and the programme for the occasion tells us that it was produced by Harriett Buck, with characters including a grandmother, mother, father, child, hoodeners and carol party, without listing the names of the cast. Photographs of the occasion show some of the performers in costume, one holding a lantern, apparently attending a staged formal party.[210]

Following an advertisement placed in the November 2001 issue of the Birchington Forum, the horse was located in the attic of one of the Guild's members without its blanket. In March 2002, at a meeting of the Guild, the horse was donated to the St Nicholas-at-Wade Hoodeners who now include it in their stable and used it for the first time during their 2002 Christmas play.

The horse was donated by the Guild to the St Nicholas Hoodeners in 2002 when Ben Jones was asked to give a presentation of hoodening, at which lines from the forthcoming play were read with a guest appearance by the author reciting the wagoner's part!

'One-Off' Revivals

Following an article in the Kent & Sussex Journal, the Godmersham and Crundale Youth Club revived the customs of hoodening and the 'Seven Champions'. On the Monday before Christmas 1952, they visited a number of houses as hoodeners. The horse was made specially for the occasion by Albert Graves of Crundale House, and members took the parts of jockey, wagoner and 'Molly', together with singers and noise-makers. 'In true traditional style, the hooden horse clacked its jaws, Molly swept the ground and Christmas greetings were expressed by the whole party.' At the Club Party held on 9 January 1953, they enacted 'the Seven Champions of Christendom' with an elaborate fight scene between St George and the Turkish Knight. However, approaches to members of the cast have failed to elicit any great memory of either event. It is probable that the Crundale members only took part in the hoodening, with the big houses being visited. The two villages are three miles apart, Crundale atop the Wye Downs, with Godmersham straddling the Ashford-Canterbury road alongside the Great Stour.[211] The horse was given to the rector of the parish, Canon Stanley Brade-Birks (1887-1982), and later used by his grandchildren for their own private amusement.[212] One of these grandchildren is Edward Joyce (born 1965), and his

---

[209] Isle of Thanet Gazette, 21 October 1955, p7

[210] Isle of Thanet Gazette, 11 May 1956, p8

[211] Crundale & Godmersham Parish Magazine, February 1953; Rex Lancefield, Within Living Memory – a Hundred Years of Crundale and its Region (1990: author) p102

[212] Originally found at the website
http://samitetwo.demon.co.uk/mediawiki/index.php/Hooden_Horse_Introduction but neither this website nor any archive copy exists now

mother who lives in Cheltenham still has the horse. Mr Joyce recalls the burlesque indulged in by him and his siblings:

My Grandad (Canon Stanley Brade-Birks) owned an old wooden horse's head on a pole and he brought it to us. It looked like a fearsome kind of hobby horse with a black head and white teeth. I took the horse and tried to ride it like a hobby horse, but was told to hold the horse in front of me. There was the remainder of a black piece of cloth that had almost frayed away attached by a nail and it was put over the head. The string below the jaw was pulled down to make a click-clacking sound. Since the cloth was worn, it was replaced with a large silver sheet, we were then all given our parts in a ritualized performance; Katherine was the horse, Andrew the rider, I was the wagoner, and Margaret was Molly – a woman with a broom. The beast was called the hooden horse and was recorded in my diary of the visit (to Godmersham)…until 1977. Then the horse was brought to Cheltenham where it remains a family heirloom to this day…I (now) live in Ealing … my Mum has the horse in Cheltenham (after the family moved there from Kent)'[213]

The local history writer Robert Goodsall wrote a short piece on the history of hoodening in his A Third Kentish Patchwork. This included two photographs: the first showing the author with the curator of Maidstone Museum holding up one of the Wingham Horses; the second showing a staged event at the author's home at Harrietsham. Further enquiries noted that:

The hooden horse ceremony was staged outside Barn Cottage, Stede Court, Stede Hill, in about 1956. My father (R.H. Goodsall) made the replica hooden horse himself. The person on the left of the photograph, in the top hat and carrying a whip is Albert Gill, our own gardener at the time. He is now very old and cannot add to this information at all, as the other people in the illustration cannot be recalled by him, or by myself.[214]

The photograph also shows a white besmocked character wearing a wide-brimmed hat, and an accordion player behind the horse.

And lastly, although it cannot be called a 'revival' as such, the East Kent Federation of the Women's Institute delivered the following commission in a London gathering in 1961.

In an attempt to send something out of the ordinary to the Women's Institute Countrywomen's Market Place at the Olympia Ideal Home Exhibition (in April 1961), organizers asked Mr W.S. Light, craftsman of Grove Cottage, Great Chart, to make models of the hooden horse. Mr Light is an

---

[213]Ed Joyce, email to the author, 25 October 2005, following an invitation to attend the Hoodening 'moot' in Canterbury the following month

[214]Robert H. Goodsall, A Third Kentish Patchwork (Harrietsham: 1970) p98; R.M.S. Goodsall, letter to the author, 23 October 2001

independent member of Ashford W.I. Market Stall. The pattern was lent by Mr Barnett Field…who liked to fashion small hooden horses of wood to amuse his daughter Zonia in her childhood. He suggested that the horses be made as collecting or money boxes – depress the tail to open the mouth to take the coins. Mr Light has carved not only a 'stable' of twelve chestnut-hued hooden horses, each gay in a scarlet trapping, but also a dozen red and blue wheeled hobby horses, rarely seen in 1961, although much ridden in Victorian nurseries.[215]

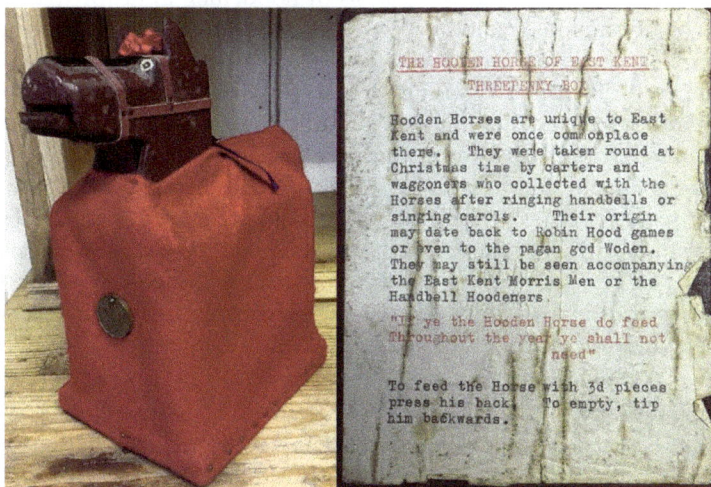

One of Light's stable of model horses

[215]Kentish Express, 10 March 1961, p7

CHAPTER 9: THE REVIVAL, 1966-2016

With so many sensitivities to assuage, this chapter aims to detail the development of hoodening since 1966, without prejudice; especially since much of its input comes from contributors who unreservedly shared confidences with the author which may differ from any conclusions drawn. Analysis of hoodening in history has shown that perceptions of 'continuous tradition' reveal more of a broken and fragmented pattern than many of us would be prepared to admit to without question. Also, both this chapter and Percy Maylam's 1909 magnum opus serve only as snapshots of the present day with acknowledgements to the past. Teams come and go due to a number of factors: work, family pressures and enthusiasm to name but three. Sometimes, teams may be over-dependent on one member to make things happen in the first place!

In the case of St Nicholas-at-Wade, for example, the team that the Rev. Bennett Smith had wind of in 1876, cannot convincingly be said to be a direct ancestor to that of 1921 when the Trice brothers gave it up. But that said, since 1966, there have been a number of revivals in East Kent, some focused as clubs, others on individuals, and most have survived the turn of the century. Envoi!

St Nicholas-at-Wade

If you were to take a walk along Shuart Lane away from the village centre of St Nicholas towards the Thanet Way, before arriving at the village cemetery, you might notice a 'compound' on the left, decorated in red, white and blue, signposted with the words 'Beware of the Dog' in different languages. This was the home of Tristan Lloyd Jones. Jones was once manager and director of The Observer newspaper. The son of a distinguished family on his father's side, he took a full part in village life as parish councillor, earning something of a reputation as an eccentric. He collected and maintained a collection of country artefacts, and was a frequent visitor to antiques shops and auctions. It was this interest that prompted the discovery of the Trice family's hooden horse in 1965.

Around that year, he raised the idea of an exhibition of rural bygones: a purely local affair since it doesn't seem to have been reported in any of the newspapers. People were asked to delve into their attics and produce old objects for display at the village school. At this event, Edmund Trice (then aged 77 years) volunteered his hooden horse, and great interest was expressed by the younger generation, who resolved to 'revive' the lapsed custom for the first time in 45 years. Among these, was Allan Garratt, himself the owner of a local antiques shop, which he retrospectively renamed 'Hoodeners Antiques' before he moved abroad to France in the 1970s. Research was conducted, and over time advice sought from all four Trice brothers, and Tom West who were still alive and living in the village. Were anyone to realize it, Steve Howland was still alive and living in Manston but, with the benefit of hindsight, the thought of finding him probably never occurred to anyone. The key characters of any performance were identified as the horse, a rider, the wagoner, Mollie, sundry actors, and a musician. Tom West mentioned that the key aims were horseplay, singing songs or telling a joke. None of this mattered in the end. As Ben Jones responded:

"the group decided they were no good at telling jokes – or even music – and hit upon amateur dramatics as something they could attempt. Reading out lines is much easier. Some had been keen on plays in any case – George Michelmore in particular." The new team for 1966 comprised Michelmore of Belle Isle who took the part of Mollie, Colin Bean of Manor Lea who was the rider, Chris Cole of Alpha inside the horse, Tristan Jones's eldest son Adam as the fiddler, and Brian Debenham, later of the Grange as the wagoner. Brian Debenham himself was formerly head of the junior school at Chatham House Grammar school, Ramsgate, and latterly head of English at Oakwood Park Grammar School, Maidstone. Seemingly, with him on board, in designing a mode of performance, a Christmas-type Mummers' play had to be involved using death and resurrection as a theme, and he would write it!

On Thursday 22 December 1966, they made their debut at Bolingbroke Farm, Sarre, where Percy Maylam had taken photographs of the Hale gang 61 years previously.

'The Hoodeners are here!' shouted someone as the door of the house opened, and in rushed the Horse followed by the Rider, the Wagoner, and the Mollie. Attempts were made to mount the horse and this was followed by the singing of country songs and carols. Eventually, the proceedings were brought to a close with the distribution of drinks and 'largesse' – which will be sent to Oxfam….So popular was the performance given on Thursday, that the hoodeners staged a repeat at St Nicholas the following day.[216]

What the newspaper didn't mention was that the whole play included four pages of script, mostly in hilarious rhyming couplets – a tradition that still lasts until today. The 'death and resurrection' aspect usually occurs when, for example, the rider is thrown from the horse, and is eventually revived after being thought dead. (Sometimes, it is the horse (as well as the rider) that dies. There might be attempts to bring the corpse back to life, or the casualty is momentarily stunned, but the theme remains the same. There is a repertoire of songs that have been attempted in the past, although the violinist usually plays for carol singing at the end of the play. The 'country songs' included those such as 'Twankydillo' by the Copper Family, or 'the Drunkard's Song' collected by Ken Stubbs from the traveller Bill 'Mousey' Smith at Edenbridge. More recently, the team have revived singing 'All Along the Rails' and 'Teach Me How to Fly' when the words and music finally came to light. The whole event in 1966 was intended as a one-off to raise money for charity, £40 being raised. Other places visited were the Sun and the Bell public houses, the junction of Downbarton Road with Summer Road, Nether Hale Farm, Chris Cole's house at St Nicholas, and also Sarre Court. Other requests came to give private shows came from 'all over Kent', and there was the offer of an expenses-paid trip to London. The story was in all three Thanet newspapers of the day. In the East Kent Times, Roger Pearson interviewed Walter Trice and photographed Edmund Trice to gauge his reaction:

Hoodening in Thanet ain't quite what it used to be though. Or, at least, so it would seem from the comments of one hardened old enthusiast from St

---

[216]Isle of Thanet Gazette, 30 December 1966, p7

Nicholas. He is one-time hoodening wagoner Walter Trice, 65, brother of the owner of the St Nicholas horse. When I talked to him at his cottage in St Nicholas this week, he said the people who had revived the custom last month were different from those who went hoodening when he was a boy. 'They're a better class of people now,' he said, 'but they're also more inhibited.' He comes from a family of nine boys and one girl, and about half of these all took main parts in hoodening parties. In those days, it was a good excuse for a 'beer up'. But Walter suspects that proceedings are a little more orderly and sober these days.[217]

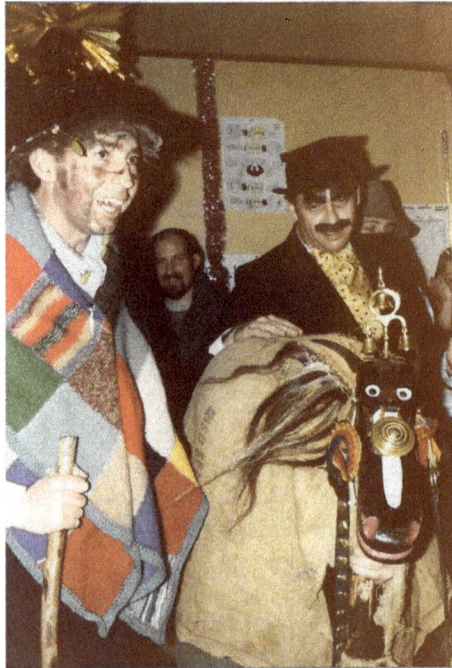

St Nicholas-at-Wade Hoodeners at the Sun Inn, December 1986

And that might have been it, had there not been any kind of clamour for a repeat performance in 1967. The local newspapers are little help in surveying what took place, and only sporadically reported the event after the 1966 revival. From 1967 onwards, the part of Mollie has been the role of David Gray, and the part of the boy that year was Martin Beale. Nobody recalls all the venues attended, apart from Sarre Court. In 1969, local antiques dealer Alan Garratt took part for the first time in an extra role created, Sam, who is usually portrayed as a besmocked yokel. Garratt became something of a spokesman for the team, summing up the performance in 1975, thus:

---

[217]East Kent Times, 18 January 1967, p9

There are six of us who perform in St Nicholas – the horse, rider, a wagoner, a Mollie, who is a young man dressed as a woman, and music maker, and Sam – that's me. We are like the Christmas Mummers of old, and from 21 December, coinciding with the winter solstice, we give two performances in 'the Bell' and about 12 shows, several a night, in private houses. The owners usually have a party on and lavish their hospitality on us – so that our acting improves as the evening goes on![218]

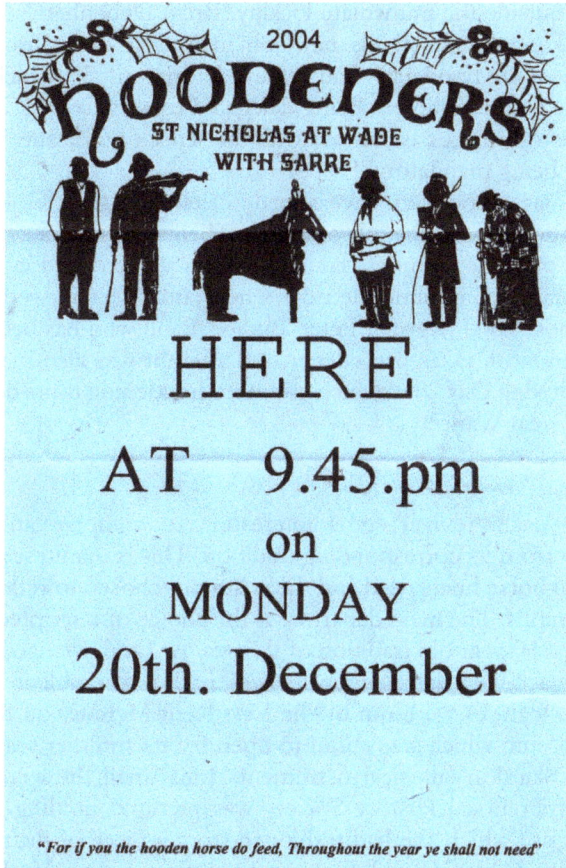

A4-size poster advertising the team

Brian Debenham wrote all the scripts up until 1979, to which Ben Jones (Tristan Jones's youngest son) commented upon compiling them for the club archive (and web site) that they were often full of biblical references and moral overtones, combined with coarse humour and local references. Sometimes scripts were only handed out on the night, and a new play was written every year to maintain the air of topicality which has always been a feature of the show. As a small boy in the early 1970s, Ben

---

[218]Kent Life, vol. 12, no. 12 (December 1975) p59

remembered the overriding personalities of Alan Garratt and Brian Debenham, and that he sat on the stairs looking through his fingers because the horse scared him.

The team that performed during the Christmas 2000 season had now done so regularly since 1993 – and have had only minor changes since. They comprise musician Ben Jones as George (who took over effectively from his elder brother Adam in 1990), David Gray as Mollie, Clive Bolton as 'Arry the wagoner, Chris Cole as the animator of Dobbin, Roy Fairbrass as Sam, and Jamie May as the boy. The actors are still drawn from the St Nicholas and Sarre village communities, and fluctuate as and when they move on to jobs outside the immediate locality. Brian Debenham's last performance was in 1978, and it is assumed his new job in Maidstone restricted his thespian aspirations. By then, the hoodeners had achieved a maturity by which they would no longer rely on one of their number being delegated to write scripts. That task is now shared around the rest of the cast; always with the sense of topicality with the dreaded rhyming couplets being mandatory![219]

The St Nicholas Hoodeners have already celebrated their Golden Jubilee, and David Gray his fiftieth year in the role of Mollie. Their story remains one of continuity, with the children of some members taking on roles vacated by long-term members, such as Simon Gray who became the rider when Jamie May moved away, and Tom Paul (the son of post-2000 wagoner Peter 'Budgie' Paul) who has been deputizing for Simon's role when work takes precedence. An attempt was also made to repeat the 'Great Walk' on Boxing Day 2016 which emulated hoodening tours described by Tom West before the Great War.[220]

Deal

In reviewing each 'revival', it is interesting to compare and contrast what influences it drew from its corresponding tradition. This is manifest at St Nicholas by way of the original horse being used and the costumes chosen to reflect those worn in Maylam's photographs. The main departure is the choice of a scripted play, which has now evolved into a 50-year old tradition of its own. At Deal, we need to consider two separate revivals, each with their own influences, each remarkable in their own right.

In May 1974, features were run by the East Kent Mercury on the Maritime and Local History Museum which was about to open for its summer season – noting the exhibition of Bob Skardon's musical instruments. Julia Small, the secretary of the Deal, Walmer and District Local History Society was pictured holding a hooden horse (christened 'Hengist') which she had fashioned from a piece of driftwood washed in front on her home in Marine Road, Walmer. In crafting it, she 'combined features of the former Deal, Walmer and Sarre horses. The creature sports a horse-brass with an appropriate anchor motif. Its mane consists of brightly coloured ribbons…as its purpose is to swallow money, it has been provided with a roomy gullet.' Teeth were also painted on to jaws that were made to open and shut, rather than comprise hobnails.[221]

The initial intention was to exhibit Julia's craftwork at the museum. However, as time drew on and the Christmas season approached, its primary use came to the fore,

[219]Ben Jones, in conversation with the author 11 April 2000; also see his website
[220]Ben Jones, email to author, 11 January 2018
[221]East Kent Mercury, 23 May 1974, p9

and £50 was raised for local charities in 1974. At Christmas the following year, more was made of the character, when the horse was accompanied by 'a small party of hooodeners in costume (who) sung carols on Christmas Eve.' Once more a collection was made for local charities, and venues included St George's church for the blessing of their Christmas tree, the Clarendon Hotel, the Queens Hotel, the Black Horse, and the Royal. A letter of thanks was published in the local paper. Julia Small tells us how the 'hoodening' came about during the 1975 season:

> The only real 'performance' of carols was in the now vanished Queen's Hotel, Deal. Someone phoned out of the blue saying he (I think it was a he) considered something should be done – but when it came to the point, 'he' had 'flu and never appeared. We were therefore reduced to myself, the chairman of the History Society, his wife, and her father. But the diners were generous in spite of our thin tones. Mr Brown was the host...[222]

Revival at Deal: Julia Small with 'Hengist', May 1974

There was some effort at dressing up. For herself, Julia Small wore white breeches, a white shirt with a large neck bow, blue close-buttoned jacket or brocade patchwork waistcoat (inspired from the traditional jacket worn by Robert Skardon portrayed in Maylam's photograph) according to season, plus a bowler hat. There was no strict

---

[222]Julia Small, letter to the author, 2 February 2000

hoodening 'season' observed, and Julia Small and her husband, Robert, took the horse out at any time of the year. She recalled visiting Sandwich with the young daughter of a History society committee member, where there was 'a kind of dancing on the village green' where 'we managed to foot it up-and-back-again with the Horse between us.'

The newspaper reported the horse being taken out every year up until 1978, before the Smalls left Deal for the West Country in 1981. During this last season, the horse took part in the torchlight procession in an entertainment that included the Deal Girl Pipers and Mary Tamm (an actress who was featured on BBC television in the popular science fiction serial, 'Doctor Who'). There was also a 'pre-Christmas pub-trot' from which £30 each was raised for four local charities. It was also noted that 'many residents who remember hoodening parties of many years ago' were encountered, although only John Burton's name was brought to mind – a regular in 'the Forester' who had 'hoodened in his youth' when the Smalls visited in 1975. Today, Robert and Julia Small live with 'Hengist' in Crieff in Perthshire.[223]

Revival at Deal: the team started by Chris & Gill Nixon, December 2000

Librarian Gill Nixon had the idea of reviving her custom after reading Geoff and Fran Doel's booklet Mumming, Howling and Hoodening. At about the same time, Deal town council were organizing a Sea Shanty Festival in the town, to which morris dance teams, folk musicians, and street theatre groups were invited. She noted her disappointment that there was 'no representation of a tradition associated with the town.' On 20 October 1997, a meeting was held at 'the Alma' in West Street among interested people, and a new revival began, their first public performance being eight weeks later. The East Kent Mercury reported:

A veritable deluge of rehearsal and costume-making has been taking place. The thirteen hoodeners will be wearing patchwork tailcoats and top hats, plus

---

[223]East Kent Mercury, 4 January 1979, p28

the horse, and the musicians will be playing traditional instruments of the time.[224]

Gill and Chris Nixon started their revival with a blank slate, so had no prejudices as to how they should go about it. As far as they could see, all that was needed was the horse, some form of traditional costume, a man-woman character or 'Mollie', and a band of music to accompany carol singing. They decided there would be no scripted 'play', since there was no historical evidence for such a thing in Deal. Their mode of performance was thus:

> Our performance consists of a Molly announcing our arrival, sweeping a path clear for us, and we sing carols and play tunes whilst the Horse wanders around snapping his jaw. We sing and play at dance speed as in the old meaning of carolling. We collect money for local causes. We sing and play both in Deal High Street and in local public houses and do venture out as far as Sandwich for one outing. The costume we all wear (except Molly) is a patched tailcoat based on Robert Skardon's garb. This departure from tradition is a deliberate move so that we would be readily identified as a 'group' when we were out and about.[225]

Their repertoire comprises songs mentioned to them as having being performed traditionally. These are the carol 'I Saw Three Ships', 'The Moon Shines Bright' and Percy French's 'Phil the Fluter's Ball'. They also include 'Here We Come a-Wassailing', a parody of 'God, Rest ye Merry Gentlemen', and 'the Boar's Head Carol' – all sung at a fair pace, without formal choral harmony, accompanied by their band (who liken themselves to the Skardon Band) who perform on melodeon, concertinas, tin whistles, banjo, violin, and percussion. Great play is made of Tor – a Belgian shepherd dog handled by member Jane Runton who bears collecting boxes around her harness. The team meet and perform all year round: with the hoodening repertoire solely for the Christmas season, and their nautical repertoire for other times, including the September Maritime Festival – the latter of which was recorded as a fundraising CD for the Royal National Lifeboat Institution.

Shortly after they were formed, they made contact with Jim and Mollie Skardon, the former the grandson of Bob Skardon, and much inspiration and background information was garnered for future performances.

The author went to see the team perform shortly after their formation. It is important to stress its work in the community, not only at Christmastime, but also at local festivals, and on commission by local charities. In 2002, the Nixons moved to Nottingham, and their most recent captain is Steve Grayland who also plays melodeon. Tracing the Deal team's progress objectively is made easier following reports in the newspaper East Kent Mercury. However, writing in December 2017, Steve says of the team's progress:

---

[224]East Kent Mercury, 27 November 1997, p1
[225]Gill Nixon, letter to the author, 24 October 1999

(We are) still doing very much the same at Deal, busking in the High Street is our main Christmas event though we have a few private and charity events on the lead up to Christmas. We have added the tune 'The Moon Shines bright on Charlie Chaplin' (also known as the dance tune 'Redwing') which some believe is the correct 'Moon Shines Bright' referred to in earlier chronicles…(but sing the original version 'to cover both possibilities') We have just celebrated our 20th birthday with a gathering of past and present Deal Hoodeners. I can report that over those years we have donated in excess of £30,000 to local charities.[226]

Whitstable

Mark Lawson's inspiration for reviving the custom of the Hooden Horse in his home town of Whitstable came after seeing Edward Coomber's horse, as we have already seen in the last chapter. At that time, he didn't know quite what a hooden horse was, until he read a number of magazine articles published in the 1950s and 1960s, which led him on an odyssey after finding there was 'a Whitstable team active in the fifties.' He tells his own story:

In the mid-seventies, I became a Scout leader. We used to go out carol singing, and I thought it would be nice to take a hooden horse along – that's what you have when you're carol singing. At that time, I still didn't know that it wasn't found everywhere. I assumed it was 'part' of Christmas – like robins and snowmen…This was in 1977.[227]

In 1980, Mark Lawson finally interviewed Edward and Margaret Coomber about their own hooden horse. At around the same time, he also saw morris dancing at the town's May Day celebrations, and read Percy Maylam's book. He learnt of the 'extra characters which we didn't have'. As a result, he modified the programme so that, in the end, what was performed 'wasn't really carol singing, but going round the pub singing some carols, but a lot of Christmas songs and secular songs as well.'

The team then comprised anyone 'whom we could grab.' My father (Raymond) was involved from very early on; various of my brothers, Bernard – he horsed and sang occasionally; my youngest brother Damien as well. My cousin Nick was certainly involved. Friends were Martin Polley, his younger brother Simon, a chap called Andy Capon, another called Ian Ritchie, who horsed. Sometimes people who turned up to accompany us found themselves with a role that evening![228]

The nascent hoodening team took part in the 1982 May Day festival in the town to 'raise public awareness.' Despite advertising, only one response came in answer to a query about the tradition in the Whitstable area. That alerted Mark Lawson to Martin

---

[226]Steve Grayland, emails to author, 6 January 2017, 5 February 2018
[227]Mark Lawson, in conversation, 15 December 1999
[228]Mark Lawson, in conversation, 15 December 1999

Beale of the St Nicholas-at-Wade team who actually lived in the town, and who did a play of all things!

Whitstable Hoodeners, May Day 1984

But the most significant event in their early career came when Dixie Lee (then Fletcher), who organized the May Day Festival, invited Mark Lawson and his hoodeners to take part in the 1983 procession. This presented something of a problem, because their repertoire only consisted of Christmas carols normally sung in pubs, and nothing of an al fresco nature! Being now aware of the Mummers' play and having heard from Martin Beale that it had at least influenced the team from St Nicholas, a brain storming session was held from which the script of the Whitstable hoodening play evolved – virtually as a result of circumstance.

> One part was 'partly based on the Antrobus Souling play from Cheshire focusing on Dick the Driver's speech at the end of the play, with the remainder of the cast improvising around this. It worked! There's bits borrowed from local sayings, customs and tradition. The bit at the end where we say 'taking it down the High Street, middling down the wall, but as we are all wallers, the buggers won't pay at all' – that was and is a local saying. Martin Polley played the mollie that year, and it was an in joke: 'My name is Polley, though they call me Mollie…'[229]

As a result, their profile was raised very quickly. They performed at the prestigious 'Dancing England' Festival at the Derby Assembly Rooms in January 1984, and again four years later. They also took part with the Graund Order of Guisers at London's Covent Garden when the Graund Order's newly-built perambulating giant Gogmagog made his debut in June that same year. The formula has remained the same for the following thirty years. The original horse – made by Mark Lawson not as a replica of the Coomber horse, but based upon his childhood memories – was 'given away' to a school in Medway in the late 1980s as the incumbent carrier (Ian Ritchie) was disproportionately tall, and a newer construct with a 20 inches long head (as opposed

---

[229]Mark Lawson, in conversation, 15 December 1999

to the original 12 inches) was made (again by Mark Lawson) to allow for this. This is the horse that is still used today, although additional horses made by Aaron Janes in around 2005 have also been used, for example at the Sidmouth event mentioned below and Alan Kane and Jeremy Deller's Folk Archive exhibition at the Barbican the same year.

Two more offshoots arose from the Whitstable team: Martin McKenna started a team at Sandgate using the Whitstable play, and Phil Bleazey from Sittingbourne started the Swale Hoodeners. Since 1999, a 'moot' of known hoodening teams has been held in mid-November, firstly by Phil Bleazey, and latterly by Mark Lawson. In 2000, this was attended by a dozen horses and their teams or minders at the Gate Inn at Marshside. To date, this still continues.

The Marshside moot in December 2000

In July 2005, the team went to Sidmouth to participate in a Dancing England 'revival' master-minded by its originator Phil Heaton with ad hoc director Gordon Newton (founder of the Rochester Sweeps Festival).

Gail Duff's Charing Heath Horse

Outside the world of folk music at the turn of the millennium, the name Gail Duff is more associated with vegetarian cookery and as a freelance journalist. In Kent, she is more widely respected for her roles in evolving some of the more innovative dance teams. In September 1974, she went to the Hop Hoodening at Wickhambreaux and met Barnett Field, conducting an interview that was to be published in Kent Life. In 1979, she produced an entertainment for the Lenham Heath and Charing Heath Village Society Christmas social.

I wrote a simple Mummers' play from various bits of plays – mainly from Berkshire as that was all I had at the time. I remembered the Hooden Horse and thought it would be a good idea to include one in the entertainment. I approached Frank Howland of Sand Cottage, Charing Heath. He had been a wheelwright and his father was wheelwright, coffin maker and carter to the village – he was about 80 years old at the time. I took him to see Barnett Field, and he took measurements of the East Kent horse and also took away a plan of its making, which, I believe he subsequently found to be not quite the same as the actual horse. He found a piece of English walnut that had been in his workshop for decades, shaped it into a head and added the glow-in-the-dark eyes. From then on it had character. He made the jaw mechanism and gave us a long piece of fur which we used for the mane and tail. I made the hood, sewed on horse brasses and gave him red, white and blue ribbons.[230]

Gail Duff at Marshside, December 2000

The horse was incorporated into the Mummers' play, and was carried by her husband Mick, 'either causing havoc or just appearing at appropriate times.' Gail visited the Whitstable May Festivities in 1984 and saw Mark Lawson's team, realizing 'there was an accessible play.' Her involvement with local Morris dance teams began in Summer 1984, when she joined the Minstrel morris dancers from Maidstone, and her horse became adopted as part of its menagerie. They folded eighteen months later, members of it joining the newly-formed Loose Women, she and her horse doing likewise. At this time, the horse was purely a supernumerary character for the Morris, and despite writing a song for a possible Christmas hoodening, opportunity for performance never arose. In Autumn 1991, Gail joined the Maenads along with Kathy and David Hall, and a hoodening play was performed at the 'Hooden Horse' public house (formerly the 'Black Dog') in Great Chart. This lasted two years, but the landlord of the pub asked Gail to continue her hoodening. Today, her present team,

---

[230]Gail Duff, letter to the author, 12 December 2000

Rabble Folk Theatre carry on these performances. Apart from dancing the very popular 'Welsh Border' morris style, Rabble indulge in all sorts of seasonal events: they do a Christmas Mummers' play, a Robin Hood play, Plough play on Plough Sunday, and a Derby Tup play. They also go wassailing. Another seasonal event participated in is the early-December 'tree dressing' at the Weald & Downland Open Air Museum at Singleton in West Sussex where the hooden horse play is performed. The words of their hooden horse play mirror those used at Whitstable, but Gail has penned lines for many of the team's plays, customizing each where necessary.

But the horse belongs to Gail and Mick Duff. Its colours reflect those of the team she performs with. When hoodening, Gail acts as the wagoner, with her daughter Lucy the rider. Mick Duff is often in the horse. Other characters comprise a Mollie and a Fool. At the November 2000 moot, Gail sang a version of the 'Derby Ram', modifying the words to mirror the anatomy of the horse rather than the eponymous sheep.

Gail says of the team's progress since 2014 (when the author last witnessed them):

Rabble are still going with the play that I updated in 2002 from the Whitstable one, but with a difference. Because Imy (13 years) and Alex (11 years) Weller wanted to be involved, we now have a Wagoner and an Apprentice Wagoner. Basically, I just split the words up between us and added a few more lines to cover the fact that we now have two horses, young Alex being in the one that I made about ten years ago for Jack Ralph when he was small. Mick (Duff) finally retired from being under the hood in the plays this year (after 38 years), but still did it at the Hoodening moot at Marshside. At the…Tree Dressing, Stuart Weller was in the horse and he will be doing it at Hastingleigh on Boxing Day and (at) Doddington on New Year's Day.[231]

Gail also fronts an arts development organization TRADS in southeast England. One of their projects was to create a one-off hoodening performance with original script by children in the Thanet-based group Pie Factory in December 2005 at the Westwood Cross shopping centre in Broadstairs and two old peoples' homes in Ramsgate.

The Tonbridge Mummers and Hooteners

If parallels are to be drawn, then the Tonbridge Mummers' raison d'etre must surely match those of Rabble, but without the dance-related activity. The Tonbridge club was formed in 1981 and perform 'traditional seasonal folk drama' including 'Midwinter Mummers Plays, Easter Pace Egg plays, Hallowe'en Souling plays, and May Games Robin Hood plays.' They also perform a hooden horse 'play', whose script was written in 1981, and incorporates all the characters from the custom that Percy Maylam reported, including a wagoner and rider with the addition of a quack doctor.

The horse itself was made by founder member Nick Miller. The actual script was put together 'by Geoff Doel and Nick Miller using several souling texts, (the) Symonsbury (Mummers play from Dorset) and much invention. It has developed extensively in one tradition – especially the puns and the jokes.'[232]

---

[231]Gail Duff, email to author, 11 December 2017
[232]Tonbridge Mummers and Hooteners publicity leaflet

Nick Miller in Marshside, December 2000

Like the St Nicholas-at-Wade play, a death and resurrection theme has been chosen, this time with the introduction of a doctor who tries to revive the horse after it has been bludgeoned to 'death' by the rider after being thrown. The character of the doctor is rare in the revival, and owes more to the familiarity of its playwrights with the Christmas Mummers' Play, and the declared need for improvisation. The play might be concluded by Geoff Doel singing 'Old Horse' – a whalerman's song adapted by Martin Carthy. Another hoodeners' play using the Doctor as a character to similar effect was written by Bishop Gundulf's morris, a mixed team from Rochester), who also perform the Christmas hero-combat type of Mummers' play, as well as a mix of Yorkshire longsword dancing and northwestern clog morris. They wrote and performed their hoodening play for the Christmas 1996 season only, writing a script for 'as many as will' with a cast that included a policeman, village idiot, as well as the doctor, minder, driver and a 'Betsy'. Ken Anderson describes their horse as being 'made out of plywood' and hadn't known what a hooden horse was when it was constructed. Ironically, he performs today with Dead Horse morris, the brother team to the Whitstable Hoodeners.[233]

Up until 2000, the Tonbridge Hoodeners homed in on 'Nellie's' – the Sunday night folk club held in or around the Tonbridge area. Very often, apart from their many requests for appearances to be honoured, they participate at lectures conducted by Geoff and Fran Doel on Traditional Culture and Drama held at or on behalf of the School of Continuing Education at the University of Kent, and at the University of London's Birkbeck College.

---

[233]Morris Ring Folk Drama Archive, file 46/D (I am indebted to Ron Shuttleworth for supplying me with a copy of the script)

Tunbridge Wells-based singer-songwriter Bob Kenward, who is also a resident at Nellie's, has also written a song 'The Hoodener's Rant' about the hooden horse inspired by the Whitstable team from his days in the Faversham folk clubs.[234]

Around 2013, Geoff and Fran Doel moved from Tonbridge to Canterbury. The Tonbridge Mummers still perform, but now rein in their performances to allow for lapsed educational demonstration bookings.

Canterbury Hoodeners

The Canterbury group was formed in 2016 by James Frost, who says: I have been performing in the Whitstable May Day parade since 2005, when I refurbished the Oyster Morris horse (originally built in the 1970s) in 2011, I constructed a new hooden horse for the Sandwich Folk & Ale Festival, now used by the Canterbury Hoodeners which I co-founded in 2016. We perform a version of the Tonbridge Mummers horse play, which was developed with the assistance of Geoff Doel…I make props and animal disguises, such as the stag for the Canterbury Hoodeners. All our plays are based on traditional and historical material.[235]

Among the hostelries visited during their 2017 season were the New Inn and Water Lane Brasserie. Photographs taken show at the horse with a Mollie, young rider and three musicians. There is also a false-bearded doctor with top hat, and surgeon with long white lab coat!

Dover Tales

Lucas Domonic is the prime mover for the Dover group. His group is part of the Dover Tales arts group which has a greater mission than just creating a hoodening custom. He adds:

I was in Whitstable about 30 years back and followed the Dead Horse Morris and the Hoodeners, (and at) that time I did Folk street theatre with the Amazing Zolas. I moved to Dover gave not much more thought until about 25 years back, I was Molly for the short-lived Sandgate Hoodeners near Folkestone. Over the last four years I have been with Dover Tales –

---

[234]Gail Duff, email to author, 12 January 2017. Gail reminded me that Bob Kenward wrote a 'hoodener's song'. In fact, I recorded Bob singing 'the Hoodener's Rant' at the former Eight Bells in Tenterden in the 1990s, although as Gail relates, she's never heard Mark or the Whitstable team ever singing it, even though it was written for them! Aaron Janes (in an email to Ben Jones, 15 March 2020) says "it was sung at most performances mainly as part of a song session in the pub after the hoodening, but was dropped from the repertoire in favour of the tune 'Hooden Horse' by Paula Jardine-Rose, which I played to start the session".

[235]James Frost, email to author, 11 January 2018

predominantly a storytelling and creative performance group with an interest in Dover Historic people and events.

We did a mystery play about St Martin of Tours (the town's saint) and dramatized ensemble stories about some events, like Webb swimming the channel.

At Christmas 2016, I wrote and put together the team to launch the Dover Hoodening play which we put out five times over that season including some three local wassailings. For the 2017 season we did four outings.

As a seaside place there is a nautical theme to the play Off White Horse [N.B. there is a White Horse pub in Dover: the oldest in the town and a Coroner's house]. (It) is called Albinus Invictus "for he is as white as Dover cliffs and the chalk that is lying 'ere bineaf". He is Hippo Mares – "a 'orse from the sea".

The Characters are locally grounded…Molly is a prostitute a favourite of Sailors; the Wagoner is the vulgar local; the Groom is Joey a hapless sailor prone to end up on his face; the Doctor is a sea captain with mystic medicines.

There is a bit of a nod to the Dead Horse Ceremony that sailors played at sea. As Skipper I lead the songs: The Blean Song, shanties 'Poor Old Man' [the dead horse] and 'Shiny O'. I also rally the play, and lead the barracking. We are also planning to revive the Dover Jack in the Green and Chummies parade which we have a historic source for and we would like to stir up a St Martinmas fayre in November.[236]

Public Houses

In the previous chapter, we met one instance of how a pub changed its name in the mid-1950s to provide a focus for teams espousing the hooden horse as part of their morris menagerie. Even though the Wickhambreaux pub only lasted another fifteen years once rechristened, there was one person who thought there to be mileage in a similar exercise.

In 1991, Canterbury restauranteur Alex Bensley perceived a niche in the public house market at a time when the recession was biting and there were plenty of free houses on the market at rock bottom prices. He took over the 'Black Dog' at Great Chart and started his chain of 'Hooden Horse' houses, with a no frills policy. 'We wanted an honest to goodness pub with plain wooden floors, tables and chairs with the sort of atmosphere that is friendly and homely as soon as you walk through the door.'[237] Also absent were juke boxes and fruit machines, and cigarette machines, although merchandise could be purchased from behind the bar. The involvement of Gail and Mick Duff giving Christmas entertainment there has already been noted.

---

[236]Lucas Domonic, email to author, 11 January 2018
[237]Kentish Express, 12 September 1991, p11

Pubs: Hooden on the Hill (Ashford), Hooden Horse (Great Chart), Hopping Hooden Horse (Paddock Wood), Very Wonderful Hooden Horse (Tonbridge)

The experiment was something of a success, and by 2000, there were eight houses in Kent alone, with four more in Hertfordshire and Buckinghamshire. It has to be admitted that only one of the twelve was in the location once known to have sponsored the traditional hooden horse; the 'Star' in Margate Road, Westwood on the western fringes of Broadstairs having changed its name to the 'Poor Ole Hooden Horse'.[238] However, such is the perversity of the local community that a number of renamed houses were forced to change their names back to their original ones, especially when the chain was sold on to new owners. The 'Hopping Hooden Horse' in Paddock Wood thus reverted to the 'John Brunt V.C.' named after a local World War Two hero. Also, the local council demanded that the 'Grand Old Hooden Horse' in Cranbrook repaint its frontage to fit in with the ambience of its olde worlde High Street – in the end, reverting back to the 'Duke of York' and being sold on in any case. Even the Westwood pub went back to being 'the Star' without any hint of its former name or local associations, then became the Grog Wench, then Falcon in rapid succession, lasting only a matter of months under each guise. Meanwhile, the Hungry Horse chain opened an eatery just around the corner, which was named 'The Hooden Horse' after a competition won by Ben Jones's suggestion.

Other teams

As noted earlier, pressures on maintaining the longevity of a team are significant. Some have lapsed by the wayside, whilst others have formed in their stead.

Sandgate Hoodeners

The hoodeners were formed by members of the extant Sandgate Morris Men around 1989. They performed in the Sandgate and Folkestone area in the run up to Christmas, with a final stand of twelfth night. Hostelries are visited, with a walking tour in Hythe on the weekend before Christmas. The characters comprise a squire, wagoner, Molly, the horse (Dobbin), Miss Whiplash, a baglady (who collects money from the public), a young rider (selected from the audience), a fool, and musicians. Writing in 1997, and in their own words: "It is pure speculation that the hoodeners perform a different play each year...it is more likely a fact that even after all this time, they still can't remember their lines!" In fact, the script is a copy of Mark Lawson's Whitstable script, evident from the line: 'My name is Mollie, although I am Polly', the Whitstable 'in joke' which has now been unintentionally transmitted into tradition.[239]

The Sandgate horse was faithfully copied by the late Martin McKenna from the Walmer horse formerly stabled in Folkestone Museum (it is now at the Deal Maritime Museum). It was given a stable mate in the unicorn Eustace, which the author saw used at the 1993 'Day of Syn' festival at Dymchurch on August Bank Holiday, when the hooden horse play was acted by the eponymous 'Unicorners'. The last known appearance of the team was in 2012, when it was photographed by Homer Sykes at various locations in and around Sandgate's public houses, led by David Rivers. Their appearances at the annual Marshside moot have since lapsed and the team are thought to have disbanded.

---

[238] Thanet Extra, 8 August 1997, p1

[239] A Day for Martin, memorial day of dance leaflet for Martin McKenna, 13 October 1997

Bishop Gundulf's Mummers

This Gillingham-based team have morphed into a Morris dance team specializing in the sword dance traditions of northeast England, although originally a Mummers team formed around 1980. The actors listed for 1996 mentioned earlier are a driver, minder, old 'orse, Betsy, policeman, village idiot, doctor, vicar and maid (chosen from the audience). Part of their script of their play resembles in part that of the Tonbridge play in the pantomime repartee where the horse is given 'intelligence test' measured by stamps of hooves and rewards of sugar lumps.[240]

Wychling Hoodeners

Unlike other teams in the ongoing revival, the Wychling group are a family unit comprising Paula and Robbie Jardine-Rose who moved to Wychling in 1998. The original horse was made before then and used to go out with Maenads Morris, around 1992/3. Paula made him, and his name is 'Arry 'Oss. They regularly perform during the week before Christmas at the Chequers Inn, Doddington and have been using the 'old horse' which has no name, since they got him.[241] The 'old' horse was given to the Jardine-Roses at Banbury by the son of a Lincolnshire farmer who had it. It is distinguished by a hessian hood upon which the name Wm Gardner, Birchington is stencilled. (see Appendix E)

The script is original, and comprises four-line stanzas, with appraisal of the horse's merits, then a plea for it to be ridden by a volunteer from the audience. Its characters comprise the 'oss, wagoner, Bessy Besom, and rider.[242]

Swale Hoodeners

The author confesses to have only seen the Swale team perform once – at the December 2000 moot – and vaguely recalled a death and resurrection scene. Its author, Phil Bleazey says:

> Back in the late 1990s some of us became disillusioned with the ethics of the Whitstable performances and so I decided to build a new horse and Alex offered to write the script. Alex is well qualified in the history of English literature as it applies to this sort of performance…The team consisted of Alex as Wagoner, Aaron Janes in the horse, Chris Janes as rider, my son Doug as fool and myself as molly with any further bodies singing and playing tunes to help it all go down.

Phil then goes on to say to comment that 'an abbreviated version of the script was used in busy pubs where the full event may not have been tolerated. The horse has upright ears and electric 'fiery eyes'.

> In 2000 my late wife Cathie and I moved to Nottinghamshire and the horse came with us but remained inactive. Following Cathie's death in 2006 I moved to Lancaster and married, Claire. Several performances were made

---

[240]Morris Ring Mummers archive
[241]Paula Jardine-Rose, emails to the author, 3 February 2018
[242]Paula Jardine-Rose, emails to the author, 30 January 2012

with the Swale horse including a skit on the original Whitstable play for Lancaster. We took the Lancaster play around the town and on one occasion even performed the Lancaster version in Scotland! The Swale horse makes an occasional appearance in associated performances, notably an adaptation of the plough boy's dream, performed as a sort of mini opera.[243]

Beyond Kent

Online viewers wishing to witness a hooden performance via YouTube will be surprised to find one in the Weymouth area of Dorset from 2008! In fact, the Frome Valley Morris Men acquired their version from Mark Lawson's group although changes were made some to it as performances developed. They have not performed it for some years due to difficulty in finding men to learn the parts which are longer than in the usual 'St George' hero-combat Christmas Mummers play.[244]

Another source of migration was Hampshire schoolteacher Mac Maclaren, who moved to Cheriton, and joined the Sandgate Morris Men and hoodeners whilst there. (The author saw him at the Dymchurch 'Day of Syn' mentioned earlier as part of the 'unicorners'). Years later, Mac moved back to Farnborough, taking the Sandgate version of the Lawson play with him, and teaching it to the Farnborough Mummers, of which he was a member. Mac says:

> ...the Sandgate Hoodeners added the squire's introduction to Mark Lawson's Whitstable version. We (the Farnborough Mummers) kept the idea of the intros, but I changed them to be a bit more relevant to the situation in which the play was performed (viz in and around northeast Hampshire).[245]

The Hooden Horse in the Morris Revival

If it wasn't for Biddy Bennett taking an interest in local tradition on behalf of the English Folk Dance and Song Society back in 1939, it seems unlikely that the folk music revival, as robust as it is today, would have had the hooden horse associations known at the time of writing. Certainly, if it wasn't for her, there would have been no reason for Barnett Field to feel the need to construct a hooden horse and, without that, there would have been no 'handbell hoodening' or 'Hop Hoodening' in the style he created. The fact that the two established Kentish teams in the 1950s both had a hooden horse amongst their menagerie served as a template for the Morris revival of the 1960s and 1970s.

The Hartley morris men from Wrotham in the west of the county were founded in the 1950s and originally had a stag type of creature (i.e. a hart) as their man-animal. Later on they had a hooden horse constructed, based on the Sarre photographs, in the early 1970s by Brian Tasker after reading Percy Maylam's book. A second horse was made around 1978 by Phil Burkin after the original was lost: both having a black wooden head adorned with horse brasses and rosettes, ears, and an opening jaw with hobnails for teeth. Like Barnett Field's horse, its function was to collect money in its

---

[243]Phil Bleazy, email to the author, 16 January2018
[244]Peter Robson, email to the author, 20 December 2017
[245]Mac Maclaren, letter to the author, received 5 February 2018

mouth.[246] Although no seasonal use is made of the horse, some of the team's members masquerading as the Darent Valley Champions performing the St George hero-combat play researched north of Sevenoaks, it does serve as a foil in the morris stick dance 'Shooting' where dancers pretend to shoot the horse, who promptly falls down dead, and pleas sent out for it to be brought back to life 'only by the kiss of a fair young maiden.' (Upon which, it is habitual for the rest of the team to similarly fall over, pleading for similar treatment!)

Ravensbourne Morris has had its descendants: the Weald of Kent morris men were formed in 1988 by Charlie Jacobs and Tim Dwyer of this Bromley-based team who had moved into the Goudhurst area, and had a horse built. Ian Hamilton of the Ravensbourne men taught the Headcorn morris dancers in their infancy – they too had a horse built for performance, although this was replaced by 'Jason', who was made by antiques dealer Terry Pearson in 1974. Its role is to accompany the dancers, harass the onlookers, dance with and through the set, and collect money.[247] None of these morris teams use the horse as part of a Christmas performance comparable with an East Kent 'hoodening', but this does not take away from them the awareness of the role of the horse in the county's folk traditions.

The East Kent morris men were formed in 1953 led by Barnett Field. Without reiterating his role in beginning the new tradition of hop-hoodening and working with Jack Laming of Walmer, his brown horse was their original horse and, despite now being stabled with Barnett's son John and presumably semi-retired, still occasionally comes to visit the EKMM's performances with their newer white horse, Invicta.[248] Invicta was also seen dancing with a visiting Mari Lwyd and mysterious 'dark horse' at Walmer Castle in the summer of 2018.[249]

James Frost tells me that he 'refurbished' Oyster Morris horse which was 'originally built in the 1970s'.[250] However, the author has witnessed and shared stands with the team on many occasions, as well as visiting Whitstable, but cannot recall them having a hooden horse. Having said that, at the inaugural town May Day in 1977, quite clearly a hooden horse was used with Wantsum Morris Man Jim Bywaters inside, taking 'a collection' – 'not strictly seasonal, of course, but most effective…'[251]

Lastly, the Rochester Sweeps Festival) series inaugurated in 1983, has also been a showcase for Morris dance horses, including those with hooden horses. Both Gail Duff and Mark Lawson were working with festival director Gordon Newton at the time, and invitations were sent out to many possible participants. In my own collection of festival photographs taken from 1984 up to the mid-noughties, there is unidentified horse with a narrow black tapered head, red hood and red and white rosette is featured with a children's group led by a melodeon playing man. It is thought to belong to a 'side who came from Deptford.'[252] Other teams performing at Rochester) and

---

[246]Terry Heaslip, letter to the author, 5 November 2000
[247]Eddie Dunmore in the Morris Dancer, vol. 3, no. 8 (2001); Ned Gayner, letter to the author, 5 November 2000; see also an archived copy of Jason's page at http://bit.ly/HorseJason
[248] Peter Brun, email to the editor, 12 September 2018
[249] Malcolm Triggs, email to the editor, 12 September 2018
[250]James Frost, https://www.jamesedwardfrost.com/hoodening-mumming
[251]Don Minifie, in English Dance & Song, 40.1 (1978)
[252]Paul Malyon via an email from Gail Duff to the author, 7 February 2018

elsewhere in Kent (or beyond) may have their own horses unknown to the author, and their continued existence indicates a healthy tradition surviving and flourishing in the present century.

CHAPTER 10: PLAYERS AND PERFORMANCE

One aim of this work has been to take Percy Maylam's work, add in various other bits and pieces, then to supply added value, using tools that would have been unavailable a century earlier. The release of the 1901 and 1911 Censuses has been helpful in this, although it is quite possible that slightly different results might be obtained in ten and twenty years' time to take into account the later survivals at St Nicholas-at-Wade, Acol and Deal.

Percy Maylam named sixteen people who actually performed in hoodening up to the time of writing his 'meisterwerk'. We can add one extra name (viz. John Beney senior) from census returns on the basis that a 'father took part'; another (H.H. Miles) in that he was prompted to start a revival of his own at Hoath; definitely Edwin Sladden, using neo-forensic information based on attendees at a funeral; and circumstantially John Smith, whose name (with Sladden's) appears in both the Thanet and St Augustine electoral registers either side of his transfer to Felderland at the request of farmer George Goodson. On the debit side, Maylam failed to cite the six people who posed for photographs for him at Sarre – that is, assuming correctly that each took part in the custom at the less clement time of year relative to that when the photo shoot took place. We are able to add back names to three of these people using the memories of an elderly resident of St Nicholas-at-Wade. Thirty-one extra names can also be added from further sources, which amounts to a total of fifty-seven performers – including those who took part in Bob Skardon's band, assuming their mutual association with hoodening at Deal at some stage. This is a paltry sum from which to deduce modes of performance of any significance, but at least it's a start!

Performance as Parody

In devising any means of performance based on traditional sources, the 'revival' teams of the 1950s onwards had little actually to go on. Some chose to devise their own scripted drama as at St Nicholas-at-Wade and Whitstable, others to use a horse as a companion to carol singing as at Birchington or musical recital as at Folkestone. Many but not all, chose to devise an entertainment centred around the key characters portrayed by Percy Maylam.

Let us first look at the performers thus represented. The costumed wagoner was set apart from the rest of the cast, complete with his top hat and tailcoat at St Nicholas. The fact that William Christian once took part as a wagoner's mate at Herne, suggests that theirs too must have comprised this senior performer. One indication was that the wagoner in real life was at least one rank above the average farm worker. Rosemary Quested writes:

In East Kent generally the wage rates of ordinary labourers were fifteen shillings per week from 1898 to 1903, when they began to rise to sixteen shillings, and in 1914 rose to 17 shillings. But in Thanet, according to a Parliamentary Commission report, they are said to have been seventeen shillings for all farm workers in 1905, including horsemen, cattlemen and shepherds. Horsemen were often given an extra four pounds at Michaelmas … From 1911 until war broke out Barzillai Sackett (at Northdown) was paying his ordinary labourers 16 shillings a week, with four pence an hour overtime and four pounds bonus at harvest. He employed 40-45 men with only ten cottages on or near the farm, so many of the men had to walk varying distances to work … Each wagoner living on the farm had to board three bachelors (covenanted yearly servants) who slept in lofts over the cottages, reached by an outside stair.[253]

At Minster, an unnamed resident recalled:

'Not everyone could work with 'orses, no. It was a specialized thing, you know, because you got to be kind man to work with with 'orses and well, they pretty near used to talk to me and I used to talk to them… The bigger the farm, the more 'orses they 'ad, you see. And there used to be the wagoner, the wagoner's mate, second boy, third man, the third boy, the works. See, so there used to be one, two, three, four, twelve, fourteen, fifteen 'orses on a big farm. But sometimes you'd 'ave a pair of 'orses for a plough and you went ploughing with two 'orses and a plough and one single for a plough. Well, then, you know, you'd combine with the wagoner, you'd have the four horses with a double plough.'[254]

This notion of hierarchy is further afforded in the next passage in the same text:

A typical working day with the horses would usually begin at four in the morning getting them ready in the stables. They used to be out in the fields by six o'clock. The men finished cleaning and feeding the horses at five in the afternoon. The wagoner generally had some veterinary knowledge and his skill was sought after by the community. One villager observes: 'When I was a boy (in the 1920s) there used to be ten or twelve 'orse and wagons come down 'ere from Monkton and the different farms up there down to the station here to unload stuff and back. Of course, they 'ad to go in strict like, the wagoner in front, wagoner's mate next, first boy, second boy, like you know. They were very strict on that. And when they come back up the hill and 'e (the wagoner) would stop and they'd all stop and go in for a beer. But nobody dared stop unless 'e did. They used to come in 'the Saddler' (public house), well, used to be summat else then, it's called 'the Saddler' now.[255]

Although evidently respected, this does not imply that the specific wagoner hired at Michaelmas was indispensable.

---

[253]Rosemary Quested, The Isle of Thanet Farming Community – an Agrarian History of Easternmost Kent: Outlines from Early Times to 1993 (Wye: 1996) p174

[254]J. Witton, Minster Remembered – Recollections of Village Life, (Margate; 1987) p26

[255]J. Witton, Minster Remembered, p26

The relative comfort of the wagoners is suggested by the fact that when a thatched cottage in Acol, inhabited by one of Val Smith's, burnt down in 1893, the insurance company paid out £85 to replace his effects. Horses and wagoners seem to have been the most treasured items on the farms, yet even a favoured wagoner could sometimes fall into disgrace. Once all of Bar's (Sackett's) wagoners and their mates came back drunk (except for the two who were teetotal) from delivering wheat to the mill in Ramsgate. One fell off his horse and broke his leg, and two young ones chased the cowmen's teenage daughters round the stackyard. The lead horses came into the yard on their own, and the head wagoner was sacked on the spot.[256]

Once more, judging by the 1891 census returns, membership of a community one year didn't guarantee a continued existence thereafter. The 1921 Thanet electoral register, and the 1901 Census returns show that many of the St Nicholas hooteners were living at cottages near the farms where they worked (presumably either renting them from the farmer or as part of their contract of work). Those whose presence has been established lived in the village centre, such as the Trices and the Wests who were related through marriage anyway.

How much the performers in hoodening acted out a parody of real life must have depended on the delegation of the roles. Two 'real life' wagoners are noted: William West was one, working at Val Smith's farm at Birchington; and Edwin Sladden was another, working for George Goodson at Cleve Court Farm before 1902, and at Felderland a few years later. Apart from the wagoner, the only other common character among many of the other teams known to have existed was that of 'Mollie' – the man-woman. 'Her' role in the affair seems to have been to prepare the way for the rest of the team by sweeping the ground with her broom and as an obvious comic figure to put aside any possible misgivings of mischievous intent. There are many parallels among other country-based calendar customs where a man dressed as a woman took part – such as the 'Mollie' or 'Betsy' in Cambridgeshire Molly dancing or northeastern longsword or rapper sword traditions, but that doesn't help us understand hoodening to any greater extent here. Typically, folk entertainment of the nineteenth century was an all-male affair given the division of responsibilities among the genders at that age, and we are mostly left to guess at the comic behaviour of Mollie in relationship to the wagoner and his entourage. William Christian of Herne describes one character as 'the driver' who presumably led the horse about – and who probably took the part of the wagoner in the case at St Nicholas.[257] Percy Maylam himself appears to have recalled the Mollie at his first hoodening experience at Monkton as a larger than life character:

All sorts of antics take place: Mollie has been known to stand on her head, exhibiting nothing more alarming in the way of lingerie than a pair of hobnail boots with the appropriate setting or corduroy trousers.[258]

---

[256]Rosemary Quested, The Isle of Thanet Farming Community, p176
[257]Maylam, p52
[258]Maylam, p3

Of the remainder of the cast, St Nicholas-at-Wade had a rider or jockey, who was usually a boy. This was certainly the case between 1917 and 1921 when Tom West (born in 1907) took part as a teenager during the last three years. His immediate predecessor was Walter Trice who was born in 1903. The boy shown in the 1905 photographs taken by Henry Beauchamp Collis for Percy Maylam was identified as one of the sons of David Gibbs, and must have been either George Gibbs who was born in 1890 or Percy who was born three years later. Edmund Trice's wife who came to live in St Nicholas in 1910, recalled her husband taking part as the rider – but seeing that Edmund would have been 22 years old at the time, one questions how such a response came to be elicited if this statement is accurate.[259] William Christian of Herne told Maylam that his team had a 'jockey', which suggests that this character had to mount (or attempt to mount) the horse's back. Christian took part 'as a boy', but described himself a 'wagoner's mate' – possibly a description of his actual work in the late 1850s rather than his role in hoodening, although the census returns for his later life suggest he turned his hand to many vocations ranging from a publican in 1881 to a wagoner in 1901.

The animator of the horse was a law to himself. Frank Trice who had been in the navy, was a physical man, and needed to be if he was to carry anyone on his back for any length of time. Obviously, the horse is key to the performance, although 'hoodening' as we have already seen isn't synonymous with the use of a horse in some locations; yet its antics when present are what made it memorable. One thinks of Henry Brazier at Lower Hardres in 1859 when his gyrations frightened an invalid lady sufficiently to resume normal adrenaline flow as a means of escape from her wheelchair (see p82)! There is also the hooden horse witnessed by the Deal Mercury newspaper reporter in 1877 (see p93). What exactly was taken exception to in its performance as to describe its antics as a 'stupid piece of foolery' which was 'decidedly wooden-headed'?[260] Most other commentators only made comment of the odd growl and the way the operator made the horse's jaws to open and shut to make its usual champing noise. More severely – and we are unaware of the exact circumstances – there was the Broadstairs incident in 1828 (see p40), when Susanna Crow was frightened to death upon seeing the horse that accompanied a team of Margate apprentices.[261] What particular movement (if any) by this character served to take the life of this fragile woman who was known to have been carrying an unborn child at the time? Or was this purely down to her state of health?

Let us now place in context the interaction of the horse with the rest of its team in examples outside St Nicholas-at-Wade. It is worth repeating Thomas Whitehead's account at nearby Birchington which took place in about 1855:

The party sang a country song, and then knocked at the door. On opening the door, the scene that presented itself was a prancing horse, opening and closing its jaws with a loud snapping noise, the groom shouting 'whoa,' the jockey attempting to mount, the old lady busy sweeping and the collector looking on. If invited into the kitchen, the acting would be continued there,

---

[259]Ben Jones's website, and sundry observations made in interviews already noted in the text
[260]Deal, Walmer & Sandwich Mercury, 29 December 1877, p2
[261]Kentish Gazette, 29 December 1828, p4; see also p40 of this book

when, of course, the success depended much upon the ability of the various performers, who, at least, amused the little folks.'[262]

Of course, this description is wholly reminiscent of Percy Maylam's in chapter four recalling the time when he stayed with his aunt and uncle at Gore Street Farm near Monkton in 1888 (see p47). It could be argued that, owing to its proximity with Birchington, even if there was no direct linkage in time and personnel, there might have been a strong common understanding of the roleplay expected. Unfortunately, we are short of the necessary data for proof of this notion.

The Horse

Without doubt, key to the success of the performance was the role of the hooden horse. But what actually comprised this character? It is quite clear that the horse itself was a parody of the real thing. It only remotely resembles the animal itself. Only a romantic would view it as little more than a carved contraption serving as the head, with a pole stuck into its base, and a shroud to cover its animator! But let us consider something of the craftsmanship and design which goes into making this ludicrous beast.

The creation of the head would depend on the tools available to its sculptor, not to mention his imagination. To enhance the illusion that this wooden being was meant to be a horse, it would be decorated with some of the trappings used in showing these beasts of burden at a fair, or taking part in a ploughing competition or other show. The hooden horse would be adorned with rosettes, usually made from braid rather than ribbon. It would boast horse brasses of various sorts. These themselves were a later innovation, only becoming popular in the late nineteenth century although 'invented' earlier as 'gypsy amulets attached to horse tack in the hope of warding off evil spirits'. On the crown of the head, there might be attached a special brass known as a 'flyer' or 'swinger'. This might comprise a tinkly sort of open-mouth bell arrangement, or a 'magic mirror' whereby a reflective metal disc would be freely mounted within a circular frame.

The shroud might comprise a simple sackcloth, although known survivors have some sort of black cloth, or even a patterned horse blanket (such as one of the two Wingham horses at Maidstone Museum).

The head was painted: usually black, perhaps with a white stripe down its nose. Features were also painted on, although it was left to the ingenuity and skill of each craftsman to fashion these by first carving an eyeball or nostril into the wooden substrate. The bottom jaw was hinged to the top either by a metal hinge or nailed leather strip. The clapping mechanism would vary, but usually involved a piece a string tied to the bottom jaw which looped through a staple in the top jaw, and out somehow through the 'throat' area to the animator beneath his shroud. The ears could be constructed from leather and stapled to the sides of the head, or comprise part of the carved structure itself. There might be a rein. In most cases, a pole would be used that fitted into a drilled hole in the head at a suitable angle, both for transporting the horse between performances, and for balancing the head during a performance.

---

[262]Job P. Barrett, in Keble's Margate & Ramsgate Gazette, 7 December 1907, p2

It is unknown whether heads were 'built to last', or crafted just for one season then thrown away. Only six have definitely survived from the period before 1921, which are discussed in Appendix E.

Performance as Christmas Entertainment

The singing of country songs and/or carols is another shared characteristic of many of the case studies we have seen. Singing is specifically stated as part of the performance at Birchington, St Nicholas-at-Wade, Ramsgate (in 1830), Walmer around the time of the Boer War, and Wingham (around 1870). Sturry and nearby Broad Oak even had their own signature: the 'Three Jolly Hoodening Boys' chant.

Carolling is mentioned at Ramsgate in the earliest account of hoodening in 1807, and might be perceived to be the chosen entertainment because of its obvious association with Christmas today. So, why is this being disputed? To answer this, let us consider the evolution of music in the rural parish church. During the time of Napoleonic Wars, what passed for sacred performance comprised the psalms of David sung in metre, the words of which were found at the back of the Book of Common Prayer of the day. These were often performed by a rustic ad hoc group of musicians in the church, stationed in a purpose-built gallery at the west end of the nave. Organs were mainly used in richer parishes or town churches. A church without such musicians or too poor to own its own organ or organist might have a barrel organ or had unaccompanied 'lining out' led by the parish clerk from the bottom tier of the pulpit. There were no 'carols' as we know them. The poet laureate Nahum Tate who put biblical psalms into a singable format, included specimen 'Hymns for Christmas' in his later versions. One of these was the ubiquitous 'While Shepherds Watched' which was basically the text of the second chapter of St Luke put into metre. This seemed to provide a root for further simulation. One hundred years after Nahum Tate's efforts, and thanks to the efforts of Charles Wesley (who wrote the words of 'Hark! The Herald Angels Sing') among many others, psalmody was complemented by hymnody where such a rigorous adherence to biblical text wasn't a precondition of publication by the Anglican church. Hymns Ancient and Modern which was first published in 1861 also acted as a watershed in church music. In short, the Christmas card image of al fresco Victorian carol singers was seemingly a late developer that might have caught on after the heyday of hoodening. One key example of this is are the hoodeners at Minster in the 1860s and 1870s, who appeared to compete with the carollers or waits, before their roles were seemingly merged. There are a few surviving hymnals and music books once used by church musicians in the area inhabited by the hooden horse, from which we could guess at what 'carols' were popular during the nineteenth century. Let us quote a few examples. At Broadstairs, words are given for 'Whilst Shepherds Watch'd Their Flocks by Night', 'Rejoice, the Promis'd Saviour's Come' and an anthem 'Comfort Ye my People, Saith Your God.[263] At Eastry, handwritten scores are available for 'Shepherds, Rejoice', two versions of 'Hark, the Herald Angels Sing' (but not the famous melody by Felix Mendelssohn-Bartholdy

---

[263] Hymns and Anthems for the Use of St Peter's Church, Thanet, 1826 (Arthur Perceval, private collection). Further background information on this and the next three references can be gauged from Appendix C.

popularly sung today).[264] There were a number of 'village Mozarts' living in nineteenth century Canterbury who composed and published music for metrical psalmody and the like. The most famous of these was Thomas Clark, a shoemaker, best-known for his tune 'Cranbook' which was adopted by a Yorkshire Glee Club for the parody 'On Ilkla Moor Bah't 'at', but also used as a melody for the ubiquitous 'While Shepherds Watched.' Another tune published in his Union Tune Book was 'Nativity' composed by Thomas Jarman, whose wonderful fuguing sections make it the second most popular melody for 'While Shepherds Watched' behind only the more sombre 'Winchester Old'[265] Another Canterbury composer was Thomas Barwick whose compositions were used at Boughton under Blean, although he only wrote one anthem for Christmas adapted from Luke, Chapter Two in his collection.[266] Quite clearly, when discussing carols as accompaniment for hoodening, those popularized by Cambridge's Kings College choristers are not the template for consideration.

The Musicians

Musicians in calendar custom tend to be a special breed. In many comparative studies, such as Morris Dance research, it was never always the case that the musician was one of the performers. He could be hired for a fee to accompany the team. Very often, ownership of a musical instrument implied the player came from a slightly different walk of life, was a village artisan rather than a mere labourer – that is to say, musical instruments cost money, only the better off could afford them. This was certainly true of many of the musicians who played in the west gallery of the village church in the days before organs took over, although the instruments played tended to comprise violins, cellos, clarionets, bassoons, serpents, and those more identified with the orchestra. That said, as at the beginning of the chapter, we are trying to draw conclusions from a list of fifty-seven names, nine of which were associated with the North Deal boatmen and might not have even been part of the hoodening party! Any survey cannot be said to be conclusive, however scientifically it might be conducted, but let us have a try!

Without doubt, hoodening was a custom often associated with music. The earliest reliable reference describing the custom in 1807 at Ramsgate mentions the use of song and handbells,[267] although this could be said to have come from a competing team of waits present in the town. The 1828 Broadstairs 'incident' (see p40) comprised 'a party with music', although nothing specific is mentioned about the use of any musical instrument.[268] The Margate reference of 1832 from an unknown correspondent to Percy Maylam, specifically stated that the party had a violin and fife. Further conclusions from this can only be speculative.[269] The brass band movement was still its infancy at this time, although the fife player may have seen service in a military band that might have included such an instrument. Indeed, Deal's musicians had to compete

---

[264]John Marbrook's Music Book, handwritten manuscript dated 1858 held at the Canterbury Cathedral Archives, CCA U193

[265]Thomas Clark and A.I. Cobbins, Union Tune Book (Canterbury: 1837)

[266]John Barwick, Harmonica Cantica Divina (Canterbury: 1783) – copy held at Canterbury Public Library

[267]European Magazine, vol. 51, p358 (May 1807)

[268]Kentish Gazette, 29 December 1828, p4

[269]Job P. Barrett, in Keble's Margate & Ramsgate Gazette, 7 December 1907 p2

with military bands at Christmas time, so this was never going to be the proverbial level playing field if competition for largesse was to be involved. No musical accompaniment was cited in either case study at Reculver in 1841 or Birchington in 1855[270, 271], but these were exceptions. The Minster tradition in the 1860s onwards was associated with all manner of singers and/or handbell ringers.[272] Henry Brazier led his team at Lower Hardres playing his 'bells on a stand, which were always struck with a stick in time and tune'[273] At Herne at around 1860, the musical instruments comprised bones and a concertina.[274] Percy Maylam recalled that the party visiting Gore Street Farm at Monkton had a concertina and tambourine.[275] This leaves us with the photographic evidence. The hoodeners and associated musicians at Deal led by Bob Skardon have already been described at length. Robert Laming from Walmer played an accordion (nowadays usually called a melodeon), as too did Walt Patterson, George Holliday and Walt Trice at St Nicholas-at-Wade. Both Walmer and St Nicholas also had a triangle player – not the puny effort often associated with children's percussion groups but something more substantial, having sides of 8 inches or more. Walmer also had a tambourine player.[276] The melodeon was about to have its heyday as a musical instrument at the time Percy Maylam conducted his research. It was comparatively cheap, and readily imported from Germany by mail order at that time. Its other assets include that it is comparatively easy to learn to play, with the only perceived disadvantage that its musical range is limited by whatever key it could play in. In general, it could thus be said that cheaper musical instruments (as opposed to those once used in church orchestras earlier in the nineteenth century) were used in accompanying the hoodeners in their singing – or possible procession in their later history. Only Bob Skardon, Murray Larkins and an unknown performer in the Margate area possessed violins, and one is reminded of the whole battery of other instruments lent to the Deal Maritime and Local History Museum by the Skardon family.

Was there a musical role for any of the other performers? Frequent references are made to the use of handbells, although the assumption to be made is that their ringing was to attract attention (e.g. like a town crier of old) rather than any coherent rehearsed consort performance using precision tuned melodic instruments. Musical prowess takes hours of practice – Henry Brazier of Lower Hardres with his bells was, after all, a solo performer.

A Costumed Performance

Many comparative calendar customs involving song, dance and performance have their participants dressed up in distinctive and sometimes extravagant costumes. In hoodening, the known use of costume is frequent, but not always a prerequisite. The newspaper reference of 1890 tells us that hoodeners at Acol wore 'quaint costumes'. Comment has already been made on the garb worn by the hoodeners at Deal, Walmer and St Nicholas-at-Wade, if only because photographs are available of them. The

---

[270]Maylam, p51

[271]Christina Hole, English Custom and Usage (London: 1941) p10

[272]Kentish Gazette, 7 January 1868, p4 (for example)

[273]Maylam, p53

[274]Maylam, p52

[275]Maylam, p3

[276]Maylam, p8

description of the hoodeners at Ash in around 1825 bears repeating, if only to enhance the extraordinariness of their performance:

> A party of hoodeners from Ash used to come round on the day before Christmas Day. Some of the party were dressed as fools and there was with them a Maid Marian ... One of the party has a kind of black rug thrown over him, and carried a horse's head, which kept nodding about ... the hoodeners (were) knocking one another about with sticks and bladders on the green at the back of our house.[277]

Nowhere a scripted play is mentioned, and even the example at Herne Bay in 1888 – if accepted as a bona fide hoodening – shouldn't be interpreted as proof of one. To repeat the text:

> ...the 'mummers' had performed the old tragedy of the defeat of the dragon by St George. ... As presented in Herne Bay, the affair was simply ludicrous.[278]

The newspaper text fails to elucidate who the other actors might have been. It is the author's assumption that the 'dragon' was a de facto hooden horse, rather than a participant in the Christmas mummers play of the Seven Champions of Christendom. One could deduce that the eyewitness saw the horse fall over under the apparent volition of another actor, assumed to be St George. Neither costuming nor spoken text is cited, but there must have been something distinctive about the party to have first drawn the journalist's attention to their clamour in performance.

There is a further observation to be made here, albeit focusing on two specific examples from twelve locations over a century. Both Bob Skardon of Deal and the St Nicholas musicians are dressed differently from the rest of the team.[279] Is there a reason for this? Unfortunately, no one had the presence of mind to ask the relevant questions. William West is featured on photographs of the St Nicholas team of 1921 wearing a remarkable rig resplendent with outsize bow tie and curly wig crammed beneath a black top hat, reminiscent of a clown – perhaps this was the function intended? Bob Skardon's jacket is a patchwork affair, possibly harlequinade – and imitated by the present-day revival team. This brings to mind the character 'Harlequin Billy' and his band who performed with fife, triangle and drums in the streets of Ramsgate during 1866. The fife player 'Billy', whose real identity remains a mystery, was arrayed in 'a most peculiar combination of Life Guard and Lancer uniform', whilst the rest 'of this group were dressed in a most fantastic and grotesque manner.' Not the classic impression of harlequinalia, but of course, there was never to be any proven unimpeachable link with hoodening using this 'evidence' beyond the portrayal of the musician here as an extraordinary character. The entertainment 'Harlequinade Billy Taylor' was composed in 1851 as incidental music (as well as similar entr'actes) to

---

[277]Maylam, p92
[278]Herne Bay Press, 29 December 1888, p5
[279]Maylam, plates A-F

more substantial burlesques in the Victorian theatre as the 'Grand Transformation Scene' to hide the sound of stage machinery![280]

Finding a Theatre

In conventional drama, the audience visits a theatre, whether it be in a town or even a village hall, for example. The cast has a base camp; the audience has to leave home to witness the performance. The reverse is true in hoodening. The performers tour the locality to gather largesse, proceeding from venue to venue. The 'stage' could be unpredictable; its lighting dubious.

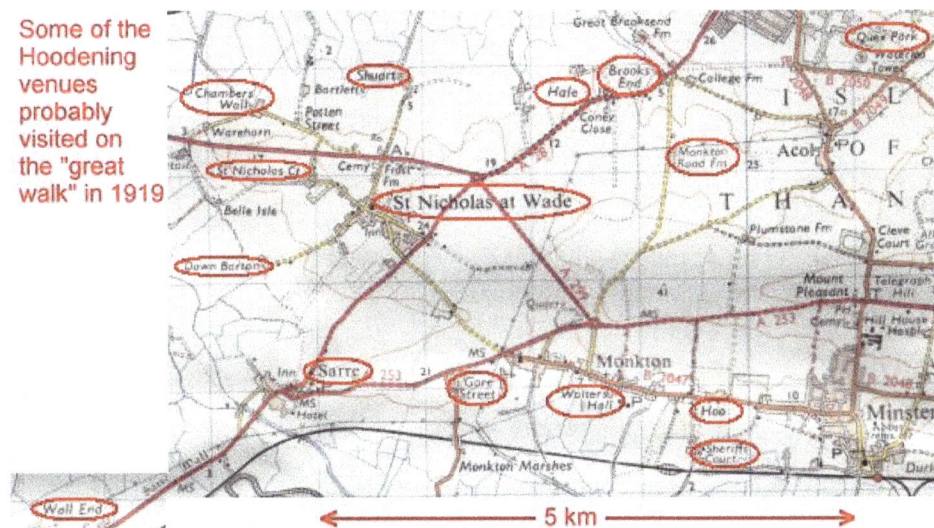

Some of the Hoodening venues probably visited on the "great walk" in 1919

Map of the Great Walk

All manner of places would be visited: country houses, farms, public houses, shops, rectories - even the open air, if payment was in the offing. At St Nicholas-at-Wade, a wide area would be visited, and we are told a list of locations where the hooodeners would tour. In St Nicholas itself, there would be Shuart Farm, Chamber's Wall Farm, Down Barton Farm, St Nicholas Court, the Bell, the draper's shop, the bakery, the big house at Brook's End, and Ropeyard Farm. At Sarre, they would visit Bolingbroke Farm, Sarre Farm, the King's Head, and the Crown. The journey might be extended into Upstreet, where they would visit Wall End Farm, stopping short at crossing the Stour at Grove Ferry. They would also visit the Birchington environs including the Powell-Cotton house at Quex Park, Brook's End, as well as Crispe Farm, Road Farm, and Hale. Hoodening took place on two nights in Christmas week, one night being devoted to shops, pubs and big houses in St Nicholas. The second night was the 'great walk' to Sarre and beyond. On another occasion, Tom West specifically stated that one night was spent at Monkton, where Gore Street Farm, Monkton Court,

---

[280]Chris Goddard, Music in the Victorian Theatre before 'Ivanhoe', archive copy at http://bit.ly/ChrisGoddard

Monkton Parsonage, the White Stag (then called the New Inn), Walters Hall Farm, Sherrif's Court Farm, and Hoo Farm would be visited.

What seems clear is that this is a litany of options where the hoodeners could rather than did visit. It is hypothesized that what Tom West described as 'the great walk' was ten miles in length and specific to the period just after the Great War. Clearly from the range of venues possible, to do justice to a performance then progress on to the next, only a limited number of locations would be visited during the course of an evening. The men would agree an action plan, convene at a mutually agreed point (this is not difficult, because they all worked within a few miles or so from each other), then do the tour. Tom West also said they started in the evening when the 'shops were still open'. Even allowing for a 6 p.m. start, a brisk walking pace, and adequate time to perform and enjoy the hospitality of their hosts, the hike concerned looks like a challenge for getting home by midnight, with work beckoning the following morning.

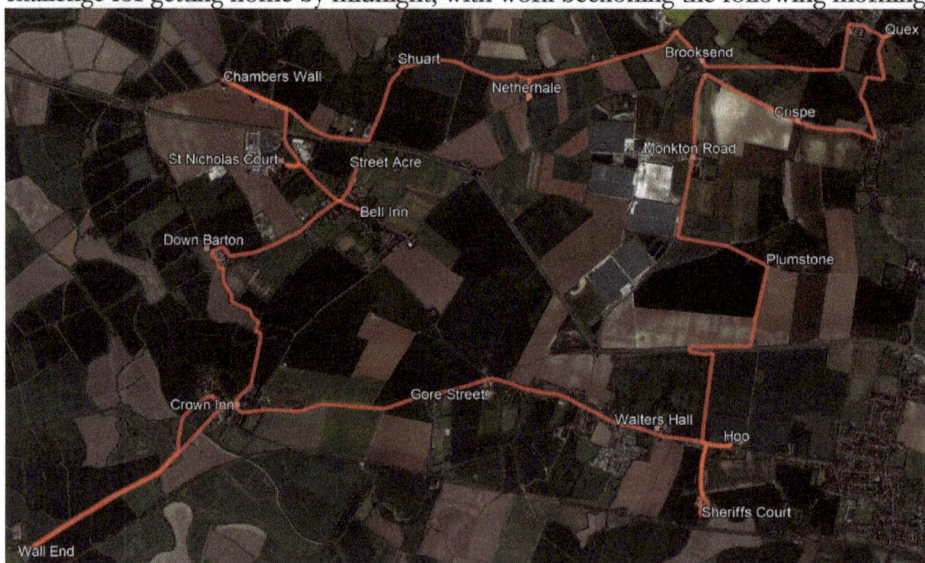

Great Walk: 2016 route

To judge by Percy Maylam's assessment of the party at Lower Hardres, their 'catchment area' offered something more testing. The country houses included Mystole at Chartham, Kenfield at Petham, and Lower Hardres rectory. Farms visited included Sextries and Winter's Farm at Nackington, and St Lawrence Farm House on the edge of Canterbury, with the suggestion they went as far afield as Waltham, Stelling Minnis, and Upper Hardres. In Canterbury itself, they entertained parties of soldiers in public houses. Percy Maylam himself commented after interviewing John Brazier that 'they went round for a week or ten days at Christmas time and must have covered a wide district.' There are plenty more houses, farms and rectories in the same area that may also have provided a welcome to the hoodeners, and Edward Mantle of Stelling clearly remembered them with some fondness. But let's put a little of what Percy Maylam discovered into perspective. In listing the participants in the practice, it is evident from public records that the same actors didn't carry on from the earliest citation of activity through till the custom lapsed in 1892. The Noble brothers had moved away by then, and Henry Fairbrass had died long before. Let the feet do the walking. If you were to get off the railway train at Chartham, take in the Fagge Arms and other pubs in the village itself, progress on to Mystole House, perhaps include Kenfield House and Petham village en route before returning to Lower Hardres, then that is a three to four-hour stint along unlit country lanes even allowing time for performance and hospitality. Presumably, there would be a 'southern' tour comprising Upper Hardres, Bossingham, and Stelling Minnis one night, and a 'northern' tour that included Nackington and Canterbury on another. Maylam doesn't cite any village to the east such as Bridge, Bishopsbourne, Bekesbourne or Patrixbourne as possible venues. The feet that have pounded the route say that it's a long long way from Chartham to Bekesbourne railway stations with the farmsteads well spaced apart astride the Nailbourne, with largesse more likely in the village centres.

We are told that for a decade or so at Deal, the custom was kept up by Elbridge Bowles who lived for a time at Great Mongeham (although by 1908, he was back in Deal continuing his decorating business). Only he and one other man went round with the horse, himself playing the tin whistle whilst the other man was inside the horse. Bowles's business contacts permitted them to explore a wider campus than just North Deal – which they also did. At the turn of the nineteenth century they were reported to have visited Finglesham, Ripple, Tilmanstone, Eastry and Betteshanger. As an aside, Northbourne isn't specified although the hamlet of Finglesham is, but it is a cross-country footpath route between the former and Betteshanger. This is also the period before collieries were set up in the district, so that is not an issue. Newspaper eyewitness accounts also mention hoodeners from Deal as visiting Sandwich. On foot, the twelve mile tour cited would be possible in one session, although it seems more plausible they were done on more than one night taking into account the grand country houses in the Betteshanger area alone. Walmer isn't mentioned as a venue – perhaps Bowles knew of the Lamings' activity in the area when he took over from Bob Skardon.

The routes of the other hoodening teams are less explicit. Edwin Sladden's team from Acol are supposed to have visited Minster, but we are not sure where else. When he moved to Felderland, the team he formed visited Woodnesborough, but whether they travelled on to Eastry, Sandwich or Worth is unknown. The inference from Maylam's talks with the Laming family at Walmer is that their team kept to within the village and farming community of the village itself. This seems unambitious, but we do not know what other factors prevented them from extending their tour. Perhaps it was viewed as an imitation of the ongoing custom at Deal, and they were anxious not to impinge on their territory. The Laming family were incomers from Ringwould, a village just three miles down the road to Dover, a village that never knew the custom itself according to published sources. We also know that their horse was made by Robert Laming's father Edward David (born 1822), so the antiquity of the custom at Walmer can be guessed at as extending to the first half of the nineteenth century.

Continuity in Community

To the onlooker, customs such as hoodening could be thought of as having taken place since time immemorial. Students of such topics realize that even these have a perceived life with changes in performance and practice over their span. Profiles of each of the performers in agricultural districts indicate that over the seventy-year period from 1841 to 1901, judging by census returns, it was seldom the case that the hooders were drawn from a static population – Deal being one notable exception. There is the impression left of a hiring fair by which workers were selected by a farmer or his bailiff for the approaching year in true Thomas Hardy fashion. Let us focus on the St Nicholas-at-Wade performers and see how this bears up to examination.

I recall once hearing a claim that the St Nicholas horse had been in the Trice family for over 150 years, but this was clearly an exaggeration. Speaking to the East Kent Times in 1966, Edmund Trice estimated it to have been made about 'a hundred years ago'[281]. But even that story was qualified to state that its creator was 'Chuck' Bolton, who was born in 1871.[282] This is the horse that was used in Percy Maylam's photographs so, assuming that Bolton grew up with the custom as a youngster in St Nicholas, it could only have been made in the 1890s or later. Chris Cole, who played the part of the horse for many years, when available, claims that the style of a repair to the main pole indicates that it might be around 200 years old, although the tip of the pole does seem to be a different colour possibly indicating new wood.[283] An interpretation of this could be that repairs were made to parts of the horse as and when necessary, rather than a new one constructed per se. As mentioned earlier in this chapter, although the Trice family may have been pivotal in sustaining the tradition at St Nicholas throughout the first two decades of the twentieth century, their paternal grandfather was born six miles southwestwards at Staple and their father George (1858-1911) at Woodnesborough a similar distance away but southeastwards, moving to St Nicholas in the 1880s. All in all, one has the impression that St Nicholas as a farming community was a place where agricultural workers passed through rather than stayed. In 1881, the hooders' musician, Walt Patterson was working in Hackington as a bricklayer's labourer. In 1901, he dwelt in a cottage at Upper Hale Farm, and was thus identified from the 1905 photographs. His name is absent from the local Electoral Register after 1910, which would explain why his services as musician were unavailable at around that time. At his death, he was living at Stanford, near Folkestone. His place was taken by George Holliday, who moved to the village from Ulcombe where he was born. He dwelt at Brooksend Cottages throughout the war years, and was recognized in the 1917 photographs. His name is missing from the electoral register for 1919, but resurgent at Chamber's Wall Farm in 1923, which would explain why Walt Trice was pressed into service as musician in the 1921 photographs.

Tom West was interviewed on many occasions during his long lifetime. At his death, a two-page obituary was published in the parish magazine which gives us great detail into his early life and also the progress of his father as an agricultural labourer.[284] Will West was born in September 1879 at Sarre, although his own father was born five miles away at Chislet – neither place being very far away from St Nicholas. Although he lived at Brooksend Cottages (presumably working on the farm of that name) during the 1890s, as a young man he had evidently moved to Garlinge (between Birchington and Margate) where Tom was born in 1907. Soon after this, the family moved to Flint Cottage, Canterbury Road, Birchington, with the explanation 'his father (i.e. Tom's

[281]East Kent Times, 18 January 1967, p9

[282]Tristan Jones, notes from an interview with the Trice brothers and Tom West, 19 January 1977

[283]Ben Jones, in conversation with the author, 11 April 2000

[284]St Nicholas-at-Wade Parish Magazine, November 2001

father Will) was a wagoner and changed jobs frequently around Michaelmas, which was the custom in those days.' During the next ten years, Will found work at Bowerland Farm at Chartham and later at Chilham Castle before moving back to St Nicholas after the Great War, working at Ambry Court. Moving home was frequent and 'Tom recalled … that he has lived in more houses in St Nicholas than anyone else! His first job was on the farm and he had to lead a horse round, but the horse kept standing on his foot, so Tom decided that agriculture was not for him!'

APPENDIX A: SONGS USED IN THE TRADITION

Deal

The authority on the repertoire of Bob Skardon's Deal hoodenening group is his grandson Jim Skardon, who wasn't actually born until around the time the team ceased. Therefore it must be assumed that Bob told Jim all about the horse and hoodening in the North Deal area during his lifetime. In conversation with Gill and Chris Nixon, these three songs were specifically mentioned:

I Saw Three Ships

This well-known carol has more or less identical words in three Kentish versions. One collected by Cecil Sharp from Alice Harden at Hamstreet in 1911, another from Gravesend and published in 'the Kentish Note Book' in 1888, and a third citing singing by children at Herne Bay in the 'Canterbury Journal' of 31 December 1887. That said, since the version in the 'Oxford Book of Carols' was used in 'Chrystmasse in the olde Tyme' which was first performed in Dover in 1906 and later at Deal (see comments on 'Phil the Fluter's ball'), it is quite plausible that that was used.

collected by Cecil Sharp

As I sat on a sun - ny bank, A sun - ny bank, A sun - ny bank, As I sat on a sun - ny bank, On Christ - mas Day in the

morn - ing.

As I sat on a sunny bank,
A sunny bank,
A sunny bank,
On Christmas Day in the morning.

I spied three ships come sailing by,
Come sailing by,
Come sailing by,
On Christmas Day in the morning.

And who should be with these three ships,
With these three ships,
With these three ships,
But Joseph and his fair lady!

Oh, he did whistle, she did sing,
And all the bells on earth did ring,

167

For joy that our Saviour he was born,
On Christmas Day in the morning.

The Moon Shines Bright

This version was collected by Cecil Sharp from James Beale at Warehorne in 1908, and was part of a local carolling tradition there along with 'I Saw Three Ships'.

The Moon shines bright, and the stars give light,
A little before it was day,
The Lord our God, he calls on us,
And bid us awake and pray.

Awake, awake, good people all;
Awake, and you shall hear,
Now our Lord our God died on the cross,
For us he lov-ed so dear.

In yonder garden green doth grow,
As green as any leek,
Our Lord our God he waters us
With his heavenly dew so sweet.

So teach your children well, dear man,
It's whilst that you are here,
It will be the better for your soul, dear man,
When you are gone from here.

Today you might be alive, dear man,
And worth ten thousand pound;
Tomorrow you might be dead, dear man,
And your corpse lie underground.

The turf all at your head, dear man,
And another at your feet;
When your good deeds and bad deeds
Before the Lord shall meet.

There is also a parody on "Pretty Redwing" sung about Charlie Chaplin which might have been the correct words that Bob Skardon told his grandson Jim about in reference to 'the Moon Shines Bright.' The chorus goes:

Oh the moon shines bright on Charlie Chaplin,
His boots are crackin' for the want of blackin',
And his baggy trousers they want mendin',
Before they send him, to the Dardanelles.

Phil the Fluter's Ball

'Phil the Fluter' was written by Percy French in 1903. In 1927, it was still being used for the local entertainment 'Chrystmasse in the olde Tyme' which was first performed in Dover in 1906.

Percy French

Have you heard of Phil the Fluter, of the town of Ballymuck?
The times were going hard with him, in fact the man was broke.
So he just sent out a notice to his neighbours, one an all
As to how he'd like their company that evening at a ball.
And when writing out he was careful to suggest to them,
That if they found a hat of his convenient to the door,
The more they put in, whenever he requested them
The better would the music be for battering the floor.
With the toot of the flute, and the twiddle of the fiddle-oh.
Hopping in the middle, like a herring on the griddle-oh.
Up! Down! Hands around, crossing to the wall.

169

Oh! Hadn't we the gaiety at Phil the Fluter's Ball.

There was Mister Denis Docherty, who kept the Running Dog;
There was little crooked Paddy, from the Tiraloughett bog;
There was boys from every Barony, and girls from every "art"
And the beautiful Miss Bradys, in a private ass and cart.
And along with them came bouncing Mrs Cafferty,
Little Micky Mulligan was also to the fore,
Rose, Suzanne, and Margaret O'Rafferty,
The flower of Ardmagullion, and the pride of Pethravore.
First, little Micky Mulligan got up to show them how,
And then the Widow Cafferty steps out and makes her bow,
I could dance you off your legs, says she, as sure as you are born,
If you'll only make the piper play, "The hare was in the corn".

So Phil plays up to the best of his ability,
The lady and the gentleman begin to do their share;
Faith, then Mick it's you that has agility,
Begorrah! Mrs Cafferty, you're leaping like a hare!
Then Phil the Fluter tipped a wink to little Crooked Pat,
"I think it's nearly time," says he, "for passing round the hat."
So Paddy passed the caubeen round, and looking mighty cute.
Says, "You've got to pay the piper when he tooters on the flute".
Then all joined in with the greatest joviality,
Covering the buckle, and the shuffle, and the cut;
Jigs were danced, of the very finest quality,
But the Widow bet the company at "handling the foot".

St Nicholas-at-Wade

Various interviews were conducted between Tristan Jones and others with the Trice brothers and Tom West as to the mode of hoodening before 1921. One imagines country singers as having passed down songs orally through generations, but in conversation, the hoodeners of the day were quick to mention how they cribbed theirs from Felix McGlennon's song sheets bought at F.W. Woolworth, or by repeated hearing gramophone records containing them. Vive la tradition!

Tree in the Hole

Tom West recalled a version of the folk song 'Rattling Bog' which ended with the line 'and the green grass grew all around'. This version was part of the musical 'Baby Bunting' which was on at the Shaftesbury Theatre in London in September 1919 around the time 'Teach Me How to Fly' was recorded. It was composed by Nat D. Ayer, with words by Clifford Grey, although obviously from traditional roots.

A little hole
In the ground
And the green grass grew all around, all around,
And the green grass grew all around.

Now in this hole
There was a little tree
Oh, the cutest little tree
That you ever did see.
The tree in the hole
And the hole in the ground
And the green grass grew all around, all around,
And the green grass grew all around.

Now on this tree
There was a little branch
Oh, the cutest little branch
That you ever did see.
The tree in the hole
And the hole in the ground
And the green grass grew all around [etc.]

[Repeated with the following additions:]
Now on this branch, there was a little leaf…
Now on this leaf, there was a little fuzz…

Now on this fuzz, there was a little skeeter [mosquito]…
Now on this skeeter, there was a little wing…
Now on this wing, there was a little elephant…
Now on this elephant, there was a little trunk…
Now on this trunk, there was a little suit…
Now on this suit, there was a little button…But there wasn't any button hole!
And the green grass grew all around, all around, And the green grass grew all around.

Teach Me How to Fly

The variety performer Florrie Forde, best known for songs like 'Down at the Old Bull and Bush' and 'I am a Lassie from Lancashire' recorded this in 1919. But in fact, the song was recorded a year earlier by Miss Vera Wootton and written and composed by Maurice Scott. Tom West recalled this song with obvious fondness, but it seemed remarkably obscure when unearthed at the British Library over eighty years later.

Maurice Scott

Maud had a sweetheart, an airman was he,
And she'd watch him fly all the day
Diff'rent stunts on the plane he would do
Loop the loop and some other tricks too

Isn't it wonderful she cried, in ecstacy,
And one night, placing her arms round his neck,
She said coaxingly:
[Chorus:]
Teach me how to fly, dear, in your aeroplane
Up to the clouds we'll go
All of a sudden we'll drop down again
It's so exhilarating, sailing towards the sky,
Hi! Joe, Joe, don't say no,
Teach me how to fly!

Oh! How exciting, to chase all the clouds,
There's not a game like it on earth,
When the rain's coming down pit-a-pat,
Think how soon we can fly above that!
When we are married, dear, what wondrous times there'll be,
We spend our weekends at Venus or Mars
Only you and me.
[Chorus]

All Along the Rails

This version was found in 'Feldman's Fourth Comic Annual' which was published in 1898. The words and music were written by by A.J. Mills and F. Carter, and performed by Billingsgate fish porter Charles Deane (1866-1910) who took on a career on the stage in 1890 until his death.

The other night I journey'd with some dear old pals of mine
Into a little pub, a small harmonic club;
A fellow there who thought himself a singer, if you please,
Tried to sing "The Anchor's Weighed" in thirteen different keys.
We cried "Encore!" told him he was fine,
Just because he bought us lots of wine.
At half past twelve, a little bit insane,
Sixteen good boys made for home again.

[Chorus:]
All along the rails – what a lively gang!
Shouting out the chorus of every song we sang.
We laughed, we chaffed, and told some fairy tales;
Playing the harp at two in the morning
all along the rails.

I acted as the leader, for I thought I knew my way,
So shouted out with glee, "Now, boys, you follow me."
We came across a policeman who was having forty winks;
Tried to sneak his helmet and to make him toss for drinks.
We'd no gamps, so for nearly half an hour

173

We tramped and tramped all through a lovely shower –
When all at once I tumbled, I declare,
We walked fifteen times around a square.

[Chorus]

I clutched hold of some railings that were painted overnight,
Got covered all serene with such a lovely green;
The servant girl was waiting up, the saucy little saint!
I cuddled her, and marked her cotton dress with spots of paint.
The wife found out, there was a row, of course –
Sacked our girl, and said she'd have divorce.
But afterwards I made it right. What ho!
And swore a swear that never more I'd go…

[Chorus]

Words and Music by A.J. Mills and F. Carter

The oth-er night I journ-ey'd with some dear old pals of mine In - to a litt - le pub, a small har-mon - ic club, A fell - ow there who thought him-self a sing - er, if you please, Tried to sing "The An-chor's Weigh'd" in thir - teen diff - rent keys. We cried "En - core!" told him he was fine; Just be - cause he bought us lots of wine. At half past twelve, a litt - le bit in - sane, Six - teen good boys made for home a - gain. All a - long the rails, what a live - ly gang! Shout-ing out the Chor - us of ev - e - ry song we sang. We laughed, we chaffed, and told some fai - ry tales; Play-ing the harp at two in the morn-ing All a-long the rails.

Sussex by the Sea

Composed in 1908 by W. Ward Higgs, a solicitor from Bersted near Chichester, for the Royal Sussex Regiment. The song was obviously current when the Trices first went hoodening in around 1910. According to the Sussex-based singer Bob Lewis in

174

conversation with the author at Sidmouth in 2003, 'Sussex by the Sea' was immensely popular even up to the 1950s and, in Sussex at least, "everybody knew the words". Perhaps this was so in Kent as well. This would explain why any chauvanism for Kent might be overlooked when the Trices did the rounds singing this song and seeking largesse.

W. Ward Higgs

Now is the time for march - ing, Now let your hearts be gay, Hark to the mer - ry bug - les Sound - ing a - long our way. So let your voic - es ring, my boys, And take the time from me, And I'll sing you a song as we march a - long, Of Suss - ex by the Sea! We're the men from Suss - ex, Suss - ex by the Sea. We plough and sow and reap and mow, And use - ful men are we; And when you go to Suss - ex, Who - ev - er you may be, You may tell them all that we stand or fall For Suss - ex by the Sea! Oh! Suss - ex, Suss - ex by the Sea! Good old Suss - ex by the Sea! You may tell them all that we stand or fall, For Suss - ex by the Sea.

Now is the time for marching,
Now let your hearts be gay,
Hark to the merry bugles
Sounding along our way.
So let your voices ring my boys,
And take the time from me,
And I'll sing you a song as we march along,
Of Sussex by the Sea! For …

[Chorus:]
We're the men from Sussex, Sussex by the Sea.
We plough and sow and reap and mow,
And useful men are we;
And when you go to Sussex,
Whoever you may be,
You may tell them all that we stand or fall

175

For Sussex by the Sea!
Oh Sussex, Sussex by the Sea!
Good old Sussex by the Sea!
You may tell them all that we stand or fall,
For Sussex by the Sea

Up in the morning early,
Start at the break of day;
March till the evening shadows
Tell us it's time to stay.
We're always moving on my boys,
So take the time from me,
And sing this song as we march along,
Of Sussex by the Sea. For...
[Chorus]

Sometimes your feet are weary,
Sometimes the way is long,
Sometimes the day is dreary,
Sometimes the world goes wrong;
But if you let your voices ring,
Your care will fly away,
So we'll sing a song as we march along,
Of Sussex by the Sea. For...
[Chorus]

Light is the love of a soldier,
That's what the ladies say,
Lightly he goes a wooing,
Lightly he rides away.
In love and war we always are
As fair as fair can be,
And a soldier boy is a lady's joy
In Sussex by the Sea. For...
[Chorus]

Far o'er the seas we wander,
Wide thro' the world we roam;
Far from the kind hearts yonder,
Far from our dear old home;
But ne'er shall we forget my boys,
And true we'll ever be
To the girls so kind that we left behind
In Sussex by the Sea. For...
[Chorus]

176

A Farmer's Boy

The Millen Family from Bethersden have this in their repertoire of country songs and glees, as did Charlie Bridger of Stone in Oxney, but the song is well known across England. This version comes from a Francis and Day's song folio, but it is equally likely that the Trice brothers learnt theirs from one of Felix McGlennon's song sheets bought from Woolworth's.

words: Robert Bloomfield; tune: traditional

The sun had set beyond yon hill,
Across the dreary moor,
When weary and lame, a boy there came,
Up to the farmer's door,
'Can you tell me wher'ere I be.
And one that will me employ?
To plough and sow, to reap and mow,
And be a farmer's boy, And be a farmer's boy.

The farmer's wife cried 'Try the lad,
Let him no longer seek.'
'Yes, father, do,' the daughter cried,
While the tears rolled down her cheek.
'For those that would work, 'tis hard to want
And wander for employ.'
Don't let him go, but let him stay,
And be a farmer's boy, And be a farmer's boy.

The farmer's boy grew up a man
And the good old couple died,
They left the lad the farm they had,
And the daughter for his bride;
Now the lad that was, the farm now has,
Of the thinks and smiles with joy.
Oh, happy day he came that way,
To be a farmer's boy, To be a farmer's boy.

177

Walmer

Jack Laming commented to Barnett Field that his hoodeners only sang 'South African War' songs, without actually stating what they comprised. Newspapers of the day cite 'Absent-Minded Beggar' and, to a lesser extent 'Soldiers of the Queen' as being the most popular at local concerts and fundraising parties.

Absent-Minded Beggar

This song in particular was key to the war effort. Broadsides containing Rudyard Kipling's words were sold to public acclaim at the start of the campaign, later to be supplemented by Sir Arthur Sullivan's score towards the end of 1899.

Rudyard Kipling and Arthur Sullivan

When you've shouted 'Rule Britannia', when you've sung 'God save the Queen',
When you've finished killing Kruger with your mouth,
Will you kindly drop a shilling in my little tambourine
For a gentleman in khaki ordered South?

He's an absent-minded beggar, and his weaknesses are great –
But we and Paul must take him as we find him –
He is out on active service, wiping something off a slate
And he's left a lot of little things behind him!
Duke's son – cook's son – son of a hundred kings
(Fifty thousand horse and foot going to Table Bay!)
Each of 'em doing his country's work
(and who's to look after their things?)
Pass the hat for your credit's sake, and pay – pay – pay!

There are girls he married secret, asking no permission to,
For he knew he wouldn't get it if he did.
There is gas and coals and vittles, and the house-rent falling due,
And its more than rather likely there's a kid.
There are girls he's walked with casual. They'll be sorry now he's gone,
For an absent-minded beggar they will find him,
But it ain't the time for sermons with the winter coming on
We must help the girl that Tommy's left behind him!
Cook's son – Duke's son – son of a belted Earl
Son of a Lambeth publican – it's all the same to-day!
Each of 'em doing his country's work
(and who's to look after the girl?)
Pass the hat for your credit's sake, and pay – pay – pay!

There are families by thousands, far too proud to beg or speak,
And they'll put their sticks and bedding up the spout,
And they'll live on half o' nothing, paid 'em punctual once a week,
'Cause the man that earns the wage is ordered out.
He's an absent-minded beggar, but he heard his country call,
And his reg'ment didn't need to send to find him!
He chucked his job and joined it – so the job before us all
Is to help the home that Tommy's left behind him!
Duke's job – cook's job – gardener, baronet, groom.
Mews or palace or paper-shop, there's someone gone away!
Each of 'em doing his country's work
(and who's to look after the room?)
Pass the hat for your credit's sake, and pay – pay – pay!

Let us manage so as, later, we can look him in the face,
And tell him – what he'd very much prefer
That, while he saved the Empire, his employer saved his place,
And his mates (that's you and me) looked out for her.
He's an absent-minded beggar and he may forget it all,
But we do not want his kiddies to remind him
That we sent 'em to the workhouse while their daddy hammered Paul,
So we'll help the homes that Tommy's left behind him!
Cook's home – Duke's home – home of a millionaire,
(Fifty thousand horse and foot going to Table Bay!)

Each of 'em doing his country's work
(and what have you got to spare?)
Pass the hat for your credit's sake, and pay – pay – pay!

Sons of the Sea

The words and music to this were by Felix McGlennon, who we have already met
in connection with the song sheets bought by the Trice family, from which they learnt
material for use on their rounds in the St Nicholas-at-Wade district. In fact,
McGlennon was a musical entrepreneur, publishing song collections at the height of
the Music Hall boom at the turn of the century.

Felix McGlennon

Have you heard the talk of foreign powers,
Building ships increasingly?
Do you know they watch this Isle of ours,
Watch their chances unceasingly?
Have you heard the millions they will spend,
Strengthening their fleets, and why?
They imagine they can break or bend
The nation that has oft made them fly
But one thing we possess, they forget, they forget
The lads in blue they've met, often met, often met.

[Chorus:]
Sons of the sea, all British born
Sailing every ocean, laughing foes to scorn
They may build their ships, my lads
And think they know the game
But they can't build boys of the bulldog breed
Who made old England's name.

Do you know they threaten to combine
Three to one's their bravery?
Do you know they'd like to sweep the brine
Bind us lads in slavery?
Have you heard they think that plates of steel
Plates of steel and guns will do?
But we know 'twas British hearts of oak
In every battle pulled us safely through
For one thing we possess, they forget, they forget
The lads in blue they've met, often met, often met.

[Chorus]

If they'd know why Briton rules the waves
If they'd solve the mystery
If they'd know the deeds of Britain's braves
Let them read their history
Let them search the bottom of the seas
Where their battered hulks now lie
Let them build their puny ships of war
We build men prepared to do or die
There's one thing we possess, they forget, they forget
The lads in blue they've met, often met, often met.

[Chorus]

APPENDIX B: GAZETTEER

Location	Grid Ref.	Last Performance	Classification	Bibliography
Acol	TR3067	1929?	THMC	Pharos, 1907b
				Saunders, 1890
				Frampton coll.
Ash	TR2858	1875	THSC	Maylam, 1909
Betteshanger	TR3152	1908	VHM	Maylam, 1909
Birchington	TR3069	1907?	THSC	Pharos, 1907b
				Frampton coll.
Blean	TR1260	1859	S	Maylam, 1909
Broad Oak	TR1661	1869	HS	Maylam, 1909
Broadstairs	TR3967	1828	HM	Saunders, 1890
Canterbury	TR1457	<1865	VHM	Maylam coll.
Challock	TR0150	1890s	TH	Frampton coll.
Chartham	TR1054	<1873	VHM	Maylam, 1909
Chestfield	TR1366	1857?	VHMC	Maylam, 1909
Chislet	TR2264	1888	TH	Lombard, 1891b
				Maylam, 1909
Cliftonville	TR3770	<1907	H	Pharos, 1907b
Deal	TR3752	1934	THMSC	Lombard, 1891b
				Maylam, 1909
				Frampton coll.
Eastry	TR3154	1908	VHM	Maylam, 1909
Elham	TR1743	<1820	H	Maylam, 1909
Evington	TR1145	<1860	TH	Maylam, 1909
Eythorne	TR2849	1890s	S	Moore, 1892
Finglesham	TR3353	1908	VHM	Maylam, 1909
Garlinge	TR3369	<1907	H	Pharos, 1907b
Godmersham	TR0650	1736	C	Maylam , 1909
Goodnestone-next-Wingham	TR2554	1890s	H	Frampton coll.
Great Mongeham	TR3451	1908	VHM	Maylam, 1909
Guston	TR3244			see Goodnestone
Harbledown	TR1358	1859		Maylam, 1909
Herne	TR1865	1888	THMC	Lombard, 1891b
				Maylam, 1909
Herne Bay	TR1767	1888	VHC	Frampton coll.
Hoath	TR2064	<1910?	TH	Lombard, 1891b
				Maylam, 1909
Hythe	TR1634	1930s	H	Frampton coll.
Lower Hardres	TR1553	1892	THM	Maylam, 1909
Margate	TR3571	1865	THMC	Maylam, 1909
				Pharos. 1907a
Minster	TR3064	1882	THS	Thanet Advtr 1864
				Kent Gazt 1868
				Saunders, 1890
				Frampton coll.
Monkton	TR2865	1921	VHSMC	Maylam, 1909
				Jones coll.
Mutrix				see Garlinge
Nackington	TR1554	<1892	VHM	Maylam, 1909
Northdown				see Cliftonville
Petham	TR1251	1892	VHM	Maylam, 1909
Preston-next-Wingham	TR2561	1889	VH	Maylam, 1909
Ramsgate	TR3865	1885	TMC	Euro Mag, 1807
				Maylam, 1909

Reculver	TR2269	1889	TH	Hole, 1937
				Maylam, 1909
Richborough	TR3160	1824	THSC	Maylam, 1909
Ripple	TR3449	1908	VHM	Maylam, 1909
Rushbourne	TR1963			see Hoath
St Lawrence	TR3665	1839?	THSC	Saunders, 1890
				see also Ramsgate
St Nicholas-at-Wade	TR2666	1921	THSMC	Maylam, 1909
				Parish & Shaw, 1887
				Frampton coll.
				Jones coll.
St Peters	TR3868	1839?	THSC	Saunders, 1890
				see also Broadstairs
Sandwich	TR3258	1907	VHMS	Frampton coll,
Sarre	TR2565	1921	VHSMC	Jones coll.
Sittingbourne	TQ9063	<1903	H?	Tooley, 1903
Stelling Minnis	TR1446	<1892	VHM	Maylam, 1909
Stourmouth	TR2562	1882	VHC	Maylam, 1909
Sturry	TR1760	1869	VHS	Maylam, 1909
Swalecliffe	TR1367	1857?	VHMC	Maylam, 1909
Tilmanstone	TR3051	1908	VHM	Maylam, 1909
Upper Hardres	TR1550	<1892	VHM	Maylam, 1909
Upstreet	TR2263	1889	TH	Maylam, 1909
Walmer	TR3750	1906?	THSM	Maylam, 1909
Waltham	TR1148	<1892	VHM	Maylam, 1909
Wingham	TR2457	1871	HS	Frampton coll.
Woodnesborough	TR3056	1908	VHSM	Maylam, 1909
Worth	TR3356	1908	HC	Maylam, 1909
				Frampton coll.

The convention used is one based on Dr E.C. Cawte's Ritual Animal Disguise published in 1978.

Maylam, 1909	Percy Maylam, the Hooden Horse (Canterbury: 1909)
Pharos, 1907a	Job P. Barrett, in Keble's Margate & Ramsgate Gazette, 16 November 1907
Lombard, 1891b	Peter Lombard, in The Church Times, 23 January 1891, p78
Thanet Advtr 1864	Thanet Advertiser, 31 December 1864, p3
Kent Gazt 1868	Kentish Gazette, 7 January 1868, p4
Saunders, 1890	Charles J.H. Saunders, in the Bromley Record, 1 January 1890, p15
Frampton coll.	George Frampton, private collection
Jones coll.	Ben Jones, private collection. Ben is the archivist and secretary of the St Nicholas-at-Wade Hooveners; see also his website at http://hoodening.org.uk
Euro. Mag.	European Magazine, vol. 51, p358 (May 1807)
Hole, 1937	Christina Hole, English Custom and Usage (Batsford, London: 1941) p10
Parish & Shaw, 1887	Parish & Shaw's Dictionary of the Kentish Dialect (1888)
Tooley, 1903	Sarah A. Tooley, 'Old Christmas Customs in the Counties' in The English Illustrated Magazine, vol. 30, p270 (December 1903)

Classification (cited only if known to be present)

- T   place of origin of team
- V   venue visited
- S   singing/carolling involved
- H   use of horse
- C   costumed performance
- M   use of musical instruments acknowledged

Notes

Gazetteers are useful in giving a geographical depth and breadth of a subject, but less so when the temporal dimension is concerned. With limited information available, I have prioritized classification 'T' where both incumbent and visiting teams were known over an undisclosed timespan, e.g. Chislet was thought to have an extant team in 1888, but the Hale Farm team from St Nicholas included it on their rounds in 1921 – hence its classification. Where no mention is made of music, singing, or costuming is made, classification is omitted rather than assumed, aiming to avoid misleading the reader. Tabulation of similar related calendar customs use an 'extant' year (best year of definition) rather than date of last known performance. Once more, due to the limited data used, some of which says 'about fifty years ago' or, in one case 'donkeys' years', it is difficult to be more authoritative.

Map showing the geographical distribution of hoodening in East Kent[285]

A 'clickable' version of this map can be found online on the Ōzaru Books website

APPENDIX C: TRADITIONAL PERFORMERS

Entry Format

In each case, the name of an identified performer has been taken, and presented thus;

[A] Name

[B] Birth (or baptismal) and death dates, plus location of each if different from key locus. Quarter of birth/death cited if unknown

[C] Address when active as a hoodener.

[D] Occupation

[E] Performance Role

[F] Father, and place of birth if kinship relevant

Where it has been beyond reasonable cost to identify the quarter of the year concerned, dates have been entered as e.g. JM2000 = January to March 2000, AJ = April-June, JS = July-September, OD = October-December, etc.

Acol and Birchington

Castle, William Frederick (1875-1942)

born 27 March 1875; died 25 October 1942, aged 67

4 Grosvenor Cottages, Acol

farm labourer at Quex Farm

musician, 1922-29(?)

son of William Castle, agricultural labourer (born 1848 at Hoath)

Denne, Charles (1904-1988)

born 15 June 1904; died 25 May 1988 aged 84

6 Mill Cottages, Mill Road, Birchington

unknown, assumed to be labourer at Quex

member of William Castle's team, 1922-29(?)

son of Charles Denne, horseman on farm (born 1859 at Sarre)

Port, John Downs 'Doddington' (1847-1929)

baptised 21 February 1847 at Birchington; died 23 November 1929, aged 83

2 Manchester Villas, Crescent Road

gardener at Quex Park

'captain' of William Castle's team, 1922-29(?)

son of William Port, jobbing gardener (born 1814 at Birchington)

Harris, Leonard (1883-1958)

born JS1883; died JS1958 aged 75

2 Park View, Acol

occupation unknown, assumed to be labourer at Quex

musician for William Castle's team, 1922-29(?); and later in 1945 and 1953

Burton, William Edward (1875-1956)
born AJ1875 at Bow; died 13 March 1956, aged 81
1 Park View, Acol
gardener
member of William Castle's team, 1925-29?
son of Charles Burton (born 1843 at Bethnal Green)

Sladden, Edwin Alfred (1873-1951)
born AJ1873 at Monkton; died 11 January 1951, aged 77
2 Grosvenor Cottages, Acol in 1902; The Bungalow, Felderland Lane, Worth in 1908
wagoner for George Goodson at Cleve Court, and later at Felderland
maker of horse and leader of team at Acol before 1902, and at Worth ca. 1906
son of Thomas Sladden, agricultural labourer (born 1836 at Chislet)

Smith, John (born 1868)
born JM1868 at Minster; died JM1947 or JM1948 at Folkestone
Church Street, Acol in 1902; Felderland, Worth in 1908
agricultural labourer
member of Edwin Sladden's teams at Acol and at Worth
son of John Smith, agricultural labourer (born 1835 at Minster)

Terry, Stephen 'Mouser' (1877-1963)
born OD1877 at Margate; died 10 March 1963 aged 85
3 Mill Cottages, Birchington
plasterer's labourer; workshop at Quex
active as a hoodener in the 1890s?
son of Robert Terry, innkeeper at the Acorn (born 1848, at Birchington)

Wood, Alfred Henry Wood (1897-1989)
born 12 March 1897; died 2 May 1989
1 South End Cottages, Canterbury Road (1910-29 electoral register)
occupation unknown
maker of 1954 horse, originally a hoodener before WW1?
son of William Wood, carpenter (born 1859 at Hamstreet)

Deal

Beney, John Ashley (1810-1856)
interred 27 June 1856 aged 44
King Street in 1841; 120 Lower Street in 1851
mariner
hoodener
son of Charles Beney, general dealer (born ca. 1801 at Deal)

Beney, John James (1832-1907)
> died 15 September 1907 aged 74; uncle of R.J.T. Skardon
> 6 Fisherman's Row (1871); 2 Kings Arms Alley (1881); 7 Alfred Road, Deal (1891)
> boatman, later fishmonger
> fiddle player
> son of John Ashley Beney (see above)

Bowles, Elbridge Eugene (1870-1940)
> born JS1870 at Ramsgate; died 18 July 1940 aged 71
> 49 Middle Street, Deal
> painter and decorator
> tin whistle and horse for Deal team. Leader 1888-1905?
> son of William Bowles, decorator (born 1833 at Ramsgate)

Chawner, Henry Charles 'Harry' (1855-1906)
> baptised 27 January 1856; died OD1906 aged 52
> 104 Middle Street, Deal
> farm servant
> piccolo for Deal team
> son of Henry Chawner, carter/farm labourer (born 1818 at Deal)

Skardon, Charles Ramsay (1824-1878)
> baptised 19 June 1825; died 19 July 1878 aged 54
> 8 Alfred Row, Deal
> labourer; worked for a Mr Prescott, carrier?
> "a former hoodener"
> son of Samuel William Skardon, surgeon (born 1786 at Deal)

Skardon, Robert John Thomas (1857-1951)
> baptised 21 October 1857; died 1 February 1951, aged 94
> 104 Sandown Road, Deal
> carrier, fishmonger
> musician (concertina and bugle) and leader of Bob Skardon's North Deal Band
> son of Charles Ramsay Skardon (see above)

Lill, Richard Talbot 'Dick' (1875-1955)
> born ca. 1875 (no entry cited in births/baptismal registers); died 12 April 1955
aged 80
> 8 Church Road, Deal
> lifeboatman on the Frances Forbes Barton
> member of Bob Skardon's North Deal band
> son of Richard S. Lill, coastguard and boatman (born 1833 at Devenport)

Burton, John Frederick (1898-1981)
> born 12 January 1898; died 9 July 1981 aged 83
> Sydenham Road, Deal

occupation unknown
"hoodened in his youth"
son of Thomas Burton, carpenter (born 1873 at Deal)

Larkins, James (1801-1866)

died 2 December1866 aged 65
9 Middle Street, Deal
shoemaker
fiddle player?
son of George Larkins (born 1774 at Deal)

Larkins, Murray (1846-1903)

baptised 6 March 1846; died 3 August 1903 aged 58
4 Primrose Hill, Deal in 1891
servant at the time of the 1861 Census
fiddle player
son of James Larkins (see above)

Larkins, Henry Horatio 'Cock' (1847-1933)

baptised 19 April 1848; died 27 March 1933 aged 86
9 Oak Street, Deal
fishmonger
leader of rival band to his brother Murray's
son of James Larkins (see above)

White, Reuben Henry (1839-1923)

born JM1839 at Wandsworth; died 8 August 1923 aged 84 at Guildford
17 Gilford Road, Deal
carpenter
fiddle player
no information as to father

Revell, George Arthur (1892-1963)

baptised 27 April 1892; died 6 September 1963 aged 71
95 Middle Street, Deal
boatman
used horse to frighten a young Jim Skardon in 1953 – scant evidence of hoodening
son of George William Revell, general labourer (born 1859 at Dover)

Elham

File, Stephen (c. 1784-1873)

died in winter 1873
the Row, Elham
agricultural labourer

role as hoodener unknown; possible father of Eliza Clayson (c.1819-1908), whose father told her that he hoodened when young

son of Thomas File (born c.1753-1755 at Elham)

File, Thomas (1776-1859)

buried 17 April 1859 aged 83 at Elham

Elham

agricultural labourer

role as hoodener unknown; possible father of Eliza Clayson (c.1819-1908), whose father told her that he hoodened when young

parentage unclear

Herne, Swalecliffe and Chestfield

Christian, Henry William (1837-1909)

chr. 25 June 1837; died OD1909 aged 69 at Faversham

Herne Common

wagoner's mate (?), licensed victualler in 1881

wagoner's mate in play (?)

son of William Christian, agricultural labourer (born 1806 at Herne)

Hoath

Miles, Herbert Henry (1883-1971)

born 10 April 1883; died JS1971

Millbank, Hoath

carpenter

made horse for a revival in 1906, kept for many years at the Gate Inn, Marshside. Commissioned by Percy Maylam to find hoodeners for photographs (see entry for St Nicholas)

son of Frederick Miles, farmer (born 1852 at Herne Hill)

Lower Hardres

Brazier, Henry (1801-1890)

born c. 1801 at Elmsted; died JM1890, aged 88

Three Horseshoes Cottages, Lower Hardres

agricultural labourer

horse, and player of bells

possibly son of Thomas Brazier, agricultural labourer (born 1766 at Elmsted)

Brazier, John (1845-1928)

chr. 3 August 1845 at Bishopsbourne; died JS1928 aged 84

Nightingale Cottages, Lower Hardres

agricultural labourer

role in hoodening unknown

son of Henry Brazier (see above)

Fairbrass, William Henry (1801-1876)

born 7 November 1801?; died OD1876 aged 75
Pett Bottom, Lower Hardres
agricultural labourer
role in hoodening unknown
son of Edward Fairbrass, agricultural labourer

Noble, George (1817-1904)

baptized 30 March 1817; died 19 January 1904 aged 86
Little Broxhall, Upper Hardres
agricultural labourer
'Old George Noble' who made the horses in 1860
son of Robert Noble, labourer, and Mary *née* Filmer; relationship to Henry &
William Noble unclear

Noble, Henry (1829-1888)

born or chr. 26 April 1829; died 9 June 1888 aged 60 at Canterbury
The Greenway, Lower Hardres; 36 St George's Place, Canterbury at death
agricultural labourer; carpenter in later life
role in hoodening unknown
son of William Noble, labourer

Noble, William (1833-1887)

born or chr. 27 November 1833; died 19 October 1887 aged 54 at Sellindge, miller
The Greenway, Lower Hardres; Hodiford Mill, Sellindge at death
agricultural labourer; miller at Sellindge in later life
role in hoodening unknown
son of William Noble, labourer

Minster

Kemp, Richard (1847-1926)

baptised 31 January 1847 at Bridge; died 23 April 1926 at Wingham, aged 79
address at Minster unknown; lived at Chalkpit Farm Cottages, Bekesbourne from
1874
labourer (farm bailiff at death)
role in hoodening unknown, but he kept the horse
son of Brice Kemp, labourer (born 1813 at Reculver)

St Nicholas-at-Wade

Miles, Herbert Henry (1883-1971)

born 10 April 1883; died JS1971
Millbank, Hoath

carpenter

role at St Nicholas unclear. Percy Maylam commissioned him to find some hoodeners for photographing, then started his own team at Hoath (q.v.)

son of Frederick Miles, farmer (born 1852 at Herne Hill)

Patterson, Walter (1865-1938)

born JM1865 at Hackington; died 10 September 1938 at Stanford
Upper Hale Farm Cottages, St Nicholas
ordinary agricultural labourer
musician (accordion) in 1905
son of George Patterson, agricultural labourer (born 1833 at Sutton)

Bolton, Arthur David (1871-1950)

chr. 11 June 1871; died 23 June 1950 aged 79 at Capel le Ferne
Chapel Yard in 1901, St Nicholas
yardman/cattleman in 1901 at Upper Hale Farm
maker of the horse
son of Francis Bolton, agricultural labourer (born 1826 at Chislet)

Gibbs, George William (1890-1966)

born 7 August 1890; died 16 March 1966 aged 76
Rose Cottage, St Nicholas
agricultural labourer assumed
the rider
son of David Gibbs, agricultural labourer (born 1853 at St Nicholas)

Gibbs, Percy Ernest (1893-1961)

born 6 June 1893; died 7August 1961 aged 68
Rose Cottage, St Nicholas
agricultural labourer assumed
the rider
son of David Gibbs, agricultural labourer (born 1853 at St Nicholas)

Trice, George (1858-1911)

born 1858 at Woodnesborough; died 16 September 1911 aged 53
The Street near Home Farm, St Nicholas in 1901
agricultural labourer
wagoner in 1905?
son of Thomas Trice, agricultural labourer (born 1827 at Staple)

Trice, George (1890-1974)

born 6 December 1890; died OD1974 at Canterbury
The Street, St Nicholas in 1901
horseman at St Nicholas Court Farm
Molly in 1919-21
son of George Trice, agricultural labourer (born 1858 at Woodnesborough)

Trice, Frank 'Podger' (1897-1980)

born 24 January 1897; died JS1980 at Chatham
St Nicholas Court Cottages in 1919; Thanet View (in 1966)
horseman at St Nicholas Court Farm
horse in 1919
son of George Trice, agricultural labourer (born 1858 at Woodnesborough)

Trice, Ernest (1900-1985)

born 7 October 1900; died February 1985 at Maidstone
The Street, St Nicholas in 1901
horseman at St Nicholas Court Farm
sundry character, tambourine player/collector
son of George Trice, agricultural labourer (born 1858 at Woodnesborough)

Trice, Walter (1903-1973)

born 29 May 1903; died 19 August 1973
The street, St Nicholas in 1901; 2 Jubilee Cottages, Downbarton Road in 1966
horseman at St Nicholas Court Farm
jockey before 1914; wagoner after 1917; musician (accordion) in 1921
son of George Trice, agricultural labourer (born 1858 at Woodnesborough)

Trice, Edmund (1888-1974)

born 4 July 1888; died JM1981 aged 92 at Chatham
St Nicholas Court Cottages in 1905; 3 Thanet View in 1966
horseman at St Nicholas Court Farm
horse in 1921
son of George Trice, agricultural labourer (born 1858 at Woodnesborough)

West, William Henry (1879-1958)

born 14 September 1879; funeral 6 March 1958 aged 78
Elm Cottage, Sarre in 1919; Manor Cottage, St Nicholas at death
wagoner at Ambry Court Farm, St Nicholas-at-Wade
accordion player before 1914; 'clown' in 1921
son of William Henry West, agricultural labourer (born 1855, at Chislet)

West, Thomas William (1907-2001)

born 7 September 1907 at Garlinge; died 14 September 2001
many addresses in St Nicholas area; Myrtle Villa, Manor Road, St Nicholas at
death
labourer 'leading a horse round'; slaughterman in butchery trade
jockey
son of William West (see above)

Holliday, George Austin (1882-1946)

born AJ1882 at Ulcombe; died OD1946
Brooksend Cottages until 1914

cowman at Chamber's Wall Farm
melodeon player in photographs
son of Richard Holliday, labourer (born 1838 at Hastingleigh)

Howland, Stephen John 'Steve' (1890-1970)

born 16 December 1890; died 8 March 1970 aged 79 at Manston
Prospect Place, St Nicholas in 1923; 18 High Street, Manston at death
agricultural labourer
wagoner in 1921
son of John Howland, agricultural labourer (born 1863 at Sholden)

Walmer

Laming, Robert Richard (1860-1947)

baptised 20 July 1860 at Ringwould; died 7 March 1947 aged 86
3 Granville Terrace, Great Mongeham in 1891; 52 Mayers Road, Walmer (1908)
wagoner at Walmer
leader of the Walmer team
son of Edward David Laming, agricultural labourer (born 1822 at Ringwould),
who made the Walmer horse

Laming, Edward James (1883-1971)

baptised 4 March 1883; died 8 July 1971 aged 88
6 Woodnesborough Road, Sandwich
agricultural labourer
musician (triangle), but only according to one (disputed) Kentish Express report
son of Robert Laming

Laming, Joseph Percy 'Jack' (1886-1959)

born OD1886; died 26 July 1959 aged 72
54 Mayers Road, Walmer
agricultural labourer
musician (tambourine)
son of Robert Laming

Laming, William Henry (1866-1939)

baptised 28 October 1866 at Great Mongeham; died 4 October 1939 aged 75
Dover Road
grocer's assistant
musician (triangle)
son of Edward David Laming, agricultural labourer (born 1822 at Ringwould),
who made the Walmer horse

Axon, Harry (1877-1951)

born JM1877; died 9 January 1951 aged 79
3 Granville Terrace, Great Mongeham; Castalia Cottages, Walmer

agricultural labourer, boatman, odd job man
horse
son of James Henry Axon, mariner (born 1829 at Deal) and brother-in-law of Robert Laming

APPENDIX D: TIMELINE

690   Archbishop Theodore's Penitential condemning the practice of those 'who on the kalends of January clothe themselves with the skins of cattle and carry heads of animals'

1450   St George plays in use in the towns on Romney Marsh and East Kent

First pageant of St Thomas at Canterbury, including use of perambulating giant

1589   Morris dancers tour Canterbury and villages north of the Stour

1735-6   Rev. Samuel Pegge, vicar of Godmersham, refers to Hooding (houding): 'a country masquerade at Christmas time'

1773   Sturry – men in ragged dress with 'large black dog' robbing boy just before Christmas. Probably nothing to do with hoodening!

1782   Woodnesborough – men with blackened faces trying to force an entry at a farm. Also probably nothing to do with hoodening!

1807   Ramsgate – first mention of hoodening involving an effigy of a horse cited in the European Magazine

before 1809 Elham – tradition of horse with wooden head: the earliest eyewitness account extrapolated from Percy Maylam's contacts

before 1820 Ramsgate – Maylam's great-aunt sees the custom (later telling his aunt Ann Lacy)

1820s   Hoodening at Ash reported to include a Maid Marian figure

1824   Richborough – eyewitness account by George Solley

1828   Broadstairs – death of Susanna Crow, frightened by the sight of a hooden horse, cited in text as a 'bear'

Lower Hardres/Stelling – Edward Mantle's first memory of the horse

1830   Captain Swing uprising in Kent and the southeast

1832   Ramsgate – the horse's head is cited as being wooden, albeit obliquely

Margate – a resident remembered hoodening occurring this year

Deal – birth of John Beney who had known of the custom 'all his life, and (whose) father had also taken part'

1834   Ash-next-Wingham – Thomas Vickers's mother (Mary Marsh) recalled the horse 'when she was a little girl'

1838   Chartham/Lower Hardres – horse recalled in same year as rick-burning possibly associated with the Courtenay uprising (or with the Swing riots of 1830)

1840   Hoath – a man recalled being frightened (when a young boy) by a candle showing through two eyes bored into the horse's forehead

1846   Hoath, Herne & Chislet – horse and rider at least used in hoodening

1849   Ramsgate – hoodening noted as having been replaced by carolling

Walmer – Henry Page moved to Walmer Court Farm and sees the horse, acknowledging its presence up until (at least) 1903

Herne/Swalecliffe – Henry Christian first took part as the boy

1855   Margate – newspaper account recalling the horse in a party with 'various musicians who passed round the hat'

195

Birchington – in 1907, Thomas Whitehead gives an elaborate description of a performance in about 1855

Margate – eyewitness accounts by J. Meadows Cowper and Alice Tomlin

1857   Deal – Robert Skardon born; he told Maylam in 1909 that he'd 'always known of the custom'

Lower Hardres – earliest reference to hoodening in the district, although John Brazier says his father Henry had done so "for a great number of years before"

Ramsgate – acknowledgement of a horse whose head was 'carved in wood', together with ringing of handbells

Thomas Wright describes 'Hodening' as 'an old custom […] now discontinued, but the singing of carols is still called hodening'

1859   Lower Hardres – incident of the wheelchair-bound lady who was 'so frightened of the horse that she leapt up and dashed for cover.' The custom at Lower Hardres continued until 1892.

Blean – use of the song 'Three jolly hoodening boys' recalled by Edward Cladish

Sturry – performances recalled by Edward Fleet at Hawe Farm

Harbledown – hoodening 'party' noted at Wingate Farm

before 1860 Evington – eyewitness account by Thomas Vickers, senior

1860s   Herne, Chestfield, Swalecliffe – Henry Christian's memories

1862   Minster – earliest reference to hoodening here including the horse, noted regularly until 1882

1869   Sturry – Thomas Culver's eyewitness account at Broad Oak, Sturry

1871   Wingham – newspaper account of 1896 says that 'twenty-five years ago (the custom) was last seen at Wingham'

1872-1882   Stourmouth – visit to Dean Farm

1875   Minster – last specific mention of a hooden horse at Minster

before 1876 St Nicholas-at-Wade – Rev. H. Bennett-Smith, describes a horse having a wooden head – 'custom long since ceased'

1877   Deal – newspaper reference to a 'wooden headed…horse'

1882   Walmer – circumstantial evidence that Robert Laming from Coldblow Farm first took round a horse, independent of the one at Walmer Court Farm

Minster – latest reference to hoodening at Minster

1887   Hoath, Herne & Chislet – Church Times reference to the last outing of the Hoath horse – discontinuation of hoodening noted 'for the next 20 years'

Deal – the hoodening team noted in a newspaper text, with the names of the musicians in two separate bands

1888   death of George Noble of Lower Hardres, maker of the local hooden horse and 'the only man in the district able to do so'

Monkton – Percy Maylam sees his first hoodening whilst a guest at Gore Street Farm

1889   Preston-next-Wingham – evidence that hooden horse visited

Isle of Thanet in general – Charles J.H. Saunders, in Bromley Record listing that St Peters, St Lawrence, Minster, St Nicholas, Acol, Monkton and Birchington had the custom, with Minster which was the 'headest and toppingest for it', also relating the story of the woman frightened to death at Broadstairs

Deal – Robert Skardon discontinues his involvement with the Deal hoodeners in favour of his band; continued thereafter by Elbridge Bowles and an unknown tin whistle player

1890   Lower Hardres – death of Henry Brazier

1892   Lower Hardres – last outing of the hoodening party

before 1893 Birchington – Job Barratt reported that attempts to continue the hooden horse at Christmas seem to have died out

1895   Eythorne – Alfred Moore describes carolling in the village, known locally as hoodening

1899   Acol – George Goodson moves from Cleve Court Farm to Felderland (near Worth), taking a horse.

1904   Worth – George Goodson's wagoner follows him to Worth, and continues the tradition.

1905   Sarre – Bert Miles recruits the Hale group to be photographed out of season, by Henry Beauchamp Collis on behalf of Percy Maylam at Bolingbroke Farm

1906   Hoath – revival by Bert Miles over this and the next two years

Walmer – Percy Maylam visits to view the hoodening

Sarre – eyewitness account by Alfred Loft, Crown Inn, Sarre

Birchington – a revival by some hooligans calling themselves the Birchington Hoodeners, who terrorized the village (people used to barricade their doors) and were led by an infamous character called Steve 'Mouser' Terry – so-called because he used to bite the heads of mice as a party trick!

1907   Walmer – Percy Maylam takes photos of Robert Laming's Walmer hoodeners

1908   St Nicholas-at-Wade – Percy Maylam once more witness to the custom

1909   Deal – Percy Maylam photographs the Deal horse with Bob Skardon
            death of Henry Christian (Herne)

1910   Publication in February of Percy Maylam's book: *The Hooden Horse, An East Kent Christmas Custom*

St Nicholas-at-Wade – Edmund Trice's wife comes to St Nicholas and sees the hoodeners

1911   death of George Trice (St Nicholas-at-Wade)

1912   Walmer – Robert Laming's horse stowed away at Coldblow Farm, not to be rediscovered until 1955

1917   St Nicholas-at-Wade – revival by the Trice brothers including Will and Tom West

1920   Deal – eyewitness account by A.M. Williams

1920s   Deal – eyewitness account by Mrs Naomi Wiffen

1922   Acol – revival by William Castle, Len Harris and others throughout the 1920s

1928   death of John Brazier (Lower Hardres)

1932   Deal – letter by Beatrice Patterson concerning hoodening when she was a child, stating that the 'custom still continues'

1934   last outing of the Deal horse when Bob Skardon retired

1939   death of Percy Maylam

Aylesford Priory EFDSS festival, when a replica horse operated by Balgowan School (Beckenham) appeared

1945   Acol – Len Harris's horse previously used in the 1920s part of a fancy dress tableau at VJ Celebrations

1947   Balgowan horse given to the Ravensbourne Morris Men

c. 1950   discovery of hooden horse at 'Guston' – possibly a misnomer for Goodnestone-near-Wingham

1950   death of Arthur Bolton – creator of the St Nicholas-at-Wade horse

1951   death of Robert Skardon (Deal)

Revivals by boys from St Stephen's School touring Canterbury under the tutelage of Edward Coomber

Albert Graves's hooden horse paraded around Crundale and Godmersham

1953   Folkestone – Barnett Field first parades his hooden horse at the Coronation celebrations

Acol – Len Harris's horse used as part of a tableau in village Coronation celebrations

Folkestone – inauguration of handbell hoodening

1954   Birchington – inauguration of the hooden horse as part of carol singing festival by the Birchington Evening Townswomen's Guild, Christmas week 1954

1956   acquisition of two hooden horses from the Wingham district by Maidstone Museum

Birchington Evening Townswomen's Guild perform Once They Lived in Our Town with their hooden horse at the Granville Theatre in Ramsgate

Wickhambreaux – 'Swan Inn' is renamed the 'Hooden Horse' in accordance with brewery instructions

Walmer – rediscovery of Robert Laming's horse

Whitstable – Edward Coomber's horse processing in a party along High Street by members of St Peter's church

Harrietsham – a one-off performance at Stede Hill, Harrietsham at the home of Robert Goodsall using a horse he had constructed

1957   first Hop Hoodening festival in Canterbury district

1959   death of Jack Laming (Walmer)

1966   St Nicholas-at-Wade – Arthur Bolton's hooden horse rediscovered and displayed at a fete of rural bygones in the school

          revival of hoodening at St Nicholas-at-Wade

1967   Folkestone International Folklore Festival produces a giant Hooden Horse (14 feet high)

1973   death of Walter Trice (St Nicholas-at-Wade)

1974   Deal – first season of the Deal Hoodeners under Julia Small until 1981

1980   death of Frank Trice (St Nicholas-at-Wade)

1981   inauguration of hoodening by the Tonbridge Mummers

death of Edmund Trice

1982   formation of Whitstable hooadeners

1984   death of Brian Debenham (St Nicholas-at-Wade)

1990   death of Edward Coomber (Whitstable)

death of Tristan Jones (St Nicholas-at-Wade)

1997	revival at Deal, led by Chris & Gill Nixon
2000	death of Barnett Field
2001	death of Tom West

APPENDIX E: THE HOODEN HORSES THEMSELVES

At the time of writing, six existing horse heads have been verified as coming from the period before 1921. Two are in the possession of the St Nicholas-at-Wade Hoodeners, one of which appeared appeared in Maylam's photographs of 1905. The two 'Wingham' horses are kept in the store rooms at Maidstone Museum. The Walmer horse is currently on display at the Deal Maritime and Local History Museum. The Hoath horse fashioned by Bert Miles was kept for many years behind the bar at the Gate Inn at Marshside, but when Chris Smith retired he returned it to Miles's grandson Bernard Miles, who then passed it to his daughter Rosamund in Bedfordshire. It occasionally returns to Kent for events such as the Hoodening moot.

St Nicholas-at-Wade

'Dobbin' is the main horse of the St Nicholas Hoodeners, which was used at the turn of the century and 'rediscovered' in 1965. Ben Jones comments that the style of a repair to the main pole indicates that it might be around 200 years old, although the tip of the pole does seem to be a different colour, perhaps indicating new wood, judging by the 1919 photographs. It has also been said that it was given to the Hoodeners by Arthur Bolton and made by him. This would date the horse as being from the turn of the nineteenth century, since Bolton wouldn't have been old enough to experience the practice of hoodening before then. The tacks holding the brass decorations on the reins kept on catching on the clothes of the bearer, thus a second leather layer was added by Ted Lawrence shortly after the 1966 revival. At one stage in the post-1966 revival, a bone was also attached to the top of the head. A copy was used in 1994 as 'The Third Horse'.

This horse has all the classic features of the archetypal subject. The head comprises a carved wooden 'joist' that has been painted black, with a white stripe along the snout. Its eyes and nostrils have been sculpted in and painted. Its jaw comprises a semicircle of hobnail teeth. There is one horse brass along its snout just below its eyes, and there is a flyer comprising three brass free-swinging open-bells on its crown. Its ears are leather and not part of the head structure. From around the crown, braids depend. There is a hessian shroud, and the horse is led by two leather reins with brass shields along its length fixed to a leather strap.

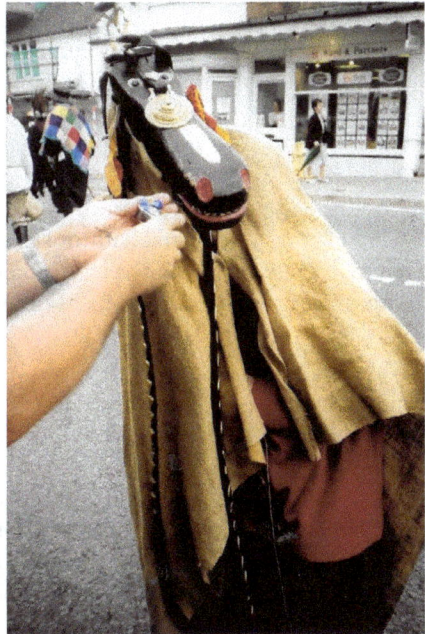

Wingham

As mentioned in chapter six, two horses' heads were donated to Maidstone Museum by Wye Agricultural College (now part of Imperial College, London) on 1 May 1956. It is unrecorded as to their exact origins. Graham Hunter, the curator of Maidstone Museum in 1977 dated them, saying 'the more elaborate dates from 1900 to 1910. The plain one dates from about 30 years earlier.' One supposes the method used for dating was guesswork, rather than anything more scientific.

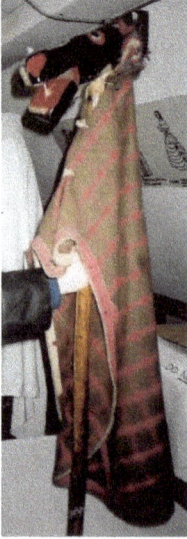

The 'more elaborate' horse also has the classic features of the archetypal subject, having a full-sized pole and possessing a (broken) string. It also has hobnail teeth and a horse brass on its forehead. It also has a studded belt. Its canopy comprises a red chequered cloth on a faded green background – possibly an old horse blanket. There are also rosettes on either side of its head, with a streamer depending from its centre.

The 'plain' horse, as said, lacks its pole, but one can quite clearly see the drilled socket inside the head into which one might fit. There is also a circular brass surmounted upon the crown with a vertical mirror-like disc hanging down from an annular frame (a 'magic mirror') – a distinctive brass matched by other hooden horses in the region. The horse is smaller than the first one, having leather ears, with nostrils sculpted and eyes indented and painted black, red and white. It further has a blanket covering and jaw that is pulled open and shut with a string, with hobnails fixed in the jaw to create the snapping noise.

Walmer

Caroline Bell, the daughter of Edward Mowll donated the Coldblow Farm, Walmer horse to Folkestone Public Library, which was moved to the Deal Maritime and Local History Museum when the former was redecorated and enlarged. This horse was used in Walmer in 1906 and rediscovered in 1955. A 'colt' made by Jack Laming in 1956 is also displayed (see also photo on p117).

Unlike the horses attributed to Wingham and 'Dobbin', the Walmer horse has a much longer jaw. This is hinged and made to open and shut similarly using a string attached to the bottom jaw, looped through a staple in the top jaw, and threaded through to the back of the 'throat', out and down through an opening in the hessian cover under which it may be be operated. There is a flyer comprising three swinging bells attached to the top of the crown between carved wooden ears. There are two rosettes either side of the head, made using red, white, blue, yellow, and red braid (from outer to inner). The hood is nailed to the head via a green leather strap. The head is painted black, with a black leather noseband

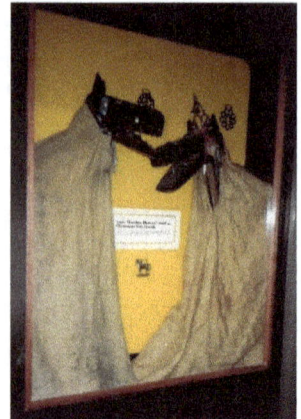

having five small brass bosses upon it. The eyes are painted on, but not made to stand out, which is the opposite of Laming's 'colt' which has glass eyes that appear to 'glow in the dark'. Horse brasses are also absent. There are four hobnail teeth on both top and bottom jaws, mounted inside an unpainted mouth.

Hoath

The Gate Inn, Marshside had for many years a horse that was found hanging in a barn in Hoath in 1974. It was said to have been made in the village around 1900 and is very similar to the St Nicholas horse 'Dobbin'. Common opinion has it that this is most likely to be a copy crafted by Bert Miles (i.e. H.H. Miles) in the revival noted by Maylam in 1907. Ben Jones adds that 'it is possible that it also physically 'inherited' part of the St Nicholas horse (the disc on top) as a way of imbuing it with life.'

The head is painted black with a short white flash on the nose, and carved nostrils painted red. The eyes are sculpted and painted to give the appearance of a black pupil within a white outer circle. There are no horse brasses; these being replaced by one large latten or morris bell on the forehead. Two leather ears are nailed to the forehead. The bottom jaw is short and hinged, and surmounted with fourteen hobnail teeth with a mouth whose inside is painted red. The pole remains attached to the head within a black shroud. For effect, the horse is further adorned with a sprig of hops to convey the ambience often found inside Kentish public houses.

Deal

What is known about Deal's horse is derived purely from one photograph, the description by Percy Maylam, and information gauged from Jim Skardon at the time of the 1997 Revival. Maylam's black and white photograph shows Elbridge Bowles crouched beneath the horse and totally hidden – so even his feet were concealed. The bottom jaw is similar to that of the Walmer horse in that it is longer than those of Hoath and St Nicholas, to make it look more like a 'crocodile' in opening and shutting. There are two rather large 'tear-shaped' eyes painted with a black pupil and possibly carved, if only because they appear to stand out compared to eyes painted flush with the wood's surface. The head is painted black. The are isoscelean-shaped ears pointing forward on the crown with what looks like a wheel-shaped rosette mounted

vertically between them (described by Maylam as a substitute for the usual 'swinging brass disc'). The green hood referred to in the text is attached to the head with rosettes at their join behind the eyes. There is also a short stumpy tail, which is a feature apparently unique to the few horses under discussion. It is difficult to tell whether teeth are present from the photograph alone. With the exception of the young Naomi Adams who described a long row of teeth snapping at us with its wooden jaws, all other eyewitness recalled only the clapping sound made by such manipulation.

It is curious that so many revival teams have used the Deal horse as a template for their own. Barnett Field adapted his without using teeth, so that the bottom jaw was grooved and made to 'swallow' money placed in its mouth, which would then slide down inside into a money bag. He also decorated his effigy with brasses. The modern Deal horse has a shorter jaw, no brasses or rosettes, but is simply decorated with streamers attached to its head and shroud.

'Satan'

Which brings us to an assessment of the second St Nicholas horse, known variously as Black Beauty, Young Dobbin, Scarlet or Satan. This horse was found in a Canterbury antique shop in 1976 by the late Tristan Jones, and labelled '18th century Italian hat-snatcher', but the proprietor subsequently agreed that it was English. In turn, it had been bought from Post Boy Galleries in Kilndown (now a motel complex on the main London to Hastings road) on the Sussex border near Tunbridge Wells two years before. It is unknown as to how this horse arrived in the Weald of Kent rather than the region associated with hoodening. It is known that Post Boys Galleries was owned by the actress Margaret Lockwood (1916-1990), although its day-to-day management was by an Alan Vidler. It is doubtful whether either had East Kent connections by which one might hypothecate the horse first coming to Kilndown, so its origins remain a mystery.

This horse is much heavier than 'Dobbin', and its head is quite different from the five previously considered. The top jaw is made to open and champ on a fixed bottom jaw each having a horseshoe-shaped white-painted metal plate into which grooves are cut to give the impression of teeth. This is reminiscent of how the jaw operates in the welsh 'Mari Lwyd' custom where a horse's skull is used, although Mark Lawson comments that the use of a skull made to open and shut thus would hasten its demise on the sheer dynamic of the champing action! Its ears are mounted on a lever system which can be moved forwards and backwards to give the impression of being waggled. The head is painted black with a long white band from between the eyes to between its carved red-painted nostrils. The eyes are painted on protrusions raised from the head, which has been carved to give a tapered effect – more like a true horse's head. There is a flyer with two free-swinging brass bells. There is a bridle, with a rosette made from red, white, blue and yellow braid attached to the harness. A short pole is fixed to the bottom jaw, to which the bulk of the head is hinged, and a hessian sack beneath which the bearer crouches hidden.

The Birchington Horse

Before June 2002, a horse was presented to Paula Jardine-Rose of the Wychling Hoodeners by a friend of her family who lives in Nottinghamshire. He had cleared out the house of his late father and found what appeared to be a traditional Kentish hooden horse. It has hessian sacking with the imprint 'Wm. J. Gardner Ltd., Birchington, Thanet. On Hire' upon it, together with the familiar logo of the horse associated with the county of Kent. It is known that William Gardner was active as an agricultural merchant from 1908 until his death in 1956, and a former employee remembers such sacks being used for goods transported as far afield as the East Midlands. The dates might infer an unidentified revival or survival at some time in the first half of the twentieth century. Alternatively, there is the possibility that the horse was used in a local Plough Monday play, although few survivals existed during this time span. Although it would seem unlikely that there would be any plausible reason to construct a horse merely for the sheer enjoyment of the exercise, the daughter of the owner (thought to be a George Henry Hope (1910-2001)) said she thought she remembered him making it sometime in the 1980s. She also added that her father never left Lincolnshire in his life!

The horse itself superficially resembles the Hoath horse, but slightly cruder. The head is a flat pine joist, with the bottom jaw cut out in the manner of the Thanet horses already considered. Its nostrils are carved and painted red, but its eyes are painted onto the face without being countersunk: black pupils within white circles. It has one horse brass in the middle between eyes and nostrils – almost the width of the head. There are isoscelean leather ears nailed to either side of the head, from which small braid rosettes in pink and blue are attached. The jaw mechanism is familiar but rustic, the bottom jaw linked to the main frame by a metal hinge. A string is attached to the inside of the bottom jaw, and threaded through a staple in the top jaw, and out to the operator. There is a semicircle of hobnail teeth fixed to each jaw which fail to provide a full 'dentition'. Between the ears is a magic mirror type of flyer. The hessian sack is nailed to the head, and there is a silver birch post inserted into a roughly chiselled hole in the base of the head.

Post-1950s Horses

Birchington (Townswomen's Guild)

Despite a newspaper report that a Mr Wood had made the horse used at guild pageants in the 1950s it was impossible to track down his family. However, the horse remained the property of the Guild until 2002, when it was presented to Ben Jones of the St Nicholas Hoodeners at a club meeting in Birchington.

Whitstable & Canterbury (the Coomber horse)

After serving many Christmases throughout the 1950s and early sixties, the horse remained the property of the Coomber family with whom Mark Lawson made contact when investigating the town's custom via a newspaper request. This was forgotten about until the Coombers moved house, whence the horse is thought to have endured a number of house clearances. According to yet another version of the story (see p125), Mark Lawson was alerted to a 'children's hobby horse' which lay in the corner of a household garage on the outskirts of town. This he instantly recognized as the Coomber horse, although in poor condition, and it then entered his safe keeping.

Current Hoodening Groups

Canterbury Hoodeners

Dover Tales (hoodening group)

Deal Hoodeners

Wychling Hoodeners

Whitstable Hoodeners

Sandgate Hoodeners

Tonbridge Hoodeners

Gail Duff's 'Rabble' horse

Pie Factory horse

Jim Bywaters's Whitstable May Day horse (before its refurbishment by James Frost)

Some Morris Dance Horses

East Kent Morris Men

Weald of Kent Morris

Headcorn Morris

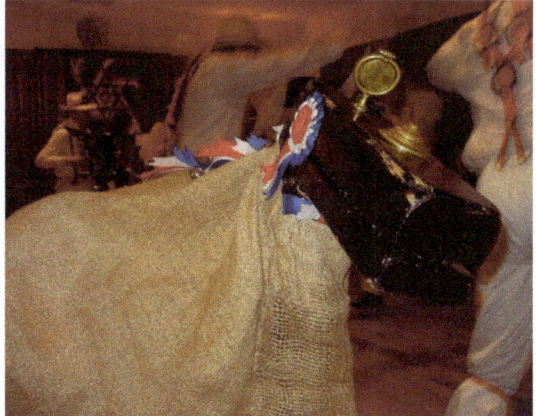

Hartley Morris Men

...and?

The Rochester Sweeps Festival), hatched in 1983, brought dozens of morris dance teams into the city. There were also many children's groups: schools, cubs scouts, beaver packs, etc. This red horse is unidentified, but thought to belong to a Deptford group, led by a melodeon-player. In this photograph, he is being 'fed' by City Crier, Peter Saddler.

APPENDIX F: TWENTY-FIRST CENTURY MUMMING TRADITION

This article was originally published in Living Tradition in December 2013, and aimed to portray how some 'traditional' Mummers' plays had been changed, to present them afresh every year, by updating to reflect current events – much as the St Nicholas team do annually. Of course, the onus is for the actors to learn their lines with minimal prompting for the season, rather than resort to recalling the same words year-in-year-out. The irony is, the year after the article was published, the Woodchurch Morris Men abandoned the idea of an annual Christmas play. C'est la vie!

Twenty-First Century Schizoid Men – New Mummers Plays for Old!

"In comes I, King Crimson. Welcome, or welcome not…" are lines you wouldn't expect to hear on a cold crisp Boxing Day outside a Hampshire pub. Indeed, with apologies to Bob Fripp of the eponymous prog rock rhythm combo, they are yet to make their debut!

'Tradition' for me once encompassed following the wallpaper trail on a cold crisp Boxing Day lunchtime through the lanes of Crookham Village and Dogmersfield in Hampshire, ending outside a country pub where Morris dance icon Roy Dommett would be leading his sons and friends in the time-honoured local Mummers play. The action itself would last about twenty minutes, in which Father Christmas would firstly introduce the actors: King George, Bold Slasher and Turkish Knight. Boasting, then battle would ensue between George and his two protagonists who, in turn, would be 'slain'. The services of a doctor would be summoned, 'surgery' performed and the vanquished accordingly resurrected. Little John Jack (with his wife and family on his back) would then appear, offering to fight King George, but an emboldened Father Christmas takes him on instead only to fall beneath the underdog's seemingly inferior might. All very jolly, and a fine way to complement one's Christmas, and thoroughly unique, so I thought…

As time rolled by, I have seen more or less similar fayre, either as tipteering plays at Guildford and Rusper near Horsham; champions' plays at West Malling and in the villages near Sevenoaks; pace egging at Middleton in Manchester; and a wooing play at Whittlesey. Most of the characters are the same, give or take a Beelzebub, Bold Roomer, Dame Jane and sundry combatants. King George might be St George, the Turkish Knight might be Turkey Snipe, and Johnny Jack might be Twing Twang (the right and left man of the press gang). Whatever! I was left musing about my 'unique' play seen at Crookham back in the mid-1980s. I thought then: "Write a new Mummers' play script, and the world will beat a path to your door!"

So, there I was acting as cheer leader for 'the Tradition' at Sidmouth Folk Week in 2005 when the offer came to me to stage the Sidmouth Mummers play inside The Volunteer Inn during Sunday lunchtime, this time by members of the Exeter Morris Men. The original lines were recited verbatim to Peter Kennedy and Sidbury head teacher Win Humphries by local builder Arthur Baker in 1954 and is unusual in that it has a full cast of fifteen performers. Baker recalled seeing it in his schooldays in the 1890s. However, it is suspected that the roles were added to by Nelson and

Collingwood for the Sidmouth Carnival of November 1905 which celebrated the centenary of the Battle of Trafalgar, and stayed as full cast members. Essentially, the storyline is the same as elsewhere, supplemented by all participants clashing swords in a chorus reminiscent of that of the Yorkshire longsword dance. For Sidmouth Folk Week of 2006, I made the acquaintance of Henry Piper of the Sidmouth Traditional Mummers group, and asked them to do their version of the play. Whilst ostensibly the same as the Exeter men's, it was more noticeable in its ribaldry. Six years later, I saw the same team perform outside The Anchor, and it had progressed from merely being amusing to outrageous! The character 'Merman' was now a French aristocrat who chased his assailant with 'le bomb' (pronounced 'berrmm', of course!) which exploded, putting the local seagull population to flight. (In 2013, he fired a cannon!) It also dawned on me, the script had progressively departed from the lines recited by Arthur Baker over half a century earlier. What had transpired was 'traditional' without being a reflection of the historical snapshot it once was – and far more entertaining than before!

Meanwhile, back in Tenterden just before Christmas 2000, the Woodchurch morris men made their entrance at the monthly song and music session in the former Eight Bells pub (now Café Rouge). I recognized all the old lines, characters and plot lines of the Crookham play, but somehow, that too had changed. Scroll on eight years, and the morris men had taken their play a few more illogical steps forward. One or more of the party also belonged to the local amateur dramatics society, and they had persuaded the others to literally write their own play with the hero-combat/death and resurrection scenes somehow incorporated into it. Local pubs were postered with 'Biggles Flies Undone', and a packed public bar at The Eight Bells in Woodchurch was to witness every aviation gag imaginable with Bigglesworth and Algey at the helm, before our hero was shot down by enemy flak, and brought to life by the 'fair maiden' – whom, it is hoped, had bothered to shave before her kiss of life! In 2012, the same troupe entertained us with a skit from Victorian London entitled 'Jack the Sniffer Strikes Again' written by member Richard Fair who is also a member of the local 'amdram' group. I was told the team had been performing an annual play in this fashion each year since 2002, however, the local newspaper 'The Kentish Express' with which the team often advertises itself makes no note of this, although their performances since 2008 are featured. This takes away nothing from the hilarity it brings to many, and the thousands of pounds raised for local charities in so doing speaks volumes.

Sporadic attempts took place to revive the East Kent tradition of the Christmas hooden horse in the 1950s. The St Nicholas Hoodeners were formed in 1966 by five people interested in local drama who lived in this Thanet parish. During the year, Tristan Jones, a noted local antiques collector and director of 'The Observer', began a village hunt for bygones in the wake of the popular BBC television antiques programme 'Going for a Song'. One object produced was a horse's head on a pole, which was found in the attic of a member of the last gang who took round the horse in the 1920s. Jones then interviewed 77-year old Edmund Trice, and other surviving members of the team to find out more of the custom. Canterbury solicitor Percy Maylam researched the topic, publishing his book 'The Hooden Horse: an East Kent Christmas Custom' in 1909. However, only his photographs and description of the characters portrayed, gave any clue as to what mode of performance ensued. This comprised 'barging' into someone's house, mimicry, a boy or rider trying to mount an obstinate horse, a few country songs or carols, and begging largesse. Then off to the next big house in an effort to raise much-needed cash at a low time of year for the farm workers taking part. One of the 1966 team, Brian Debenham, head of English at Chatham House Grammar School in Ramsgate, was forthright about what to do with this mimicry. He would write a play: short topical verse, with hilarious rhyming couplets. This was the template for future plays, Tristan's son, Ben Jones, who today acts the part of farm labourer 'George' and musical accompanist on violin' remarked to me that Debenham's initial efforts were moralistic in their aspect. Not content with writing the original play performed in December 1966, he wrote a new one the following, year, and another in the year after that. This guaranteed its topicality, parodying events of the year, both locally and nationally. Following his own death in 1984, script-writing became a collective by the remaining actors, but retaining this topicality. The play written by current script-writer Annette Paul in 2006 had off-beat references to Wayne Rooney, Katie Price, prime minister of the day Gordon Brown, and 'Celebrity Come Dancing' – nothing was sacred. The cast today reflects that of the Maylam photographs: the horse, his rider, Moll (a man-woman, who since 1967 has been played by local man David Gray), the wagoner, farm worker 'Stinky Sam', and 'George' the musician. All actors must live in St Nicholas or have some inscrutable connection with the village – and only one has any 'form' as a morris dancer! This is a community performance not one imported by the wider 'folk' community, and one which too, like the Woodchurch men, raises thousands for charity.

As we approach the fourteenth year of the century, the challenge in Kent is to find venues. The circuit where the St Nicholas team perform comprises local hostelries and private parties in an effort to raise money for local charities. Dwindling numbers of country pubs and their clientele, are forcing the team to become more selective in seeking locations. In 2011, the team performed during the daytime at Gadds' brewery in Ramsgate and the touristy old Town Hall market square in Margate, not far from the Turner Contemporary gallery. The Woodchurch men are facing a similar plight on the fringes of Romney Marsh, especially when new owners taking over the surviving pubs make no attempt to 'understand' the good intentions of the money-raising principle behind the mummery. It would be interesting to hear whether any other groups up and down the country have taken up the challenge of 'writing their own play' based upon the hero-combat/death and resurrection themes of old to uphold what I perceive to be a living tradition. I say, good on 'em!

APPENDIX G: GOODENING

[This article was submitted and published in Bygone Kent in December 2000 as 'Doleing for St Thomas'. When conducting research into Christmas customs in East Kent newspapers, several items headed 'Goodening' were encountered, which have no relationship to 'hoodening' other than the approximation of their names, the season involved, and the coincidence that both goodening and hoodening took place in Harbledown. Also, the custom was more widespread in the county than hoodening is or was. Some explanation is required.]

The custom of the Christmas 'box' for milkmen, refuse collectors or other house callers, may or may not be on the proverbial way out, but over hundred years ago, one might have had an entire procession of unexpected house-callers hoping for some form of largesse. In Kent, one such day was St Thomas's Day – 21 December – where the custom was known as 'doleing' in the area around Maidstone, which the historian William Hone described in volume two of 'Hone's Works' as 'an annual solicitation for charity', either for the poor or for widows. Without going into any greater detail, this form of doleing can best be described as 'petitioning and peripatetic', rather than 'institutionalized', where a gift is bestowed and administered by some charitable concern to designated recipients. The best example of the latter that springs to mind in Kent, is the Easter Monday distribution of bread and cheese at Biddenden in commemoration of the conjoined Chulkhurst sisters, a charity which is reputed to have twelfth century origins. Even today, you can still witness the queue of elderly people outside the White House waiting for its side window to open and receive their benefits.

So far as 'doleing' on St Thomas's Day was concerned, Hone gives three instances cited by an 'obliged friend' who signed himself 'W.W.' in 1825.

> At Loose, Mr T. Charlton gives the poor of the parish certain quantities of wheat, apportioned to their families, in addition to which, his daughters give the widows a new flannel petticoat each; who at the same time, go to the other respectable inhabitants of the place to solicit the usual donation, and it is not an uncommon thing for a family to get in this way six or seven shillings. The custom is also prevalent at Linton an adjoining parish; and I am also informed that Lord Cornwallis, who resides there, intends giving to the resident poor something very considerable. At Barming, C. Whittaker, esq. is provided with 100 loaves to distribute to the resident poor on this day, which to my knowledge is annual on his part; they likewise go to the other respectable inhabitants, who also give their alms in the way they think best.

A Mr Ellis who wrote to Hone and published in volume one, described the custom as 'gooding' and prevalent in the Maidstone area which, of course, Loose, Linton and Barming must rank.

These examples seem to overlap both 'petitioning' and 'institutionalized' categories. Alfred Moore of Eythorne described one 'petitioning' form of the custom at greater length in a weekly column he wrote for the 'Kentish Express' in the 1890s. Under the general heading 'Kentish Odds and Ends by Highway and by Hedgerow', he described the custom falling within his experience and from a pool of contacts in his column of 6 April 1895, under the title 'Goodenin'. He begins by saying that, in 1895, he believed the custom to be common to the whole of Kent, but 'generally discontinued'. He defines 'Goodenin' as 'the going round just before Christmas of poor people to the residences of more wealthy neighbours to solicit small gifts of money (occasionally of meal or flour also) the request being generally put in the formula of 'Please remember the goodenin' and the doles being called goodenin' gifts.'

In Leeds, Moore continues, the custom was also known as 'dawdlin' according to an 'old gentleman at Willesborough who has kindly sent some interesting notes on the subject'. This veteran was a native of Leeds and was an eyewitness to the custom in 1845, adding that it was continued there for some twenty years longer, being finally given up about 1865. The practice was said to have remained strong at Newington-by-Sittingbourne according to Parish and Shaw in their 'Dictionary of the Kentish Dialect' published in 1888, where a house-to-house collection was observed. A similar pursuit was followed at Elham where 'it was a great institution a century ago', and at Tenterden where 'eleven poor women – widows all of them – collected over three guineas, or about six shillings apiece.'

Although the Leeds custom clearly falls within the 'petitioning' category, Moore also notes examples where it was more institutionalized. His mother, who was a native of Eythorne also recalled the custom, where 'a private gentleman named Fector used to give away a couple of pounds or so in sixpences on St Thomas's Day as goodenin' gifts, which my grandmother had the distribution of. The old folks came from far and near to receive the money and use to say "Thank Mr Fector fer de goodenin', mum" when they took their sixpences. One old man used to walk all the way from Buckland to Eythorne to get his goodenin', and sometimes rather perplexing claims for a second sixpence used to be advanced, the genuineness of some of which were occasionally 'not proven', for instance when an old dame wished to take "Another goodenin' for old Master Gambrill's son's widow's brother down in 'the bottom'." It was rather a difficult matter to decide whether to give or to withhold the second coin, though I do not think there were many refusals – the sum to be distributed being (within reason) practically unlimited. Another gentleman in Eythorne (Mr Sayer of 'Street End', or as it is now called Elvington House) used to keep the same custom, encouraging "goodenin'" on St Thomas's Day.'

Returning to the 'dawdlin' at Leeds, Moore writes that in 1845, 'the gooderers (who were either widows or poor women with large families) met at a gate opposite the Ten Bells Inn at ten o'clock on the morning of St Thomas's Day. An old widow who was known as Granny Hicks was chosen 'Queen of the Gooderers', after which election they started on their 'dawdling' as it was there called. The party was under the entire control of its queen, calling only at such houses as she thought proper, the first being to Burgess Hall where 'Granny made a deep curtsey to Farmer Hodsell with a "Please remember the gooderers" and was rewarded with a coin of the realm. Crossing the fields and calling at most of the houses, they reached Fulling Mill Farm where "Mr Betts gave old Granny half-a-crown and a peck of wheat which was his regular custom." Crossing more fields, the party came out into the Maidstone and Ashford Road and on into the parish of Broomfield to Leeds Castle, where all the gooderers standing together curtsied to the squire, wished him a Merry Christmas and were presented with five shillings, after which they gradually worked their way by another route back to the place from whence they had started, where they arrived at about three o'clock in the afternoon after a perambulation of some six miles of more. The money which had been collected was here shared out, but I regret to say that it only amounted to eight pence for each member of the expedition in which about thirty gooders took part.'

Moore then makes comment on a passage in Brand's 'Observation on Popular Antiquities' quoting 'the Gentleman's Magazine' of 1794 where it was stated that the custom 'is still kept up in the neighbourhood of Maidstone'. He then went on to make a brief comparative study with similar customs elsewhere in the country, then to theorize on the derivation of the words 'goodening', and its correlation with St Thomas's Day. Before making further comment on that, I will describe one more specific case study which lasted to the turn of the nineteenth century – that at Harbledown, which was occasionally featured in the Canterbury newspapers. This is curious as a case study since, although it appears to be an 'institutionalized' example, its recipients actually receive largesse from a third party who do the collecting or petitioning!

The first extract appeared in the 'Kent Herald' on 10 January 1862, and is described thus: 'Three or four of the most nimble of the 'goodies' go round the parish and neighbourhood, and collect money on St Thomas's Day, which is put in a box, the contributors also placing the amount they give in a book. It is at length brought to the school where the box is broken open, the money counted, and the amount is supposed to tally with the book; this done, it is found how much each is entitled to. This year 60 received 2s. 3d. each, and 20 received 1s. 3d. each; these were young married people, or those without children. A small reserve was kept back, and this has since been given to the widows, aged and sick people of the parish. It is scarcely necessary to say that all answered to their names when the roll was called.' The passage seems to infer that younger people were the recipients of such charity, which is curious and is at odds with successive newspaper references to the custom. Perhaps the 'young married people' were the 'goodies' who did the collecting rather than the beneficiaries. What is clear, however, is that this same newspaper extract noted that 136 poor persons of Harbledown received a hundredweight of coals as a New Year's gift from George Neame, esq., and that the 'brothers and sisters of St Nicholas's Hospital as well as the inhabitants of 'the Mint' always share in this benefit.' To whom the donations to the 'brothers and sisters' stated were intended is unknown, since the St Nicholas's hospital's inmates at one time comprised those suffering from leprosy, rather than the poor and/or elderly.

By the 1880s, the Harbledown custom had clearly evolved, and was overseen by local farmer, Mr Edward Pillow. In 1882, he undertook this task 'for the twenty-fifth time', and was still doing it three years later when he was assisted by Mr Whorlow, the schoolmaster (later the Canon Alfred Whorlow). In the former instance, the 'goodening' was for 'the distribution of the subscribed fund to about seventy of the old and needy parishioners'. In 1885, 'a number of old and deseving persons of both sexes received sufficient money to buy them a Christmas dinner'.

So why 'goodening' on St Thomas's Day? Alfred Moore claimed that 'old Kentish people used to say that St Thomas had to pay for his determined doubt and that the custom had been appointed…in memory of this, for we should remember the doubting Apostle and give to the poor as a thank-offering because that through his incredulity our faith has received the greater confirmation.' The major books on folklore fail to forge any connection with the saint, so Moore's theory seems as good as any.

As to the derivation of the words, I would suppose 'dawdling' is a dialectic version or corrupt pronunciation of 'doleing' which is the preferred description of many similar customs, such as the Biddenden example, or even the Tichbourne Dole of Winchester where largesse is given to travellers to that ancient capital of Wessex. Moore also supposes that the word 'goodening' shares the same root as East Kent 'hoodening' which is an activity usually involving carolling for which money is also expected. The root concerned is that related to Woden or Odin, who was one of the old Teutonic or Scandinavian divinities commemorated at the great annual winter festival of Jol, and that the custom might have been pinched by the Christian church. That said, one would have to forge a link covering 800 years of English history between that and the Victorian custom, or dismiss it as mere speculation. Elsewhere in the country, the word 'gooding' or 'going a-Thomassing' is used.

Either way, we are grateful to William Hone and to Alfred Moore for painting so graphic a picture of a charitable concern from over a hundred years ago, to record a more unusual form of Christmas-based calendar custom than that previously noted.

This article was written and published in the December 2000 issue of Bygone Kent with minor amendments. Although not mentioned in the article above, it's worth noting that Maylam too discussed 'goodening' and the theories regarding its possible connection with 'hoodening' (theories which he discounted) in his book.

ABOUT THE AUTHOR

George Frampton is a Hampshireman, but was seduced by Kent culture upon seeing the Seven Champions Molly Dancers perform at Sidmouth in August 1979. He joined them in September 1982 on a part-time basis before moving to Marden in 1985, bringing with him a deeply-rooted knowledge and love of folklore and musical tradition, both as a performer and researcher, and continuing with the Seven Champions as a dancer and musician until 1992. From 1993 to 2005 he then joined the highly unusual and bizarre Fabulous Fezheads, a self-proclaimed unit of sand dancers, as concertina player, during which time he played for the team on the Goodwin Sands, and once performed as musician in front of 13,500 spectators at Watford's Vicarage Road stadium! Next he then followed his daughters and joined Rabble Folk Theatre, followed in turn by his wife Flirby – she as dancer, he as a musician. There he long resisted the temptation to participate in their hoodening activities for fear of perverting an established format (also being 'rubbish at learning lines!') – although this latter attribute qualified him to guest as an 'honorary member' with the St Nicholas Hoodeners. In between times, he formed the Thomas Clark Quire as researcher and singer, performing the music of rural parish churches of Kent discovered from the period 1780-1830. He is also well-known as a singer and researcher of traditional song in Kent, and has even served time playing for barn dances with the Surrey-based band Stockbroker's Belt.

He has researched, written and delivered lectures on a variety of folklore-related topics, and is author of a number of booklets on Plough Monday customs in East Anglia (fostered by his involvement with the Seven Champions) as well as books on Great Wishford's Oak Apple Day custom, and on Kent life in general, published through Faversham Papers. He was a frequent contributor to the magazine Folk in Kent and Bygone Kent, and still writes for Morris Matters and Living Tradition.

While in Kent, he was Artistic Director for the Kent Gathering in Frittenden, and even now he is chair of In the Tradition at Sidmouth Folk Festival. He is a member of the Folklore Society, English Folk Dance & Song Society and Traditional Song Forum.

Today, George lives in Whitley Bay, but still values his time in Kent and his many contacts there. He is grateful to Ben Jones for rekindling his interest in hoodening, discovering that life does not stand still, and proud that the old custom is still very much a 'living' tradition in itself.

INDEX – GENERAL

The larger categories – teams, locations, names and publications – have been split off into separate indices.

A

J

K

L

M

INDEX OF TEAMS

INDEX OF LOCATIONS

INDEX OF NAMES

L

Lacy, Ann, 39, 195
Laming family, 109, 164
Laming, Edward David, 109, 164, 193
Laming, Edward James, 107, 109, 193
Laming, Jack (Joseph Percy), 104, 107, 108, 109, 110, 117, 121, 122, 151, 178, 193, 198, 201
Laming, Robert, 101, 105, 106, 107, 109, 110, 160, 164, 193, 194, 196, 197, 198
Laming, William, 107, 109, 193
Land, John, 77, 80
Lardy Dooks, 96
Larkins, Henry Horatio 'Cock', 96, 188
Larkins, James, 96, 188
Larkins, Murray, 95, 96, 160, 188
Lawrence, Ted, 200
Lawson, Bernard/Damien/Raymond, 139
Lawson, Mark, 12, 122, 125, 126, 139, 140, 141, 142, 148, 150, 151, 203, 205
Lee, Dixie, 125, 140
Light, William, 129
Lill, Dick, 97, 104, 187
Linington, Edmund Sidney, 46
Lockwood, Margaret, 203
Loft, Alfred, 51, 62, 197
Lombard, Peter, 71, 99, 106, 182, 183
Ludlow, John/Annie/Dan, 87
Lynn, Mick, 12

M

Machin, Noel, 75
Maid Marian, 30, 90, 91, 161, 195
Mantle, Edward, 84, 163, 195
Marsh, Mary, 90, 195
Martin, G.S., 115
Martin, Phil, 59
May, Jamie, 135
Maylam family, 16
Maylam, Clark, 16, 48
Maylam, Elizabeth, 48
Maylam, Morris, 16
Maylam, Percy, 13, 15, 16, 17, 20, 39, 47, 51, 58, 105, 106, 112, 153, 195, 196, 197, 211, *(and throughout)*
Maylam, Richard, 12
Maylam, Robert, 16, 119

Maylam, William & Jane (*née* Bensted), 15
McGlennon, Felix, 66, 67, 170, 177, 180
McKenna, Martin, 141, 148
Michelmore, George, 132
Miles, Bert (Herbert Henry), 20, 74, 75, 76, 153, 189, 190, 197, 200, 202
Miles, Ethel, 75
Miles, Rosamund, 200
Miller, Nick, 143, 144
Millington, Peter, 31
Mockett, John, 40, 41
Molly, 45, 47, 49, 50, 63, 64, 65, 67, 77, 85, 90, 94, 105, 106, 110, 122, 123, 125, 126, 128, 129, 131, 132, 133, 134, 135, 138, 140, 143, 145, 146, 148, 149, 155, 191, 212
Moore, Alfred, 21, 77, 86, 182, 197, 213, 216
Mowll & Mowll (solicitors), 16
Mowll, Caroline. *see under* Bell
Mowll, Edward, 107, 108, 109, 201
Mowll, John, 109

N

Neame, Edward/George, 53, 215
Nixon, Gill, 12, 104, 137, 138, 167, 199
Noble, 'Old' George, 83, 190, 196
Noble, Henry, 82, 83, 164, 190
Noble, William, 82, 83, 164, 190

O

O'Connor, Feargus, 85
Oliver, Sydney, 122

P

Page, Henry, 105, 195
Page, Vaughan, 105, 106
Paice, Don, 121
Parker, Kate, 102
Parker, Louis Napoleon, 17
Patterson, Beatrice, 102, 197
Patterson, Walter, 50, 51, 160, 165, 191
Paul, Peter 'Budgie', 135
Paul, Tom, 135
Payne, Jessie, 126
Pearch, Kate, 16

Pearson, Roger, 132
Pearson, Terry, 151
Pegge, Rev. Samuel, 21, 80, 195
Penny, Robert, 43
Pharos, John, 52, 183
Phillpott, Violet, 59, 62
Polley, Martin, 139, 140
Polley, Simon, 139
Port, Doddington, 59, 185
Prescott, Richard, 94, 187
Prout, Carol, 75

Q

Quested, Rosemary, 153

R

Ralph, Mr, 61
Rashleigh, Rev. George/Maria, 82, 84
Reed, Fanny, 126
Revell, George, 104, 188
Ritchie, Ian, 139
Roach, Ruth, 126
Roberts, Charles James, 108
Roberts, Joy, 87
Robin Hood, 29, 31, 91, 143
Roper, Anne, 119

S

Sackett, Barzillai, 154, 155
Saunders, Charles J.H., 41, 44, 52, 183, 196
Scamp, Brian, 122
Schwartz, Wilhelm, 33, 36
Scott Robertson, William Archibald, 30
Sharp, Arthur, 31
Sharp, Cecil, 105, 167, 168
Sheppard, Joseph Brigstocke, 29
Skardon, Bob, 20, 87, 93, 94, 95, 96, 97, 99, 100, 102, 104, 112, 135, 136, 138, 153, 160, 161, 164, 167, 169, 187, 196, 197, 198
Skardon, Charles Ramsay, 94, 187
Skardon, Jim, 99, 104, 138, 167, 169, 188, 202
Skardon, Mollie, 104, 138
Sladden, Edwin Alfred, 49, 58, 153, 155, 164, 186

Small, Julia, 104, 135, 136, 137, 198
Smith, Bert, 51
Smith, Bill 'Mousey', 132
Smith, Chris/Carole, 74, 75, 76
Smith, John, 58, 153, 186
Smith, Val, 66, 67, 155
Smith, William, 67
Solley, George (jun./sen.), 90, 91, 195
Sperling, Charles Brodgen, 108
St Augustine, 23
St Christopher (Salisbury giant), 24, 25, 112, 121
St George / King George, 25, 29, 77, 78, 79, 128, 150, 151, 161, 195, 210
St Nicholas, 30, 32, 34
St Thomas, 27, 28, 195, 213, 215
Strickland, Ray, 121
Stubbs, Ken, 132
Sullivan, Arthur, 110, 178
Swannack, John, 61
Swing, Captain, 84
Sykes, Homer, 148

T

Tasker, Brian, 150
Terry, Steve 'Mouser', 59, 186, 197
Theodore, Archbishop, 20, 23, 195
Thom/Tom, John Nichols. see Sir William Courtenay
Thomas, Charles Russell, 87
Thomson, Richard Edward, 83, 84
Tomlin, Alice (née de Vaynes), 46, 196
Tooley, Sarah, 79, 80, 183
Trice family, 50, 51, 60, 62, 63, 65, 66, 67, 68, 131, 155, 165, 170, 174, 177, 180, 197
Trice, Edmund, 50, 51, 62, 63, 64, 65, 67, 131, 132, 156, 165, 192, 197, 198, 211
Trice, Ernest, 63, 67, 192
Trice, Frank, 62, 63, 67, 68, 156, 192, 198
Trice, George (junior), 63, 65, 67, 191
Trice, George (senior), 191, 197
Trice, Walter, 63, 65, 67, 132, 133, 156, 160, 165, 192, 198
Tuff, Lady Helen Constance née Denne, 101, 122
Turnbull, Mrs, 126

INDEX OF PUBLICATIONS

Z

OTHER PUBLICATIONS FROM ŌZARU BOOKS

Ōzaru Books is a boutique publisher based in the Thanet village of St Nicholas-at-Wade. Our primary focus is on books with a local connection, ranging from creative writing by East Kent authors to (occasionally niche) scholarly tomes about Kentish history, but we have a secondary interest in works in translation, particularly from Eastern languages, and also tales from East Prussia. Some of our profits go to support gorilla charities, which is the origin of the name Ōzaru ('Great Ape') and our logo.

Animal Guising and the Kentish Hooden Horse
James Frost

Published to accompany a four-month exhibition at Maidstone Museum, this book builds on Maylam's "The Hooden Horse" and Frampton's "Discordant Comicals" to expand the field of study into East Kent's unique folk custom: what hoodening was, what the hooden horse is, and how it can be seen in the national context of animal guising. It covers historical records and artifacts, revival groups, "Autohoodening" performances which reimagine the old tradition in a modern context, and related practices such as the Mari Lwyd, Obby Osses, various northern beasts, and stag guising. Appendices contain the text of numerous contemporary verses and plays.

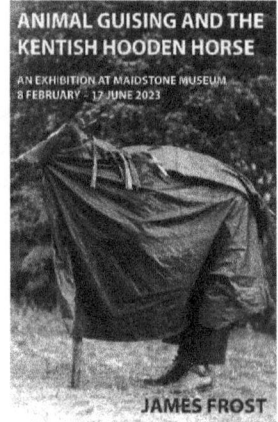

ANIMAL GUISING AND THE KENTISH HOODEN HORSE

AN EXHIBITION AT MAIDSTONE MUSEUM
8 FEBRUARY - 17 JUNE 2023

JAMES FROST

The author, James Frost, is a Lecturer in Performing Arts at Canterbury Christ Church University, as well as a Senior Fellow of the Higher Education Academy. He has also made numerous hooden horses and similar beasts, and performed with the Canterbury Hoodeners.

The book features over 60 full colour illustrations, many never seen before in print.

"[an] essential purchase [...] generously and informatively illustrated [...] a fascinating volume that at once informs, intrigues and entertains" (Tykes' Stirrings)

"stands alone as a scholarly re-examination of the Kentish ritual ... a detailed account ... beautifully and extensively illustrated ... right up to date ... fascinating and absorbing ... a comprehensive bibliography and an extensive appendix [with] a beautifully evocative first-hand account of what it is like to be a hoodener" (Folk London)

ISBN: 978-1-915174-06-2

The Hooden Horse of East Kent – Annotated Edition
Percy Maylam

Percy Maylam's "The Hooden Horse: an East Kent Christmas Custom" was long the definitive work on Hoodening – indeed, the only full-scale study of the custom. It covered the current practice in Thanet at the start of the 20th century, past printed records, theories about its possible demise, similar customs in other parts of England and Germany, and speculation about its ancient, possibly pagan origins.

Although Frampton has arguably superseded Maylam as the authority on Hoodeners and their activities, his book still takes Maylam as a basis to explore what happened since his time. Maylam's original work is indispensable even now, but the first format is very rare, as only 303 copies were printed, and only a reduced edition appeared later.

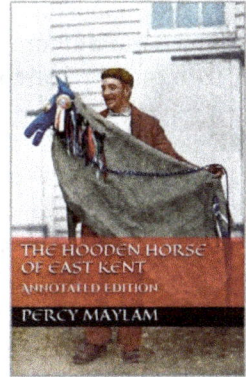

This new eBook includes the whole of Maylam's text, with numerous features to help those wanting to push the research further – even those lucky enough to have a copy of the 1909 hardback. There are copious annotations, internal hyperlinks, images of and external links to original sources, and appendices with contemporary reviews. The eBook naturally allows readers to search the whole text, yet the page numbers are still present to enable cross-referencing to Frampton and others (N.B. some of the functionality may vary, depending on the device used to read the book). The list of subscribers (which was omitted from another edition) is present, along with brief biographical notes on many of them, to show who was reading Maylam and what impact he would have had at the time.

The book is therefore a vital source of information for anyone interested in folk drama, including mumming. It is rigorously academic by the standards of the day, but also remains readable for general fans of the genre. This edition also contains updated versions of the early 20C photographs.

Available on Kindle

Misadventures at Margate – A Legend of Jarvis's Jetty
Thomas Ingoldsby
illustrated by Ernest Jessop

This lavishly illustrated facsimile edition comprises a humorous story about the adventures of a 19th century London gentleman visiting the seaside resort of Margate. There he naively befriends a poor 'vulgar boy', only to have his trust betrayed... A quaint fable from the Victorian era, or a cautionary tale for modern-day DFLs coming 'down from London' to explore Thanet's nooks and crannies (and crooks and nannies)? Some of the faces depicted in Jessop's wonderful cartoons can still be found in the side streets around Margate Pier and the Turner Contemporary art gallery! The verse – in rhyming couplets throughout – forms part of the ever-popular Ingoldsby Legends. An appendix also explains the witty references that pepper the poem, and some terms that may be unfamiliar to modern readers.

ISBN: 978-0-9931587-9-7

The Margate Tales
Stephen Channing

Chaucer's Canterbury Tales is without doubt one of the best ways of getting a feel for what the people of England in the Middle Ages were like. In the modern world, one might instead try to learn how different people behave and think from television or the internet.

However, to get a feel for what it was like to be in Margate as it gradually changed from a small fishing village into one of Britain's most popular holiday resorts, one needs to investigate contemporary sources such as newspaper reports and journals.

Stephen Channing has saved us this work, by trawling through thousands of such documents to select the most illuminating and entertaining accounts of Thanet in the 18th and early to mid 19th centuries. With content ranging from furious battles in the letters pages, to hilarious pastiches, witty poems and astonishing factual reports, illustrated with over 70 drawings from the time, The Margate Tales brings the society of the time to life, and as with Chaucer, demonstrates how in many areas, surprisingly little has changed.

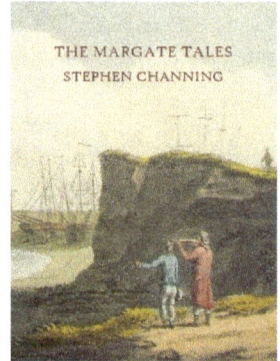

ISBN: 978-0-9559219-5-7

Turner's Margate Through Contemporary Eyes
The Viney Letters

Stephen Channing

Margate in the early 19th Century was an exciting town, where smugglers and 'preventive men' fought to outwit each other, while artists such as JMW Turner came to paint the glorious sunsets over the sea. One of the young men growing up in this environment decided to set out for Australia to make his fortune in the Bendigo gold rush.

Half a century later, having become a pillar of the community, he began writing a series of letters and articles for Keble's Gazette, a publication based in his home town. In these, he described Margate with great familiarity (and tremendous powers of recall), while at the same time introducing his English readers to the "latitudinarian democracy" of a new, "young Britain".

Viney's interests covered a huge range of topics, from Thanet folk customs such as Hoodening, through diatribes on the perils of assigning intelligence to dogs, to geological theories including suggestions for the removal of sandbanks off the English coast "in obedience to the sovereign will and intelligence of man".

His writing is clearly that of a well-educated man, albeit with certain Victorian prejudices about the colonies that may make those with modern sensibilities wince a little. Yet above all, it is interesting because of the light it throws on life in a British seaside town some 180 years ago.

This book also contains numerous contemporary illustrations.

"profusely illustrated...draws together a series of interesting articles and letters...recommended" (Margate Civic Society)

ISBN: 978-0-9559219-2-6

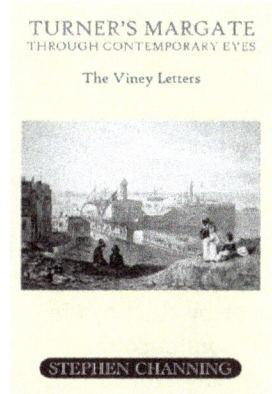

Watch and Ward
A History of Margate Borough Police 1858 to 1943
Nigel Cruttenden

A comprehensive history of Margate Borough Police from its inception in 1858 until its amalgamation into Kent County Constabulary in 1943. It covers the origins of the modern police force, detailing the influence of local councillors, JPs, solicitors and freemasons, as well as central government and world events such as the Boer War and two subsequent world wars.

Alongside its new prosperity, the up-and-coming Victorian seaside resort also had an underbelly watched over by the boys in blue. The borough's residents and visitors encountered issues similar to those of today, ranging from nuisance dogs and speeding vehicles through to mental health, alcohol abuse, domestic violence and assault – even the occasional murder. This book therefore also serves as a social history of East Kent, offering local, social and police historians copious material for research. Whenever an incident occurred in Margate, a policeman would be lurking nearby: a police man, indeed, as there were no warranted female police officers until after amalgamation. Women did however also play an important role within Margate Police, as the book shows.

This is also an invaluable reference work for genealogists or other enthusiasts researching family history in and around Thanet. Family Trees are all very well, but they do not put the flesh on the bones, and even internet searches are quite limited. Full indices make it easy for modern Margatonians and Thanetians to check whether their ancestors might have been 'involved' with the police – on whichever side!

"without a doubt this book raises the bar ... a well-researched and comprehensive account ... serious students ... will not be disappointed" (Police History Society)

ISBN 978-1-915174-03-1

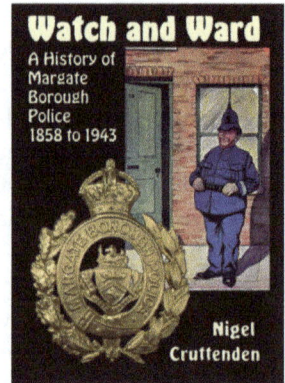

A Victorian Cyclist
Rambling through Kent in 1886

Stephen & Shirley Channing

Bicycles are so much a part of everyday life nowadays, it can be surprising to realize that for the late Victorians these "velocipedes" were a novelty disparaged as being unhealthy and unsafe – and that indeed tricycles were for a time seen as the format more likely to succeed.

Some people however adopted the newfangled devices with alacrity, embarking on adventurous tours throughout the countryside. One of them documented his 'rambles' around East Kent in such detail that it is still possible to follow his routes on modern cycles, and compare the fauna and flora (and pubs!) with those he vividly described.

In addition to providing today's cyclists with new historical routes to explore, and both naturalists and social historians with plenty of material for research, this fascinating book contains a special chapter on Lady Cyclists in the era before female emancipation, and an unintentionally humorous section instructing young gentlemen how to make their cycle and then ride it.

A Victorian Cyclist features over 200 illustrations, and is complemented by a fully updated website.

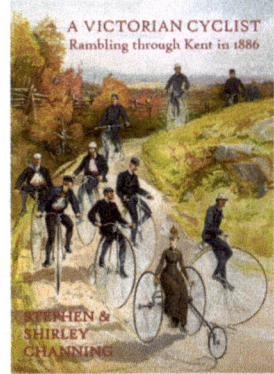

"Lovely...wonderfully written...terrific" (Everything Bicycles)

"Rare and insightful" (Kent on Sunday)

"Interesting...informative...detailed historical insights" (BikeBiz)

"Unique and fascinating book...quality is very good...of considerable interest" (Veteran-Cycle Club)

"Superb...illuminating...well detailed...The easy flowing prose, which has a cadence like cycling itself, carries the reader along as if freewheeling with a hind wind" (Forty Plus Cycling Club)

"a fascinating book with both vivid descriptions and a number of hitherto-unseen photos of the area" ('Pedalling Pensioner', amazon.co.uk)

ISBN: 978-0-9559219-7-1   Also available on Kindle

Bicycle Beginnings

The Advent of the Bicycle or Velocipede… and what people of the 19th century were really saying about it

Stephen Channing

Cycling is such a natural activity for millions of people around the globe now, it is difficult to imagine that a little over a century ago many regarded it as reprehensible, revolting, or indeed revolutionary. The best way to get a feel for what early 'velocipedists' encountered is to read the words of the times, and this book gathers into one volume the most enlightening, entertaining and extraordinary insights from contemporary sources.

The mammoth work (over 190,000 words, covering the period 1779 to 1912) contains race reports, legal developments, technical innovations and inventions, records, advertisements, acrobatics, clothing, poems, arguments for and against the new-fangled vehicles, debates over women cyclists, and a long travelogue, "Berlin to Budapest on a Bicycle" capturing the excitement of a forgotten age of adventure on two wheels.

Not all the inventions were two-wheeled, however. This book also reveals the numerous variations that came into being before makers standardized on the shapes we commonly see nowadays: tricycles, ice velocipedes, water-paddle hobby-horses... These are explained with the aid of numerous illustrations, covering the gamut from cartoons to technical drawings and photographs. Even the race reports demonstrate far more variety than we are accustomed to seeing: 'ordinaries' (penny farthings) versus 'safety' bicycles versus tandems, monocycles, dwarf cycles, tricycles, double tricycles, four-wheel velocipedes, horses, ice skaters, steamships...

Rather than a single narrative to be read in one go, it is an anthology of fascinating glimpses into cycling's 'golden age', providing a new understanding of a bygone age of experimentation and much amusement, whenever the reader dips into it.

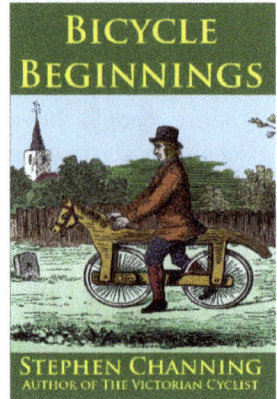

ISBN: 978-1-5210-8632-2   Also available on Kindle

The Cairnmor Trilogy
Sally Aviss

Book 1: The Call of Cairnmor   ISBN: 978-0-9559219-9-5
Book 2: Changing Tides, Changing Times   ISBN: 978-0-9931587-0-4
Book 3: Where Gloom and Brightness Meet   ISBN: 978-0-9931587-1-1

The Scottish Isle of Cairnmor is a place of great beauty and undisturbed wilderness, a haven for wildlife, a land of white sandy beaches and inland fertile plains. To this remote island comes a stranger, Alexander Stewart, on a quest to solve the disappearance of two people and an unborn child; heirs to a vast fortune.

In the dense jungle of Malaya in 1942, Doctor Rachel Curtis stumbles across a mysterious, unidentifiable stranger, badly injured and close to death. Changing Times, Changing Tides introduces new personalities, in a unique combination of novel and history that tells a story of love, loss, friendship and heroism as the characters are shaped and changed by the ebb and flow of events around the Second World War.

The final book in the Cairnmor Trilogy takes the action forward into the late 1960s. It is a story of heartbreak and redemptive love, reflecting the conflicting attitudes, problems and joys of a liberating era.

Message from Captivity
Sally Aviss

When diplomat's daughter Sophie Langley is sent to St Nicolas to care for her two elderly aunts, she finds herself trapped in an unenviable position following the German invasion. In the Battle for France, linguist and poet Robert Anderson is embroiled in an impossible military situation. From the beautiful Channel Islands to the very heart of Nazi-occupied Europe, *Message From Captivity* weaves factual authenticity into the fabric of a narrative where the twists and turns of captivity, freedom and dangerous pursuit have unforeseen consequences.

ISBN: 978-0-9931587-5-9   Also available on Kindle

The Girl in Jack's Portrait
Sally Aviss

A struggling barrister, a soldier, a divorcee, an architect, a businessman, a mental health nurse... Six people seeking an escape from their pasts and redemption in the present; six people who find their lives interwoven and their secrets revealed. But just who is the Girl in Jack's Portrait?

ISBN: 978-0-9931587-6-6   Also available on Kindle

Reflections in an Oval Mirror
Memories of East Prussia, 1923-45

Anneli Jones

8 May 1945 – VE Day – was Anneliese Wiemer's twenty-second birthday. Although she did not know it then, it marked the end of her flight to the West, and the start of a new life in England.

These illustrated memoirs, based on a diary kept during the Third Reich and letters rediscovered many decades later, depict the momentous changes occurring in Europe against a backcloth of everyday farm life in East Prussia (now the northwestern corner of Russia, sandwiched between Lithuania and Poland).

The political developments of the 1930s (including the Hitler Youth, 'Kristallnacht', political education, labour service, war service, and interrogation) are all the more poignant for being told from the viewpoint of a romantic young girl. In lighter moments she also describes student life in Vienna and Prague, and her friendship with Belgian and Soviet prisoners of war. Finally, however, the approach of the Red Army forces her to abandon her home and flee across the frozen countryside, encountering en route a cross-section of society ranging from a 'lady of the manor', worried about her family silver, to some concentration camp inmates

"couldn't put it down...delightful...very detailed descriptions of the farm and the arrival of war...interesting history and personal account" ('Rosie', amazon.co.uk)

"Anneli did not fully conform but she still survived, and how this happened is the real gem...There is optimism, humour, great affection and a tremendous sense of adventure in a period when this society was hurtling towards disaster." ('Singapore Relic', amazon.co.uk)

ISBN: 978-0-9559219-0-2   Also available on Kindle, and in German

Skating at the Edge of the Wood
Memories of East Prussia, 1931-1945…1993

Marlene Yeo

In 1944, the twelve-year old East Prussian girl Marlene Wiemer embarked on a horrific trek to the West, to escape the advancing Red Army. Her cousin Jutta was left behind the Iron Curtain, which severed the family bonds that had made the two so close.

This book contains dramatic depictions of Marlene's flight, recreated from her letters to Jutta during the last year of the war, and contrasted with joyful memories of the innocence that preceded them.

Nearly fifty years later, the advent of perestroika meant that Marlene and Jutta were finally able to revisit their childhood home, after a lifetime of growing up under diametrically opposed societies, and the book closes with a final chapter revealing what they find.

Despite depicting the same time and circumstances as "Reflections in an Oval Mirror", an account written by Marlene's elder sister, Anneli, and its sequel "Carpe Diem", this work stands in stark contrast partly owing to the age gap between the two girls, but above all because of their dramatically different characters.

ISBN: 978-0-9931587-2-8   Also available on Kindle, and in German

Ichigensan
– The Newcomer –

David Zoppetti
Translated from the Japanese by Takuma Sminkey

Ichigensan is a novel which can be enjoyed on many levels – as a delicate, sensual love story, as a depiction of the refined society in Japan's cultural capital Kyoto, and as an exploration of the themes of alienation and prejudice common to many environments, regardless of the boundaries of time and place.

Unusually, it shows Japan from the eyes of both an outsider and an 'internal' outcast, and even more unusually, it originally achieved this through sensuous prose carefully crafted by a non-native speaker of Japanese. The fact that this best-selling novella then won the Subaru Prize, one of Japan's top literary awards, and was also nominated for the Akutagawa Prize is a testament to its unique narrative power.

The story is by no means chained to Japan, however, and this new translation by Takuma Sminkey will allow readers world-wide to enjoy the multitude of sensations engendered by life and love in an alien culture.

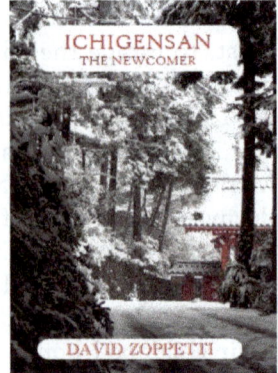

"A beautiful love story" (Japan Times)
"Sophisticated...subtle...sensuous...delicate...memorable...vivid depictions" (Asahi Evening News)
"Striking...fascinating..." (Japan PEN Club)
"Refined and sensual" (Kyoto Shimbun)
"quiet, yet very compelling...subtle mixture of humour and sensuality...the insights that the novel gives about Japanese society are both intriguing and exotic" (Nicholas Greenman, amazon.com)

ISBN: 978-0-9559219-4-0   Also available on Kindle, and in German

Sunflowers
– Le Soleil –
Shimako Murai

A play in one act
Translated from the Japanese by Ben Jones

Hiroshima is synonymous with the first hostile use of an atomic bomb. Many people think of this occurrence as one terrible event in the past, which is studied from history books.

Shimako Murai and other 'Women of Hiroshima' believe otherwise: for them, the bomb had after-effects which affected countless people for decades, effects that were all the more menacing for their unpredictability – and often, invisibility.

This is a tale of two such people: on the surface successful modern women, yet each bearing underneath hidden scars as horrific as the keloids that disfigured Hibakusha on the days following the bomb.

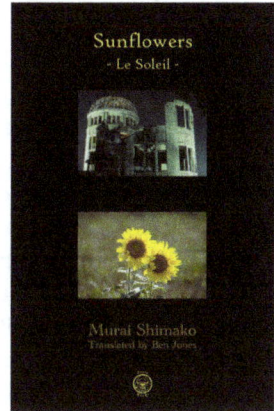

ISBN: 978-0-9559219-3-3   Also available on Kindle

The Body as a Vessel
Approaching the Methodology of Hijikata Tatsumi's Ankoku Butō
Mikami Kayo

An analysis of the modern dance form
Translated from the Japanese by Rosa van Hensbergen

When Hijikata Tatsumi's "Butō" appeared in 1959, it revolutionized not only Japanese dance but also the concept of performance art worldwide. It has however proved notoriously difficult to define or tie down. Mikami was a disciple of Hijikata for three years, and in this book, partly based on her graduate and doctoral theses, she combines insights from these years with earlier notes from other dancers to decode the ideas and processes behind butō.

ISBN: 978-0-9931587-4-2

Courtly Feasts to Kremlin Banquets
A History of Celebration and Hospitality:
Echoes of Russia's cuisine
Mikami Oksana Zakharova and Sergey Pushkaryov

Translated & adapted by Marina George

This is a book not only for lovers of food but also for those with an appetite for adventure and a thirst for the discovery of exciting gastronomic delights.

Russian history presents us with a rich tapestry of extravagant ceremony, characterized not only by the magnificent grandeur of individual courtly feasts but also by successive generations of nobility actively vying with each other to surpass the splendour created by their predecessors. Russian hospitality has always exuded a special vitality and sense of warm-hearted sociability. In Old Russia there was also a significant link between hospitality and the teachings of the Orthodox Church.

The political and social history of Russia has seen some very violent changes. The more shocking the political events of a country, the more brutal the cultural changes can be. At times, the differences between the past and the present are so extreme that one is faced with completely different worlds. Despite dramatic and often heart-breaking upheavals, we do surely have a duty to remember those distant roots that helped to nourish the present.

"Modern society contemptuously dismisses and sneers at the former way of life and deliberately breaks any connection with the past, which would always have been held to be so dear at the time." These words of writer, historian and theatre critic Yevgeny Opochinin were published in 1909 before the full horror of the revolutionary upheaval. The relevance of such remarks is surely as valid now as then.

Throughout history, special events have been an important way of imparting tradition from one generation to another, and symbolic meanings can still be found, if one knows the stories from the past. One just has to know where to look.

So, it is time to raise a toast in memory of bygone custom and tradition and to celebrate that great warm-hearted generosity of the Russian people.

ISBN: 978-0-9931587-8-0

Curling Wisps & Whispers of History
LucyAnn Curling

Vol. 1: Thanet to Tasmania

If family history is about gathering as many ancestors as possible, this book fails: it focuses on just three generations of the author's paternal side, between 1780 and 1826. At first nothing stirs the still waters of centuries of East Kent farming tradition. Men organize parish affairs, women follow domestic routines, boys attend a boarding school in Ramsgate, and only grandma seems interested in socializing or travel. Why then did Thomas Oakley Curling uproot everything and take his family on a marathon five-month voyage to Van Diemen's Land? Why leave one child behind? And where does Sir Charles Napier fit in?

Curling Wisps & Whispers of History
Vol. 1: Thanet to Tasmania

LucyAnn Curling

The genealogical quest starts naturally with a family heirloom, but soon tangential questions emerge, as multiple threads are collated and woven into one story. 'Georgian & Regency ancestors' might sound remote, removed from our reality, but the individuals' letters draw us into their world, and copious illustrations punctuate the text, animating the environments in which they lived.

ISBN 978-1-915174-02-4

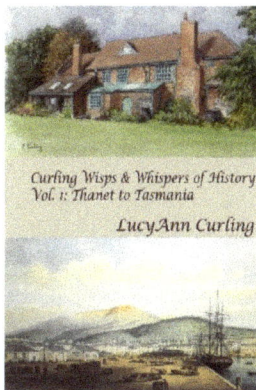

Vol. 2: Kent to Kefalonia

This second volume finds the Curling family back in England, struggling to find a financial foothold in society. Second son, Edward, has an unrewarding job in an attorney's office when Charles James Napier offers him a golden opportunity on the island of Kefalonia.

Follow the surprising twists of providence as Edward works on Napier's unusual project. What is the Malta connection? Tensions between Napier and his line manager, Sir Frederick Adam, have repercussions for Edward. Greece at this time was fighting for independence from the Ottoman Empire, and that war touches Napier's personal life obliquely but with lasting effect, while Edward's too is permanently changed by a

Curling Wisps & Whispers of History
Vol. 2: Kent to Kefalonia

LucyAnn Curling

different encounter. Edward's work journal and numerous letters in the Napier Papers at the British and Bodleian Libraries bear witness to the social pressures acting on all members of this extended clan, as their feelings come into conflict with accepted norms, and set the stage for further dramatic developments...

ISBN 978-1-915174-07-9

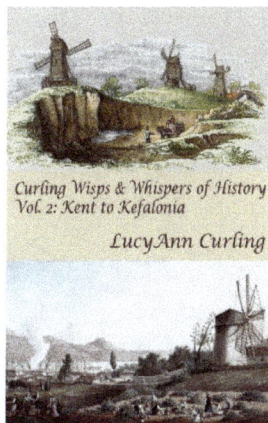

www.ingramcontent.com/pod-product-compliance
Lightning Source LLC
Chambersburg PA
CBHW051909090426
42811CB00003B/513